WHAT READERS ARE SAYING

"Laura Davis has written a brilliant memoir. *The Burning Light of Two Stars* is destined to become as much a classic as *The Courage to Heal,* her groundbreaking book on healing from sexual abuse. *The Burning Light of Two Stars,* written more than thirty years later, explores Laura's attempts to reconcile with her mother, who had previously denied that Laura had been sexually abused. Here, a mature writer looks back on the most primal and pivotal relationship in her life. Laura handles the complex emotions and interactions of mother and daughter with deep insight, clarity, and compassion. Her storytelling is compelling, poignant, and heartfelt. At times gut-wrenching, at other times hilarious, *The Burning Light of Two Stars* is a 'must read.'"

—Adrienne Drake, MD, Mission Viejo, California

"I was completely captivated by this story. *The Burning Light of Two Stars* was one of those books you start reading and feel as if you've stumbled on a treasure. Every night I found it hard to put down. I was hungry to always read more, to turn each page and consume each paragraph. The story is brilliant. There is intrigue, emotion, life lessons, and a deep connection to real family life and relationships. I highly recommend this book to anyone wanting a good read—but especially to those living with family estrangement, now or in the past."

—Yasmin Kerkez, founder of Moving Beyond Family Struggles

"I quickly ran out of superlatives for *The Burning Light of Two Stars* because so many scenes grabbed me. From the first page, I was fully engaged in Laura's world and didn't want to put the book down. It was as if she was speaking my story, her mother a mirror of my own. I am certain this wise exploration of mother-daughter dynamics over a lifetime will resonate broadly. As I pored over its pages, I didn't want this beautiful, compelling story to end. And for me, it hasn't: Laura's memoir and all of her characters have stayed with me to this day."

—Kay Taylor, author of *Soul Path Way*

"I finished *The Burning Light of Two Stars* in a bed of tears. What an eloquent and compelling story."

—Abby Stamelman Hocky, executive director, Interfaith Philadelphia

"Laura's book is a stunning achievement. I am certain *The Burning Light of Two Stars* will be used as a discussion vehicle with seniors, in groups dealing with mother-daughter issues, family estrangement, compassionate choices, Alzheimer's disease, and death with dignity, with a facilitator guiding discussion afterwards. Laura Davis has made a major contribution to the literature of aging, death, and dying."

—Etiel Herring, Santa Cruz, California

"In this riveting memoir, Laura grapples with questions that many of us struggle with: 'How do family members stay in relationship with each other when they can't agree on critical elements of their collective past?' 'How do families overcome past hurts when they need to show up for each other in their hour of need?' And 'Is it possible to risk loving someone you desperately want to be able to love, but who has repeatedly betrayed you?' As a palliative care doctor, *The Burning Light of Two Stars* put me in touch with what the caregiver experience is really like. I enthusiastically recommend this book."

—Shoshana Helman, MD, hospice and palliative medicine, Redwood City, California

"When Laura Davis and Ellen Bass published *The Courage to Heal,* it emboldened a generation of survivors of incest and sexual abuse, likely contributing to the courageous voices for many who are part of today's MeToo and TimesUp movements. In *The Burning Light of Two Stars,*

Davis allows us to know the person behind those pages, and the story behind that story. Nuanced, raw, and candid, this memoir does not designate white hat or black hat characters. Instead, it provides a topographical map through the complex landscape of the mother-daughter relationship at the heart of the story, with characters both noble and deeply flawed on both sides of the equation. This masterful heart-filling book is deeply moving and wise."

—Betsy Graziani Fasbinder, therapist and author
of *Filling Her Shoes* and *Fire and Water*

"I found *The Burning Light of Two Stars* to be riveting, an effortless read. I'm in two book groups, and at any given time I am reading or listening to two or three books concurrently. I've put them all down for this one. It's just that good."

—Olivia Bethea, Atlanta, Georgia

"Laura Davis has a unique ability to capture the details of everyday life in vivid color, as she allows the reader to shadow her on this intimate, challenging, and often humorous family journey. The emotional range of the book is a major strength: frustration, fear, rage, joy, absurdity, humor, love, hate, melancholy—it's all there. It's a fabulous read."

—Talin Vartanian, producer at *The Sunday Edition*
and creator of *Canada Reads*, CBC Radio

"Laura's story is important because it captures, with authenticity and supreme honesty, the vexed, complicated and tender mother-daughter bonds and because it doesn't hold back the daughter's ambiguity, resentments, wavering, love-hate sentiments. The sincerity through which the story is conveyed took my breath away."

—Rosa-Linda Fregoso, professor emerita of Latin American
and Latino studies, University of California, Santa Cruz, and
coeditor of *Terrorizing Women: Feminicide in the Américas*

"I've never experienced a book like this before. I was fully engrossed in every scene as if I was living it. I just couldn't put it down. I can't find words for how powerfully *The Burning Light of Two Stars* affected me. I'm a different person after having read it. My heart is full. Laura Davis addresses the complexity of family relationships like nothing I've ever read before."

—Toni Taylor, retired nurse

"In a culture that produces chasms of disconnection in our most tender relationships, and sanitizes the rawness of life, *The Burning Light of Two Stars* takes the reader on a journey that reconnects and rescues the beauty of life's messiest realities. It is a story of resistance and rebirth, one that provides myriad lessons on what it takes to transcend deep wounds. Laura Davis has written a brilliant, compelling book that I just couldn't put down. I read all night, and I do not give up sleep easily. *The Burning Light of Two Stars* fed my soul."

—Eileene Tejada, PhD, professor of English and anthropology at Napa Valley College

"I just finished this remarkable book today. My experience reading *The Burning Light of Two Stars* was profound. I found the story compelling. The writing superb. I was drawn into Laura's life story in a deeply personal way. I could not put *The Burning Light of Two Stars* down except to stop often and think about my own mother. I can honestly say I have not experienced such deep thinking about my relationship with my mother in a long time, if ever."

—Rosilyn Nesler, Oceanside, California

"I've read nonstop since I woke up, almost one hundred pages already. It's riveting and exquisitely crafted. If I didn't have things I had to do today, I'd finish it in one sitting."

—Jennifer Meyer, Eugene, Oregon

"Laura's book blew me away. It's a memoir written like a novel (no small trick, I think), which is usually my first reading choice. Laura's book reads like a mystery novel; though I sometimes dreaded what I'd learn, I couldn't wait to find out what would come next. I highly recommend *The Burning Light of Two Stars*."

—Theresa Miller, Milwaukee, Wisconsin

"*The Burning Light of Two Stars* is more than just a mother-daughter story. Laura skillfully addresses crucial human questions: 'Who am I?' 'Am I my worst moments?' 'Am I my best moments?' 'How do I move through hard places to come into a rich, full, wholehearted life?' I loved immersing myself in her journey and had a hard time saying goodbye to the characters when I reached the final page. I'd definitely recommend *The Burning Light of Two Stars* to anyone grappling with estranged relationships, aging parents or dementia, and to anyone who has wrestled with love and frustration in a family—which is all of us. It was truly a joy to read this book."

—Melissa Thomson, Unitarian Universalist minister and palliative care chaplain, Los Altos, California

"As I read *The Burning Light of Two Stars,* I felt like a witness to the unfolding of life and death and all that matters in between."

—Evelyn Hall, Soquel, California

"A powerful story, beautifully written, *The Burning Light of Two Stars* explores the journey of loss and reconciliation in vivid, gripping, moving, loving detail. Laura captures the complexity of relationships, especially relationships we don't really choose but life puts in our path. It's about a search for peace about what we can't change and the surprises of all that can change us. And, of course, mother-daughter stories are rich material. I already have a long list of people in mind who I know will just love this book."

—Lucie Eggleston, Columbia, South Carolina

"For a community trying to grasp the real and heart-wrenching truth of sexual violence, *The Burning Light of Two Stars* lays bare the life-altering and far-reaching impact of incest, sexual abuse, and assault. It strips down to the bone the deep and aching damage trauma does not only to the individual but the family as a whole. For survivors, Laura Davis demonstrates that with unending hard work and commitment one can redefine and reconcile a relationship."

—Crystal Emerick, founder of Brave Step

"Reading this book changed my heart and inspired me to pick up the phone and call my mother for the first time in eighteen years."

—Hollye Dexter, author of *Fire Season* and coeditor of *Dancing at the Shame Prom*

"I found Laura's story compelling. Throughout, Laura struggles to answer the questions: 'Can we overcome the worst betrayals and denials within family relationships, acknowledge the existence and damage it caused, and later in life, be able to love?' 'Can a heart that is walled off for good reason find ways to open again?' What a moving story about the human condition! I would recommend *The Burning Light of Two Stars* to anyone interested in mother-daughter relationships, family reconciliation, caring for elders, or understanding the effects of betrayals in childhood on family dynamics."

—Bonnie Pettus, Greenville, South Carolina

"Laura Davis crafts a raw, powerful story of her difficult relationship with her mother, from Laura's birth to her mother's passing, moving the reader easily and deftly through time like a magician. Her vivid storytelling is so credible and real that after reading *The Burning Light of Two Stars*, I feel I know her well, and the details she provides only magnify her honesty. In her public life, Laura is a teacher and hero to many who have suffered from sexual abuse. Yet she also has a private voice that is often at odds with her public persona. Like most of us, Laura is a living contradiction, and in this brave memoir, she doesn't hold back. We see her through her raging moments and in her softer ones. Fearlessly, she exposes her very private thoughts alongside her public ones. It's that internal voice that she's not afraid to use, the one most of us keep hidden, that gives *The Burning Light of Two Stars* its potency and staying power."

—Nancy Guinther, Aptos, California

"The world needs this book."

—Santoshi Wagner-Anue, Santa Cruz, California

PRAISE FOR *THE COURAGE TO HEAL*

"*The Courage to Heal* is a wise and gentle book that should be read by all people trying to recover from having been sexually misused as a child, and by all friends, family members, and professionals with a genuine desire to understand both the experience of being a victim of sexual abuse and the arduous path to recovery. *The Courage to Heal* has helped countless survivors of sexual abuse in their efforts to confront the realities of their lives and to take charge of them in the present."

—Bessel A. van der Kolk, MD, associate professor of psychiatry, Harvard Medical School

"With scrupulous care, balance, and a clear political vision, Ellen Bass and Laura Davis have written a groundbreaking book that will stand as a classic for many years to come. Clearly a labor of both love and commitment to the healing of tens of thousands of women still suffering the deep wounds of their experience, *The Courage to Heal* will find a wide, appreciative, and altered readership."

—Sandra Butler, author of *The Conspiracy of Silence*

ACCLAIM FROM SURVIVORS FOR *THE COURAGE TO HEAL*

"*The Courage to Heal* touched the deepest part of me, the part that has been walled off and silent for twenty-five years. You have spoken the words for me that I was unable to utter."

"If there was any one thing that helped me to believe in myself, and helped to reconstruct my life, it has been this book. *The Courage to Heal* has not spent a day on the bookshelf—I utilize it so often that it is a waste to put it away."

PRAISE FOR *I THOUGHT WE'D NEVER SPEAK AGAIN: THE ROAD FROM ESTRANGEMENT TO RECONCILIATION*

"Leave it to Laura Davis, who opened a whole generation with *The Courage to Heal,* to once again give us what we need—a book about how we come home to each other and ourselves. I want to buy this for everyone I know."

—Natalie Goldberg, author of *Thunder and Lightning* and *The Essential Writer's Notebook*

"Anybody who has given up on the possibility of reconciliation should read this book. Davis builds a web of hope that human beings can indeed move on, even when relationships have been painful and very destructive."

—Ron Kraybill, professor, Conflict Transformation Program, Eastern Mennonite University

"With warmth, humor and sensitivity, Laura Davis teaches us personal and practical truths about healing painful, broken relationships. She does not offer simplistic answers or tell us that there is only one way to reconcile. Her book is a tremendous gift."

—Greg D. Richardson, Restorative Justice Institute

PRAISE FOR *BECOMING THE PARENT YOU WANT TO BE*

"This unusually thorough book provides today's parents with rich and abundant insights for discerning and fostering wholeness in their children. This is an enormously helpful resource which sheds light on many issues that are not addressed in other books on parenting."

—Polly Berrien Berends, author of *Whole Child, Whole Parent*

"Through simple, direct language, touching human stories, and clear messages, the authors reveal sensitivity, understanding and in-depth knowledge of both children's and parents' development. They know what is necessary for children and parents to grow and flourish. It will become a classic among books for parents."

—Bernice Weissbourd, president, board of directors, Family Resource Coalition

"A masterpiece of wisdom! It's easy to give advice and to treat parents as if they were all alike, but they aren't. It's a challenge to respond to them in all their diversity. The authors have risen to the challenge admirably."

—Janet Gonzalez-Mena, author of *Dragon Mom: Confessions of a Child Development Expert*

8/6/23

Dear Joya,
I'm so pleased I got to know you and your resilient and joyous spirit just a little this week. I'm so glad this week worked out for you—

THE BURNING LIGHT *of* TWO STARS

In the spirit of healing—
Laura

ALSO BY LAURA DAVIS

The Courage to Heal: A Guide for Women Survivors of Child Sexual Abuse (with Ellen Bass)

The Courage to Heal Workbook

Allies in Healing: When the Person You Love Was Sexually Abused as a Child

Beginning to Heal (with Ellen Bass)

Becoming the Parent You Want to Be: A Sourcebook of Strategies for the First Five Years (with Janis Keyser)

I Thought We'd Never Speak Again: The Road from Estrangement to Reconciliation

The Burning Light of Two Stars is also available as an e-book, and the audiobook is available through your favorite audiobook retailer.

LAURA DAVIS

THE BURNING LIGHT *of* TWO STARS

A Mother-Daughter Story

GIRL FRIDAY BOOKS

Published by Girl Friday Books™, Seattle

Produced by Girl Friday Productions
www.girlfridayproductions.com

Design: Paul Barrett
Development & editorial: Katherine Richards
Production editorial: Bethany Davis

Image credits: cover photograph © Laura Davis

ISBN (paperback): 978-1-954854-16-1
ISBN (e-book): 978-1-954854-17-8

Library of Congress Control Number: 2021911736

First edition

To Karyn: For three decades of learning to love each other. Your steady love healed me and made our beautiful family possible.

"The mind creates the abyss, the heart crosses it."

—Sri Nisargadatta Maharaj, Jnana yoga master

CONTENTS

PART II

PART III

PART IV

PART V

SPARK

Summer 1956
Long Branch, New Jersey

I started life in a glass box. I lay alone, barely breathing. Eyelids thin, light stabbing. Body on fire, nerves raw. Beeps piercing my tiny ears. I couldn't swallow. I couldn't suck. Tubes down my nose, wires on my skin.

Where was she—the heartbeat that had answered my own? That soft, slippery chest pressed to mine?

For seven months, I'd held my twin in my arms. Even when we had no arms, I held her. She was always smaller, even when we were just a thought, a zygote, an embryo. She grew beside me, quarter ounce by quarter ounce, her pulse the echo of my own.

Weeks went by. Then months. She, floating in the safety of my embrace. Until the walls of our watery home began to squeeze.

Our mother was twenty-eight years old. She'd already had two late-term miscarriages. Now she thought she was losing another baby. She had no idea that we were two.

Moments after my birth, a nurse placed me on the scale: two pounds, twelve ounces. A scrawny chicken. As they rushed me to the neonatal intensive care unit, the doctor said, "Hold on, Mrs. Davis; there's another one coming!" That's how she learned about my sister.

Bone of my bone. Flesh of my flesh. The two of us identical. My twin lived twenty-four hours. I never held her again.

—~—

The rabbi advised, "Don't build a monument to someone who never existed," so my secret sister never had a memorial, a funeral, or a grave. But Mom insisted on giving her a name.

Vicki.

—~—

For six weeks after my birth, no one was allowed to hold me. And I touched no one. Doctors didn't believe in holding preemies in 1956. I spent the next six weeks in a hard glass box—an Isolette, the perfect name for my healing prison. It isolated me from the broad expanse of my father's chest, my brother Paul's laughter, my mother's eager arms.

Nurses wearing rubber gloves reached in to adjust my tubes, check my wires, change my tiny diaper. The whoosh of machines, the tick-tock of the clock, a pale shadow of the heartbeat that had sustained me, the one that I had sustained. The nurses took notes on hard brown clipboards and moved on to the next tiny baby. They did what they could and left me alone.

Babies my size weren't supposed to survive. If I made it, the doctor said, I'd probably be blind or "retarded."

If I made it, I'd be strong.

A survivor.

—~—

My whole life rolled out from that beginning. When I think back now, here's how I imagine it:

A newborn, tiny, weak, and in pain. My twin had died, and I could have followed her. Perhaps part of me wanted to just let go and disappear. But then I felt *her*—Temme Davis, the woman standing outside my clear glass box. Pulling me to her. Willing me to live. *My baby, oh my baby, let me hold you in my arms.* Beaming her life force through those hard walls. *Stay with me, darling. Please be my baby.* She pulled me into her blazing broken heart and claimed me as her daughter. *Stay with me,* she said. *Whatever you do, don't ever leave.*

And so, I said yes to life. Yes, to my mother.

I had no idea just how much of a challenge that was going to be.

PART I

"Every time I look in the rearview mirror, the past has changed."

—Deborah Fruchey

CHAPTER 1

RITUAL

Fifty-One Years Later
Santa Cruz, California

I waited until I knew I'd be home alone. Karyn and the kids wouldn't be back for several hours. This ceremony was just for me.

I pulled the giant white binder out from under the bed and carried it to the backyard, along with newspaper, an armful of kindling, and a box of Strike Anywhere matches.

The firepit in our backyard had been the center of many family celebrations. Today it would mark a different sort of occasion.

Sitting on the stone bench, I crumpled pages of the *Santa Cruz Sentinel* into loose balls and tossed them into the pit. Topped the paper with a pyramid of thin, dry pine with plenty of airspace in between.

Lit my pyre with a matchstick and watched the flames take hold.

It was early June 2008. I'd waited a long time for this day.

The binder had been handed to me the summer before at the Stanford Cancer Center after I walked in, leaning on Karyn, for our meeting with the tumor board. As we pushed our way through the front door, we encountered an incongruous, yet comforting sound—a young man playing Beethoven's Moonlight Sonata on a giant black Yamaha grand piano.

As we waited to be called, I pressed my shoulder against Karyn's shoulder, savoring the steadiness of her presence. But I couldn't look her in the eye. When I was scared, I always reverted to coping alone. So, we sat, side by side, in separate bubbles. At any moment, the doctors were going to inform us whether I'd live to see our children grow up. Lizzy was ten; Eli, fourteen. *Just let me see them graduate from high school.* That was my mantra.

In neatly divided sections, the stiff binder had laid out all the information I needed as a breast cancer patient. Now, I opened the hard plastic cover for the last time. I clicked the rings apart, crushed the first page, and tossed it onto the fire. As the carefully tallied list of medications disappeared into the flames, something tight in my chest gave way. I threw in another page. And another. I leaned in. It felt good.

I thought back to the day I'd learned that life can change, just like that.

It was supposed to be a routine annual exam. Twenty minutes max. Then back to my busy life: writing teacher, breadwinner, mother, spouse. As my doctor palpated my right breast, we chatted about our children—they'd been classmates at Orchard School, a tiny rural elementary school where kids ride unicycles to class. We were reminiscing about the potbellied pig when she felt it. Something hard. She went back and felt it again. And then again. "I'm so sorry, Laura, but you're going to need a biopsy."

I didn't hear anything she said after that. Just the word she hadn't spoken.

I wadded up the next page—contact names and numbers—and threw it onto the fire. The stiff place in my chest loosened a little more. I threw in another page. And then another. The red and yellow flames devoured them all.

It had been a year of waiting. For my diagnosis. For surgery—*just get it out now.* For the wound to heal. The pain pills to work. For my head-shaving ceremony. For nurses in lead-lined smocks to drip poison into my veins. For the nausea to end. For food not to taste like rusty nails.

I fed a dozen more pages into the fire. They sparked into the sky, and the flames drove me back. I welcomed the surge of heat.

The day my oncologist told me I was cancer-free, I floated out of her office into a warm spring afternoon. I imagined Lizzy, racing after school to climb her favorite tree. I pictured Eli, his long fingers folding origami paper into impossible shapes. I'd be here to guide them. To launch them. To see who they would become. I thought about Karyn and the life stretching out before us. The students I might teach. The things I might write. Maybe I had another book in me.

Cancer-free.

I tossed the last page onto the fire.

The empty white binder gaped open.

Where did that leave me?

Gaining back the forty pounds I'd lost, waiting to feel like myself again. Whatever that meant. I had no idea.

So, I resumed my life: carpool, shopping, laundry. My cancer blog was winding down, and my writing workshops were picking up. But underneath, nothing felt the same. How could I possibly go back to the old Laura—the doer, the manifester, the woman who added tasks she had already completed to The List of Things to Do, just for the pleasure of crossing them off?

Who am I now? That question haunted my nights and thrummed beneath the surface of my days. But no one in my family wanted to talk about cancer anymore, or the questions that survived it.

I poked at the remnants of the fire. Orange and red embers, radiating steady heat. I held my hands over the glowing coals, took a deep breath, and spoke the words aloud: "I am not a cancer patient anymore. I am open to receive whatever is next."

A deep quiet came over me when I said those words.

I watched the embers slowly fade.

It was time to discover who the new Laura might be. Maybe I'd be more present. Less driven. Less controlling. I hoped so.

I looked forward to quiet months with my family. No bombshells. No lumps. No toxic drugs. No surprises. Just a stable, steady life, so I could recover.

CHAPTER 2

THE CALL

2,179 Days

Two hours after my ceremony, I tasted my homemade tomato sauce, simmering on the stove, added basil and oregano, a generous pinch of salt. A splash of red wine. Karyn was picking up the kids on her way home from teaching reading at Watsonville High. They'd be home in half an hour.

I was about to drop a handful of spaghetti into a pot of boiling water when the phone rang. It was my mother in New Jersey. We were due for a call; we hadn't spoken in several weeks. Cradling the phone between my neck and shoulder, I dropped the pasta into the pot, stirred to separate the strands. My glasses fogged with steam. I imagined her, smoking Parliaments, curled up with an afghan on the couch in the den. She'd probably just gotten home from her poetry class or her Shakespeare class or her Course in Miracles study group. I could never track her schedule. I set the timer for thirteen minutes.

"Laurie, I've got a surprise for you."

"Oh yeah?" I was only half listening, maybe a quarter. I opened the fridge, rooted around for salad fixings.

"Why don't you guess?"

"I dunno, Mom. What's the surprise?"

"Don't you want to guess?" I pictured her lighting another cigarette, residue of the day's lipstick reddening the tip.

"Uh . . . you went to an audition and got a part in a play?"

"No, I'm afraid my acting days are over. Guess again."

"Just tell me, Mom."

"Are you sure you want to know?"

"Of course I want to know."

"Darling, I've finally made up my mind." She paused for effect. "I'm moving to Santa Cruz. I wanted you to be the first to know."

Blood rushed from my head. I closed the refrigerator. Leaned back against the door. Pictures of the kids and little square art magnets clattered to the floor.

It's true—years earlier, in a moment of generosity, I had invited Mom to move out to California "when she got old." We'd talked about it once or twice, but I never thought she'd actually take me up on it. It had been *ten* years.

"It finally feels like the right time, Laurie. New Jersey just isn't the same anymore."

That's right. Your friends are dying off, going into assisted living, or moving to be close to their children. Oh my God. That's me. My hand tightened on the phone.

My mother and I had been estranged for years. Yes, we'd forged a shaky peace, but three thousand miles still separated us for a reason. Our reconciliation went only so far.

"I love Santa Cruz. And I love your family."

"Wow, Mom. That's amazing. I mean . . . great . . . I'm so . . . happy."

"Well, that's good, darling, because I met with the real estate agent today. I've put my condo on the market. She says it's the perfect time to sell a place at the shore."

I collapsed onto one of the red cushy chairs at our yellow Formica kitchen table, stared at the black-and-white-checkered linoleum. The floor needed a washing.

"Laurie, are you there?"

"Yeah, Mom. I'm here."

"You still want me, don't you?"

"Of course I want you. We all want you. It's just that I never thought you'd actually do it."

"Well, I'm not getting any younger."

No, she wasn't. Mom was eighty years old, and her memory was failing.

"You don't sound very excited."

"I *am* excited. I'm just surprised, that's all." How could I possibly be excited? The woman who'd betrayed me at the worst moment of my life was moving to my town. And I was the one who'd invited her.

A beep reverberated in my head and wouldn't stop. Mom was talking about escrow and how hard it was going to be to pack. But I barely heard her. She was the white noise in the background. I was hovering outside my body, listening to just one voice—the one screaming in my head and taking up every inch of bandwidth: I've finally gotten through cancer, and now this? Why the hell didn't you *ask* me? How about, Laurie, do you remember that conversation we had *ten* years ago? I've been thinking about it more seriously and wonder if you still think it would be a good idea. For you? For me? For us? For Karyn and the kids? Or how about, Laurie, I know you're just getting over cancer. Is this a good time for me to move across the country to live in your town?

". . . my friends told me about this gorgeous mobile home park right at the beach in Santa Cruz. De Anza. Have you heard of it?"

"Yes, Mom."

"I'll go right from one ocean to the other. So, you'll stop by and talk to the manager?"

"Sure, happy to do that for you."

I grabbed a brand-new yellow legal pad. It had been months since I'd made a list. What would I have put on it? *"Take toxic drugs. Throw up. Smoke pot so you can eat. Grow white blood cells. Watch West Wing reruns. Survive."*

As I wrote "Find Mom a Place to Live: De Anza?" on the pristine yellow page, Mom said, "Gotta run, darling. I promised your aunt Ruth a call tonight."

Click.

She hung up on me.

The timer was still beeping. I looked into the pot. The spaghetti had congealed into a gelatinous mush. I dumped it in the compost and set a fresh pot of water to boil. As I lifted the heavy pot, I knocked my favorite glass off the counter, and it shattered on the floor.

The kids were going to walk in at any moment, and they'd be starving.

I swept up the shards and set the table for four, but I couldn't remember which side the fork was supposed to go on.

CHAPTER 3

FAME

Nineteen Years Earlier
Laura 32, Temme 61, Indianapolis

Here's how it felt to be famous. Riding to the auditorium in the back of a black Lincoln Town Car. Periwinkle leather pants on smooth leather seats. Periwinkle leather jacket. Fake pearls. Black patent leather flats. My streaked mullet spiked and gelled in place. Just enough makeup for my face to show under the lights.

Women lined up around the block, waiting to hear me speak.

A year earlier, in 1988, my coauthor, Ellen Bass, and I had published *The Courage to Heal: For Women Survivors of Child Sexual Abuse*, a six-hundred-page tome that guided women through the process of healing. From coping to survival to thriving, our book provided a road map. The first. *The Courage to Heal* galvanized a movement.

There were so many requests for us to speak that Ellen was lecturing on one side of the country while I flew off to the other.

Soon I'd be out onstage, every seat full, hundreds of faces turned toward me, drinking in my every word. The thread of excitement winding up my spine competed with the memory of vitriol from my mother's call the night before: "You and your hate book. Traipsing around the country, spreading lies about our family on national TV. You published that book just to destroy me!"

As my driver pulled up in back, a line of women snaked around the corner, standing in small clusters, holding copies of *The Courage to Heal,* waiting for the doors to open. As I slid out of the car, I could still feel the heat of Mom's rage: "You and all the other lesbians. Ninety percent of you say you've been molested. You all hate men. You hate your mothers. It's the 'in' thing. Your badge of honor. Who had it worse as a kid!" Then she hung up on me. The finality of her slam still reverberated as my host rushed up to greet me.

"Let me take you right to the green room, Laura. It's going to be a full house tonight."

I pushed the memory of my mother's voice away. I was not carrying her with me into that auditorium. Some of these women had driven hundreds of miles to hear me speak. My job was to inspire them, to let them know they weren't alone, that healing was possible. I was determined to deliver. I buried Mom's words behind a steel wall inside me.

As someone introduced me, I waited backstage, doing the vocal exercises I'd learned in seventh-grade speech class: rehearsing my first lines in a thick voice with my tongue fully extended—opening my palate, opening my voice.

To prepare myself for the intensity ahead, I pictured a roll of cotton batting wrapped around my solar plexus, protecting me from the raw pain and collective grief of the hundreds of women waiting in the auditorium. I visualized a red rose—for compassion—blossoming in my chest. I imagined my feet rooting down into the molten center of the earth, pulling heat back through my body until it glowed inside me. As I waited in the wings, sweat dotted my spine, and I grew larger. My whole body tingled. Clip a mic on my lapel and a battery pack onto the waistband of my pants, and I slipped right out of my ordinary skin. Something holy and elemental poured through me those nights as I transformed from the damaged incest survivor that I really was into the inspiring coauthor of *The Courage to Heal.*

"Let's give a warm Indianapolis welcome to Laura Davis!"

As the wave of applause peaked and subsided, I strode onto the stage into the waiting silence. An *X* taped on the polished floor told me where to stand. The stage was bare: just a tiny table, a glass, a pitcher of water, no ice. And now me. I held a small blue stack of tattered index cards in my hand. Tiny reminders of the stories I wanted to tell. We'd already done the sound check. I knew just how far the spotlight would follow me.

I took a minute to breathe and look out at the women. Some had come alone. Others held the hand of a friend. A fellow survivor. Occasionally, a husband or male survivor braved the female crowd. But mostly they were women. Women who'd been raped and taunted and threatened and filmed and sold, tortured by strangers or people who were supposed to love them. Faces of every color looked back at me. Young women, old women, all kinds of women. Baby dykes and housewives. Accountants and waitresses. Doctors, therapists, and sex workers. They came from all over. They carpooled and took buses, flew on airplanes and crossed state lines. Some had slash marks on their wrists or the inside of their thighs. They carried tearstained teddy bears and razor blades in their purses. Women told me that they held one to keep from using the other. They carried dog-eared copies of our book and were prepared to wait an hour or more for me to sign them.

I always began with my story, my cadence practiced and slow. "When I was three years old, my grandfather came into the bedroom to tuck me in. Then he stuck his hands under my nightgown and started to touch me." The only sounds besides my voice: lights buzzing, a gasp, the crinkle of a wrapper.

In the beginning, I told them, healing felt like a cruel joke. "Why did I have to live through it a second time, this time with feelings?" Heads nodded like at a revival meeting, and I always made eye contact with the woman in the audience whose head bobbed in approval the most. "It was as if I were waking up every morning with the giant letters *I-N-C-E-S-T* in my living room. I couldn't get away from it."

The whole time I was up there, an hour and a half a night, I knew I was saving lives. I knew because the women told me, "I would have killed myself if not for your book."

The Courage to Heal was a talisman. Women slept with it under their pillows. Spent months mustering the courage just to crack the spine. "I know you wrote it just for me." We heard that thousands of times. Women called it their Bible. Our post office box overflowed, some letters only addressed to *The Courage to Heal*, Santa Cruz, California, the town where Ellen was living at the time. One woman wrote that she got so enraged, she stabbed her copy of the book, and when that wasn't enough to vent her fury, she barbecued it. She assured us, "I was first in line at the bookstore the next day. I had to get a new copy."

I had no idea how to handle the weight of that responsibility.

—∾—

The moment I walked offstage, Mom's accusations pressed up from inside, but I shoved them away. Someone escorted me through the crowd to the book-signing area: a molded plastic chair and a table. Stacks of our book all around me.

I'd gone from barely paying the rent in a shared flat in San Francisco, working three part-time jobs to pay for gas, to having a bestseller and an agent booking my speeches on the road.

I'd become famous overnight for the worst thing that had ever happened to me.

—∾—

Women stood in line for me to sign their books. They often held several. One for them, one for their cousin, one for their daughter, one for their best friend. The line wound through the auditorium, and they waited patiently for their time with me, arriving with their books already open to the title page. They told me about the abuse they'd survived: "It was my stepfather." "My brother." "It happened in the car on our way to buy milk." "Then he pulled out his camera." I listened, then asked how to spell their names. I wrote a personal message to each of them. "Don't let the bastards win, Melanie." "Gina, please stick around. We can't afford to lose any more survivors. We can't afford to lose you." "Maria, the only way out is through. Hang in there. You'll make it." "In the spirit of healing, Laura Davis." They came seeking hope and to express their gratitude. I felt honored to meet them.

—∾—

Here's the part I never told anyone before:

Sometimes, the raw pain in the room was so overwhelming, it felt as if hundreds of souls were climbing on my shoulders, hoping for salvation. But I was no messiah. There was no way I could hold all that anguish. So, as I signed their books, hugged them, and reassured them, I hid my vulnerable, wounded parts deep inside me, behind a locked door.

I was the hope machine, but the hope machine was running on empty.

After the final book was signed, I climbed back into the Lincoln Town Car and rode to my hotel in silence. Alone, I ordered room service: skirt steak, a glass of red wine, chocolate cake. But I could barely taste a single bite.

After shedding my periwinkle pants, I slipped into my flannel pajamas and wiped off the makeup I wore only on the stage. As soon as the trappings of that Laura Davis were put away, a huge hole opened in my chest. Panic mushroomed in my gut. *Hold on, Laura. Hold on.*

At times like these, there was one thing I could count on: writing. As I grabbed my journal from the nightstand, a light blue envelope fell out. Addressed to me. I stared at it. Reached for it. Hesitated. This wasn't the first time I'd read it. Or the second. Or the fifth. I'd read it so many times, the creases were wearing thin. I'd promised I wouldn't do this to myself, but the letter lay on the bed, staring at me like an accusation. As I slipped the letter from its thin paper sheath, I shrank into my skin. Mom's familiar handwriting, scrawled in blue ink:

> *This is the final straw. You pile one blow on top of another on me. I have become your scapegoat for whatever is going wrong in your life. I was responsible for your father deserting you. Okay, you were a kid then. I swallowed that. Then you throw away all your academic brilliance. Another blow to swallow. Then you run away to Guru Maharaj Ji, and I become your "hated one." Then you wait for a joyous family gathering to spring your gayness on me. Gone is my motherly*

> *hope to see my daughter happily married. When I try my best to accept that, you lay on the next blow—trying to destroy the image of my dead father. Then you accuse me of not protecting you twenty-five years ago. So, I was a rotten mother even then! Keep away from me until you have something good for me. I have enough to cope with in my life without all of your shit.*

She hated me. And it wasn't just Mom. All the relatives on her side of the family had lined up against me. I'd been erased—no longer invited to weddings, holidays, bar mitzvahs. When babies were born, the birth announcements did not come.

I'd gained the world and lost my family.

I stared at the blue stationery and floated back into that Isolette where no one could touch me. I wasn't the person all those women thought I was. Not by a long shot. I was a survivor, too, and I could barely save myself. So, after those long evenings onstage, channeling Spirit or whoever it was who spoke through me those nights, I stared at the light on my hotel room wall and disappeared, just like I did as a little girl with my grandfather.

CHAPTER 4

LIFE SAVER

For the first quarter century of my life, I bragged about the great family I came from. Yes, there'd been a divorce, yes, my brother and I had joined a cult, and yes, our father had dropped out to become a hippie, but Paul and I came from a great home. Everyone said so.

Our father, Abe Davis, had been a major in the air force, stationed in France during World War II. Our mother, Temme Ross, a brainy beauty queen from an immigrant family on the Lower East Side, skipped two grades and graduated from City College of New York at nineteen. She met her future husband when her older sister married his older brother. As a teenager, Temme grew enamored of the dashing wartime photo of Abe in his military uniform. When he returned from the war, they courted and married.

My parents lived in a sixth-floor walk-up in Greenwich Village while my father studied music at NYU on the GI Bill. He became a communist, and my mother paid the bills, working as a New York City social worker. Five years later, they moved to Long Branch, New Jersey, my father's hometown, to start a family.

My father became a school band leader and music teacher. Under the baby grand piano in our living room, a dozen instruments sat ready

in their cases. When Dad's recorder ensemble met at our house, I hid at the top of the stairs in my footie pajamas, savoring baroque melodies.

Mom sang me lullabies every night, and when our family went on road trips, we sang in the car. My mother was the leading lady in our local community theater group, and when she went to rehearsal, my father dished up the veal scaloppine or hot-dog-and-bean casserole she'd left warming on the stove.

My father drew whimsical creatures and curvy designs, filling sketch pads with tiny pen-and-ink drawings and watercolor. We spent hours in the basement together, making art on the old ping-pong table. As we listened to Ella Fitzgerald and Miriam Makeba, Dad taught me to carve woodcuts and silk-screen.

I grew up in a house full of stories. My parents read to me every night, and later, I hid under the covers with a flashlight. Dad made up stories about a character named Rebopslip, and Paul invented a superhero named Frinkman who time-traveled and lived in a garbage can. We lived on a teacher's salary, but my parents invested in a brand-new set of *Encyclopedia Britannica*. In our house, education was king.

Paul and I grew up in a home with parents who loved us, wanted and planned for us. We always had a roof over our heads, clothes on our backs, food on our table. My mother helped me with homework and sewed Girl Scout badges on my sash.

—∞—

Each month, we piled into the car to drive to Manhattan to visit my mother's parents. We called it "Going to BPNY—Bubby Poppa New York." My favorite part was driving through the Holland Tunnel. The moment we entered on the New Jersey side, Paul and I had a contest to see who could hold our breath the longest. Coming out the other side, we emerged into another world. Steam billowed out of manholes in the street. Dad laughed. "The devil's having a barbecue."

The worst part was crossing the Bowery. We always got stuck there at the longest red light in the world. Men with scraggly whiskers, dirty hair, and baggy clothes lurched up to our car, spat on the windshield, and smeared it with a dirty rag, hoping for a quarter. I kept my window rolled up tight, cowering on my side of the imaginary line that divided my half of the back seat from Paul's. I couldn't wait for the light to change.

When we got to Bubby and Poppa's Lower East Side neighborhood, Mom checked and rechecked the car doors to make sure they were locked. Dad carried our big suitcase over the dirty sidewalks as I shooed pigeons out of our path. Mom called their building a tenement, a word that made me think of rats. Bad words covered the brick walls. Old ladies like Bubby talked on benches outside, wearing shapeless housedresses, black tie-up shoes, and support hose. They spoke Yiddish, which I didn't understand.

High above us, crisscrossing thc courtyard where nothing green ever grew, clotheslines poked out from windows on every floor, stitching the narrow strip of sky with a ragged web. Paul and I ran up to the building and tilted our heads back. The top was so far away, it made us dizzy.

The entrance to BPNY was solid metal, the door so heavy it took all my weight to wrench it open. When it slammed shut, it clanged. The second we got inside, I pinched my nose shut—the halls smelled like cabbage, onions, and pee.

Sometimes we took the elevator, but it was tiny, too small for four of us and a suitcase, so we usually walked up four flights. On each floor, there was a slot in the wall where people threw their garbage down into the incinerator. I imagined a big fiery monster down there—when we opened the slot, we could hear it roar.

At the end of the echoing hallway, Paul and I argued about whose turn it was to crank the doorbell—a little oblong piece of metal that made a harsh grinding sound. It took Poppa a long time to undo the bolts, the deadlock, and the chain. Standing there in the doorway with his shock of white hair, a white button-down shirt stretched over his huge belly and tucked into baggy trousers, Poppa barely tolerated our affectionate greetings. He didn't like hugging or kissing. Instead, he turned me around, reached down, and pinched my "donkey," the part of me everyone else called my *tuchus* or *tushie*. Touching my *tushie* was the way Poppa said hello. Everyone in my family thought it was funny, but my face burned. Once, my cousin and I shoved books down the back of our pants to keep Poppa's hands away. Everyone thought that was funny, too.

Bubby gave me a hug and lots of *kushenkepela*—kisses on the forehead. "So, how are you, *darlingka*?" She *kvelled* over how much I had grown and told me I was a good girl. Bubby was small and stooped and always old. Her hands, thick and transparent, like a layer of glue had been poured on them. A sparse bun captured her thin gray hair. Despite her hearing aids, Bubby still couldn't hear well. Or see very well either.

Being at Bubby and Poppa's was like visiting a museum full of unfamiliar things: books with strange letters that read from right to left. A single Yiddish newspaper strewn over a chair. Ancient sepia photos in convex frames—pictures of my great-grandparents from the Old Country. A dirty glass window latticed by metal bars. The only modern thing in the apartment was a small black-and-white TV. BPNY was a dark, serious world, with two little bedrooms, a living room, a tiny galley kitchen, and a bathroom where I accidentally burned myself on the exposed radiator. Being there was different. The smells were different. The sounds were different. Shouting voices, yowling cats, and music from transistor radios rose from the city streets below.

Bubby and Poppa were Orthodox Jews, and we weren't, which meant there were lots of rules to remember. At sunset every Friday, Bubby put a small white lace cloth on top of her head, lit the *Shabbos* candles, and sang the blessing: *"Baruch atta adonai eloheynu melech ha-olam, asher kidshanu b'mitzvo sov, vitzyvanu la hadlik ner, shel Shabbos."* Poppa stood and, swaying from the knees, chanted the *kiddush*, the ritual blessing over the wine. He sang fast. Afterward, he prayed over the *challah*, the twisted egg bread. Then Bubby tore it in pieces and handed one to each of us. It tasted like sweet yellow fluff.

Poppa was a kosher butcher, so we always had steak with potato *latkes*. While Bubby broiled the meat and grated the potatoes, Poppa yelled at her because she never did anything right.

Poppa cut the meat with a knife that was always razor sharp. At BPNY, we got to drink Pepsi with dinner, something we never had at home. After dinner, we had applesauce. Even if the dessert was something else, Poppa still called it applesauce.

As the youngest, I always went to bed first. Mom helped me into my nightgown and made me brush my teeth. After I kissed everyone goodnight, Bubby held my head in her hands and gave me a *kushenkepela*.

"Sleep well, *darlingka*." Then I headed into the back room, and Poppa came to tuck me in.

The spare bedroom, where our family slept, had twin beds pushed together, a tall wooden dresser, and a fire escape that folded up like a giant mechanical praying mantis. In front of me on the wall, an old porcelain light with a pointy bulb was lit. It was *Shabbos*, so it couldn't be turned off. That was one of the special rules.

After I climbed into bed, Poppa sat beside me. In the street below, teenagers laughed and joked in Spanish—the sounds outside always louder than the pale echo of voices from the kitchen. Pulleys screeched on squeaky wheels as mothers pulled laundry from clotheslines. Soon they'd be folding T-shirts and pants, fresh from the line.

It was story time.

In broken English, Poppa told me the story about a skunk and a railroad car. At the end, the skunk sprayed. That was the punch line. Each time he told the story, he folded the blanket back—one fold, two folds, three folds—and I sent my mind out onto the fire escape, soaring over the clotheslines. I stared at the burning light that stayed on because it was a holy time. If I stared hard enough and scrunched my eyes tight, I could forget I had a body. That way, when Poppa reached under my nightgown, I wasn't really there.

I came back as he fastened his belt and folded the blanket on top of me—three, two, one. Quiet as a stone, I watched him open the top dresser drawer to pull out our special blue roll of Life Savers. Peppermint. I opened my mouth wide, and with rough fingers, Poppa placed a single round candy on my tongue.

Paul and I each got a box of Chiclets gum when we left BPNY, but the Life Saver was special, just for me. It was our secret. Poppa never had to say, *Don't tell*. He didn't have to. The sweet melting candy was my yes. And so, I never told anyone. I never told Mom. I never told Dad. Not that night and not all the other nights. I buried the memories so far inside that I could no longer reach them.

Once the Life Saver was centered on my tongue, I closed my eyes and pretended to sleep so Poppa would go away. This part of the ritual was mine and mine alone. Lying perfectly still, I let the candy dissolve. That was my rule: Don't crunch it or bite it or crush it, even accidentally. I kept my mouth relaxed on the inside and made my tongue go slack, so the little wafer could get thinner and thinner without cracking. Swallowing was not allowed. I had to make the Life Saver last until it melted completely, but no matter how hard I tried, it always broke. Sometimes it lasted all the way till the last moment, when it was so thin, it almost disappeared, but by then there was so much saliva in my mouth that I had to swallow, and the pressure of my tongue on the roof of my mouth—even for a second—split the slight sliver in two.

—∞—

I've often wondered, What if Vicki had lived? If there had been two of us in that bed, would my whole life have been different? One girl is vulnerable. Would two have been safe? If Vicki had been with me in that back room, would I have had to drift out the window? If we'd both heard the skunk story, together in matching nighties, would he have touched us both? Even if he had, I wouldn't have been alone. With twin Life Savers on our tongues, we could have competed to see whose candy lasted longer.

But Vicki wasn't there. So, I coped as many children do, dissociating from the pain, burying the traumatic memories deep in my body where my brain couldn't find them.

Two little girls had lived inside my mother; now, two little girls lived inside me: the good one who got straight As and the broken one who hid for more than twenty years. Until one day, she came out of exile and whispered in my ear.

CHAPTER 5

AFTERSHOCK

2,179 Days

Ten minutes after Mom's call announcing her big move, Karyn and the kids burst through the front door. I pulled Karyn into the bathroom and closed the door so we could talk alone.

She looked at me, concern and exhaustion dogging her eyes. "What is it?"

"You won't believe it. Temme's moving here for good!"

"Hold on. What do you mean?"

"She put her condo on the market."

"That's great news." Karyn actually smiled. I guess I shouldn't have been surprised. I knew she loved her mother-in-law. "Can't we talk about it over dinner? Your sauce smells great."

I made no move toward the kitchen. "I don't think I can do this."

A series of expressions crossed her face: impatience, frustration, acceptance. "Laura, this was your idea. You're the one who invited her here."

"That was a dozen years ago! I never thought she'd take me up on it."

Karyn took my hand. Her grasp, warm and familiar. "You'll do just fine." But her words didn't reach the frightened child cowering inside me. "I know things were bad, Laura, but they've changed. You've got to change with them."

Easy for you to say. You're not her daughter.

Over dinner, I broke the news to the kids. Lizzy, with long straight blond hair and a tree climber's body, looked up from her plate of white food—pasta with butter and two slices of sourdough. An eager smile spread across her face. "Really? Grandma's moving here?"

Eli poked at his second serving, pushed his glasses up under a mop of straggly curls. I was still adjusting to his deep voice and the way his features had sharpened. "How long is she staying this time?"

I struggled to keep my voice light. "This isn't a visit. She's moving here for good."

Eli reached for more bread with his long, slender fingers. "Why is she coming?"

"Because she's getting old. Old people need a lot of help." Mom hadn't even left New Jersey; I had her doddering behind a walker already.

Karyn shot me a warning look and addressed the children. "Grandma Temme loves it here and wants to be near you kids."

I could see Eli calculating square footage in his head. Was he going to have to give up his room? "She's not going to live with us, is she?"

"No, Eli, definitely not." His face relaxed. He was just as relieved as I was.

A new awareness broke across Lizzy's face. "Does this mean we're not going to New Jersey anymore?"

I'd been taking the kids to the Jersey Shore to see their grandmother for two weeks every summer for as long as Lizzy could remember—eleven years. Mom's condo was at the beach, with an indoor and outdoor pool, a shuffleboard court, an elevator, snack bar, and the warm Atlantic Ocean. But every visit ended with Mom yelling and me withdrawing. The fight could start over anything: how I spoiled the children by letting them openly express their feelings; how terrible it was that we didn't have a TV; Mom commenting on Lizzy's "terrific figure."

"Grandma will be living here full-time. She won't be in New Jersey anymore." The words "full-time" felt like an anvil in my belly.

Eli chimed in. "No more Broadway shows? No more Freddie's pizza?"

Lizzy frowned. "What about Strollo's?" The best soft ice cream on the Jersey Shore.

I remembered those balmy summer nights. Three generations walking on the boardwalk with cones, ice cream dripping down our fingers. "I'll miss Strollo's, too."

"It'll be great," Karyn assured them. "Grandma will come to all your plays and events." Then she looked at me. "It *will* be great, Laura, for both of you."

I hoped she was right.

While Karyn did the dishes, Eli played his allotted hour of *World of Warcraft*, and Lizzy listened to Harry Potter cassettes, I threw on a sweatshirt and carried our portable phone out into the backyard—the only place I could speak in private. The fog had rolled in, and the temperature had dropped twenty degrees since my afternoon ritual. I sank into one of the aged Adirondack chairs that surrounded our firepit and dialed my brother's number. As I waited for him to pick up, I stared at the riot of flowers in Karyn's garden: coreopsis, lavender, and a blazing stand of orange and purple dahlias—her favorite.

I wasted no time on preliminaries. "Paul, have you talked to Mom lately?"

"Yeah, she called last night." Great. So much for "I wanted you to be the first to know."

"She didn't even ask me." I gazed over at Karyn's yurt, with its French doors and canvas walls. She used to weave rugs in it; now she used it to practice yoga.

"You and I have talked about it, Laura. We knew if Mom ever actually moved, it would be out to California."

"Yeah, well, that was theoretical."

"It *is* pretty shocking."

"It's a lot more shocking for me than it is for you."

"She'll be closer to me, too."

"C'mon, Paul. You'll still be a plane ride away. You know, I think I'd like to be that person. Maybe we should rethink this. Arizona is great for old people."

"Except I hate Arizona. I'm planning to leave."

"We had a deal, Paul."

Two decades earlier, Paul and I had gone hiking in Rocky Mountain National Park during the height of my estrangement from our mother. I'd told him there was no way I could take care of her when she got old. He'd agreed to do it. I said I'd take care of our father. And I had. I'd been there for all his heart attacks, his long, slow decline. Paul had lived a thousand miles away. "When Dad was sick, you flew in when it was convenient. Now you're going to do it again?" I stabbed at the ashy remains of my cancer notebook.

"You and Karyn are settled. You've got grandchildren Temme can still enjoy. Sonya is all grown up already. You have roots in Santa Cruz."

"Yeah, because it was as far from Mom as I could get without crossing an ocean. You've always had a better relationship with her."

"That's because our soul contract is different from yours. She's always helped me on the material plane, and I've helped her connect with spirit. That's why I incarnated as her son."

I picked up a leftover piece of kindling and jabbed the burned tip against the cement until it snapped. Paul's New Age beliefs always raised my hackles, but I was not heading down that rabbit hole. "Look, we're talking about *this* plane—who's going to take care of Mom now and for the rest of her life. The fact is, you get along with her, and I don't."

"But things are better between you now. They're good, right?"

"This isn't just a winter visit."

"You know Mom. Once she gets there, she'll get so busy with her own life, you'll hardly see her."

I swallowed hard and hugged my sweatshirt closer. "Look, Paul. I can't do this. You know our history."

"History is in the past, Laura. This is about the future. You'll be fulfilling your karmic tie with Mom. My karma with her is different." I rolled my eyes and stared out into a vibrant patch of yellow yarrow. Part of me wanted to believe him.

"Lucky you." Which sounded awfully close to "fucky you." As I gazed out at the vegetable garden, I choked up. "This is me and Mom together for the rest of her life."

"It's not like you're going to do it alone. I'm your brother. I'll be there for you."

I picked at the wood on the armrest of the chair. "You'll come when I need you?"

"Absolutely. I'll have your back."

"You promise?"

"I promise, little sister. We're in this together."

After we hung up, I stared out at the metal rooster I'd bought Karyn for her birthday. It had grown rusty. Garden art slowly disintegrating into the geraniums.

AFTER MOM'S DEATH

DISCOVERY

Two years after my mother died, I held a writers' work weekend for a dozen of my students. We holed up in a rambling home, way out in the country, where we could have uninterrupted time for creative work. Each of us defined our goals and brought what we needed, whether we were writing, rewriting, or digging through source materials. That was me—reading ancient journals and moldy correspondence.

Throughout my life, I've doggedly saved everything that documented my history: "I'm a writer. Someday I'll need this." I had no idea what I'd squirreled away, but I was writing this book, and I was determined to unearth everything connected to my mother.

The day before the retreat, after weeks—months—no, years—of procrastinating, I put on a headlamp and removed the wooden rectangle that blocks access to the hidden expanse under my office stairs. The pitch-black, musty crawl space is broad, but only a foot high; it has a rough wooden floor in places and in the farthest reaches, only dirt. It's the forgotten place where I've shoved tax receipts; medical records from my cancer; the original outline and notes for *The Courage to Heal.* One plastic box for each child, full of keepsakes they might want someday. All this and more, forgotten under the stairs—deep storage.

I rarely thought of the things in there, but once in a great while, when I needed something, I bribed one of the kids to crawl into the darkness with a flashlight. It was definitely a job for a small person who does not suffer from claustrophobia. Between the ages of seven and twelve, the kids saw it as an adventure and were willing. They did it for a dollar—later, five dollars. Now, Eli and Lizzy were grown and gone. If I wanted what was in there, I was going to have to find it myself.

I pulled on a long-sleeved shirt, a pair of jeans, and tucked my hair under a cotton bandana. I knew I'd emerge covered in bug carcasses and dust. The only way to maneuver was flat on my back, pushing off with my feet to shove my body through the darkness.

I switched on the headlamp and slid in.

I knew exactly what I was looking for: four turquoise plastic storage boxes with handwritten labels on all four sides—"Laura's Archives." Those boxes, dating back to childhood, were the deepest storage of all. My history with my mother would be recorded in those boxes. Likely, there would be a lot I didn't remember. What I'd find in those boxes, I had no idea. But finally, a few weeks shy of my sixtieth birthday, it was time to find out.

I propelled myself forward, shining my headlamp on each box in turn. Tears pressed against my eyes. *I'm too old for this. This is a fool's errand.* I slowed my breath. *You can do this. You know what you came in here for. Just find those boxes.*

I used my hands and feet to shove aside cartons I didn't want, until turquoise shone in the beam of my headlamp.

Forty-five minutes after I entered, I wedged my body back out through the portal and emerged, hair matted, clothes filthy. I ripped off the headlamp. All I wanted was a steaming bath with

Epsom salts, but first I dusted off the boxes and stacked them in the corner. Would I have the courage to open them? Was it worth the time and energy? Whatever was in those boxes was from the distant past. What difference could it possibly make now?

And what if I died tomorrow? Would I want my kids to see this stuff? To read my old journals? To be burdened by them? To learn about the humiliating love affairs and coke binges of my twenties? To read my doubts about parenting and my marriage? To see my weak, hidden places? Maybe I should just burn it all. Yet underneath the dread was curiosity.

The next morning, I carried a cloth grocery bag out to my office, grabbed eight old journals at random, and slid them into the bag. I added a torn manila envelope marked "Letters from Mom," tossed in Post-its of varying sizes, a few pens, and that was it. I had no idea what I'd just put in the bag, but this work weekend would be a good time to find out. If these notebooks and letters were all I brought, I'd have no choice but to read them.

CHAPTER 6

BEACH

2,179 Days

The night after Mom called to announce her move, I couldn't sleep. My CPAP mask—for sleep apnea—was getting old. The Velcro wouldn't stick, so a trickle of cool air kept leaking out, waking up my right eye. Karyn had a light, sweet snore going on, and we'd forgotten to pull down the shade—our neighbor's back-porch light, triggered by a marauding raccoon, streamed through the window.

On an ordinary night, I could have slept through these disturbances, but this was no ordinary night: I was going to be taking care of my mother for the rest of her life. How could I possibly sleep?

By one in the morning, I'd convinced myself that Mom's move would create the opportunity to finally build the kind of mother-daughter relationship I'd secretly wanted all my life. We'd go to the movies. The theater. She'd be a wonderful grandmother to the kids. Most important, I'd be able to dismantle the wall I'd erected decades earlier to protect myself from her—the one that kept a permanent layer of ambivalence and distance between us. With Mom in Santa Cruz permanently, we could heal our relationship the rest of the way, and I'd let down my guard for the first time since I was a teenager. Loving her would no longer be a complex minefield, but a place where I could feel safe and protected. I even imagined laying my head on her shoulder and crying in her arms, something that had been far too dangerous to consider before. And maybe right before she died, in her last moments, she'd finally acknowledge the truth about her father.

At three in the morning, I woke up in a sweat, breathing hard. Dread filled my belly. As I threw back the covers and poked my legs out, I imagined Mom's precipitous decline, her rage and unpredictability. Only this time, she wouldn't be going home to New Jersey at the end of a visit. I'd be stuck with her full-time.

My heart thudded against the walls of my chest. Sleep was out of the question.

I tiptoed out of bed, grabbed my sneakers, a joint, a lighter, my down coat, a headlamp, and half a bar of dark chocolate from the freezer. I slipped out the back door, across the railroad tracks, and walked slowly to the beach. I'd grown up a fifteen-minute walk from the Atlantic; now I lived fifteen minutes from the Pacific. That distance from Mom was intentional. It had always been intentional. Maybe the ocean would soothe me.

Breathe in, breathe out.

As my sneakers smacked against the pavement, I recalled the advice my father had once given me: "Evaluate your troubles by how far into the future they will affect you." But his wisdom couldn't help me now; my mother was staying for the rest of her life.

As I neared the ocean, the salty brine scent of seawater filled my nostrils, but I couldn't feel my feet on the ground.

I *wanted* to be a good daughter: dutiful, attentive, generous, compassionate, with a cheery sense of humor and a thick skin. I certainly wanted everyone to think I was a good daughter. But with Mom in Santa Cruz for good, I worried that I'd lose control of everything I'd worked so hard to establish: my well-ordered life with Karyn and the kids, my busy career, my reputation as a truth teller, my cherished beliefs about my virtues as a person.

I sat on the damp slats of my favorite bench and aligned my breath with the waves. Lit the joint and stared at the ocean. *What if my caregiving is a spectacular failure? Our peacemaking, a house of cards? My heart, too hard and closed to show up for her?* I'd have to face the fact that I really was the selfish, cold daughter she'd always accused me of being—a control freak who failed her dying mother because she couldn't let go of the past.

Staring at the ocean, I prayed. *Please give me what it takes to show up for her. Please, I don't know if I can love her up close without killing her. Help me become the daughter I need to be.*

I took another toke, broke off a ragged chunk of chocolate, stashed it in my cheek so its bitter sweetness might soothe me.

The waves kept coming.

CHAPTER 7

WORLD ON FIRE

Laura 13, Temme 41, New Jersey

Two weeks after I became a teenager, in August of 1969, my parents took me to Woodstock, the rock festival to end all rock festivals. It was Dad's idea; Mom was the reluctant partner. After hours in bumper-to-bumper traffic, we pitched our tent in a campground a few miles from Yasgur's farm and hiked in to hear the music. We sat in a muddy field, surrounded by people passing joints, having sex in the mud, chanting, "I've got the A. I've got the A." They were selling acid.

The next night, Mom stayed at the campground while Dad and I slogged to the festival in the pouring rain. I didn't get high while Janis Joplin sang "Ball and Chain" and Jimi Hendrix played the sunrise, but my father did. At thirteen, I wasn't a participant in Woodstock; I was an embarrassed observer. I have no memory of my parents fighting about it, but they had wildly different ideas about what was appropriate for their teenaged daughter. But more than half a century later, I still get mileage out of being able to say, "I was at Woodstock." I know Mom did, too.

That winter, before he abandoned me for college, I begged Paul to get me stoned. We climbed the rickety stairs up to the unfinished attic—Paul's pad. I wedged myself between his Fender amplifier and Jazzmaster guitar as he rolled a joint with smooth precision. He lit a match, took a deep toke, and passed it to me. "Okay, just inhale and hold it for five seconds. Then you can let it out."

I did as he told me. "Good. Now, do it again."

Pretty soon, I knew what everyone had been talking about.

Being stoned filled in the empty places, cushioned my adolescent confusion, and made me laugh. So, I started getting high with my friends.

Each morning, as I put my Thomas's corn muffin into the toaster, my parents drank their Folgers coffee, and we listened to the daily body-bag count on the radio. The endless war in Vietnam was raging, only now it had spilled over into Laos and Cambodia, with more boys being sent over every week.

More than a year since Martin Luther King had been gunned down, and the country was grieving. Bobby Kennedy had been assassinated at a campaign rally in Los Angeles. Everyone was in turmoil, and it wasn't just the hippies. Even my parents were changing. Rumors of wife swapping and marijuana wafted out of their endless cocktail parties.

To a thirteen-year-old, it was all so confusing. The world was on fire.

The following summer, Dad drove Paul to the University of Colorado and then continued west to attend an encounter group at the Esalen Institute in Big Sur, California. A month later, I got a letter from Dad, the envelope covered with whimsical drawings of imaginary creatures.

I carefully opened the envelope, leaving the art intact. A single sheet of plain white paper nestled inside:

> *Dear Laurie, I will always love you and I will always be your father, but I'm not coming back to New Jersey . . . I want to reassure you that this has nothing to do with you. I love you and miss you.*

The words "separation" and "divorce" were never mentioned, but Dad's message was clear.

An empty space opened up inside me. I knew that space, and I climbed right up inside it. It was an Isolette with smooth glass walls; when I was inside it, no one could touch me.

After Dad abandoned us to become a hippie, Mom had to pay the bills alone. She worked full-time as a school social worker, so after school, I hitchhiked home to an empty house. An hour or two later, she showed up, carrying a brown grocery bag from the A&P and a new batch of S&H Green Stamps. As she put the food away, she switched on the radio for the latest on the Vietnam War and poured herself a scotch on the rocks. While she chopped onions and sautéed mushrooms, she poured herself a second. I sat at the dining room table doing my algebra homework, dreading the clink of ice cubes I could hear beyond the open kitchen door. By the time we sat down to dinner—skirt steak, baked potato, and canned Del Monte peas, a glass of wine for her and a glass of milk for me—she was slurring her words.

I couldn't stand eating with her—the sound of her fork scraping against her teeth, the way she chewed with her mouth open. She was gross, and I hated her.

But it wasn't really hatred. I can see that now. It was terror. Was I going to lose her, too?

I wish now that I'd had empathy for what life had just handed my mother, but as a bereft fourteen-year-old, I couldn't understand her shock, her shame, her fear for our future, for *my* future. I couldn't see that everything she'd built, everything she believed in, her whole life, was in ruins. An absent husband. A son far away. A sullen, oppositional daughter. The complete devastation of her world.

I don't know how she survived it.

But Temme Davis was strong. She navigated the morass my father left behind: unpaid bills, an abandoned music studio, sixteen years of a mortgage still to be paid. My mother climbed out of her despair and built a new life. And she did it for me. She kept our sinking raft afloat and gave me something I desperately needed: someone it was safe to hate.

CHAPTER 8

DR. ASSHOLE

2,152 Days

A month after Mom's announcement, my cell phone headset buzzed as I drove up to my Wednesday morning writing class. Mom immediately launched into a rant. "I went to see Dr. Gabel for my annual exam. I'm a perfect specimen. Well, maybe I could lose a few pounds, but other than that, I'm in excellent health. The only time I've ever been in the hospital was to give birth to you and Paul . . ."

"Mom . . . MOM! I'm on my way to work. My class starts in five minutes." It actually started in twenty, but if I said that, she'd still be talking while my students lined up at the door. As I grabbed my tote, Mom kept yammering in my ear, but I wasn't listening. I hustled through the garden that surrounded the idyllic spot where I'd been teaching for years. A pond with koi and turtles and a fountain. A walking labyrinth.

Inside, the brown industrial rug was speckled with debris. I grabbed the vacuum and made a quick pass over the floor in long broad strokes. The sucking sound drowned out Mom's voice, but she continued undeterred. "I must have mentioned a little something about my memory: 'I'm getting a little forgetful, but it's just normal aging.'"

Once Mom started a story, she never stopped until she reached the end. As I reviewed my lesson plan and set up our circle, Mom kept right on talking. "Dr. Gabel sent me to a specialist . . ." That word got my attention. I listened more closely as I freshened the teas.

". . . a so-called neurologist." She spat out the word as if it were a piece of spoiled meat.

I arranged my students' name tags in alphabetical order: Carolina. Joanie. Melissa . . . "Slow down. What happened?"

"I went to see this guy, a fucking quack. He should lose his license. I should sue him!"

Pam. Tony. Valerie . . . "Just tell me what happened."

"I was in his office no more than ten minutes, and he had the gall to tell me I have Alzheimer's disease."

I froze, Vicky's name tag in my hand. "He said what?"

"Ten minutes! He barely talked to me. He had some nerve. Yes, I'm a little forgetful. So what? Everyone my age is forgetful. I should call the AMA and file a complaint!"

Alzheimer's disease? No. "Oh, Mom . . ."

I'd noticed Mom's memory getting worse, but Paul hadn't seen a change, and Karyn thought it was just normal aging. But I'd been worrying for a while. Still—ten minutes for a diagnosis? Maybe the doctor was wrong. He had to be. Mom's moving here was one thing. But Alzheimer's?

"I had to drive home alone with those horrible words pounding in my head."

"I'm sorry, Mom. The guy's an asshole. He never should have done that to you."

"Yeah, Dr. Asshole!"

"Dr. Asshole is right."

My first students were crossing the labyrinth. "I'm sorry, Mom, but I've got to go. I'll call you after class."

Half an hour later, when my students were deep into writing, the word "Alzheimer's" kept ringing in my head. I cursed Dr. Asshole. Whether he was right or not wasn't the point. What kind of irresponsible jerk was he? To just drop a bomb on Mom like that.

Mom never brought up Dr. Asshole again, but he galvanized her move to California. She felt increased urgency, and so did I. I had to move her now while she still had the capacity to build a new life.

CHAPTER 9

INITIATION

Laura 15, Temme 43, New Jersey

Soon after I started tenth grade, Paul called from Colorado. Mom grabbed the phone in the kitchen. I raced upstairs to the extension. I couldn't wait to hear what my big brother had to say.

Paul had big news: he'd become a *premie*, a follower of Guru Maharaj Ji, a thirteen-year-old Indian spiritual master. Paul was quitting college and going to India to "realize God." And by the way, could he and his friends stay with us in New Jersey for a few days on their way to Delhi?

Mom was horrified, but I was oblivious to her anguish. All I knew was that Paul was coming home, and I couldn't wait to see him. Whatever my big brother was into had to be really cool.

Paul and his *premie* friends wore white flowing clothes and were vegetarians. They cooked white blobby stuff called tofu, ate brown rice, and grew alfalfa sprouts in glass jars. They were "blissed out," their term for the joy of "practicing Knowledge." They told me all about Guru Maharaj Ji and the path of *satsang*, service, and meditation. They glowed.

The best part was that Paul no longer treated me like a kid sister who was in the way. He listened to me. Cared about my happiness.

Looking at me with those earnest blue eyes of his, he said, "You've got to learn to meditate, Laura. There's more to life than high school and getting stoned with your friends."

Two months later, Paul and his friends returned from India and stayed for a week. Each night, as soon as Mom fell asleep, I tiptoed to the living room to hear Paul play devotional rock and roll and to listen to *satsang*, their nightly discourses about Guru Maharaj Ji.

Paul's conviction that he had found the answer felt like the perfect solution to my own confusion—my father's abandonment, my mother's despair, the turmoil of the times.

Each morning, I put on my jeans, grabbed my peacoat, gathered my books, and walked to school. I looked the same on the outside, but Paul's certainty had ignited a flame. I was determined to join his spiritual family.

—∞—

That winter, a friend of Mom's invited us to attend a talk by one of Guru Maharaj Ji's closest disciples who was speaking at an auditorium in Elizabeth, New Jersey, an hour away. Mom declined, but I was eager to attend.

The hall was packed. A chair draped in white satin featured a large headshot of Guru Maharaj Ji in a gilded frame, festooned with flowers. Young Americans, women wearing long cotton skirts, red dots called *tilaks* painted on their foreheads, and men wearing white wrap-around skirts called *dhotis*, bowed down in front of the picture, lit candles, and recited prayers in Hindi. The featured speaker, Mahatma Fakiranand, was an old bald Indian man, wrapped in saffron. His accent was so thick, I could barely understand him, but I was mesmerized by the focused energy and love in the room. At the end of the night, one of the *premies* said, "If you want to receive this precious Knowledge, come back at eight tomorrow morning." I jotted the address on a scrap of paper and shoved it into the pocket of my jeans.

That night, I cracked open my piggy bank, counted out train fare, called my best friend, revealed my plan, and made her promise not to tell. At five o'clock the next morning, I crept downstairs, walked a mile to the train station, bought a round-trip ticket to Elizabeth, and hitch-hiked the rest of the way.

Two *premies* ushered me into the basement for the Knowledge Session. The room had dark paneling and an orange shag carpet. The only furniture was the satin-covered chair. Four dozen aspirants sat cross-legged, crammed together in the dark, windowless space. I was the youngest person in the room.

In a heavy Hindi accent, Mahatma Fakiranand spoke. "Humanity cries out for peace and happiness. Unless our mind is tranquil, it will not attain perfect calm. The mind is so dark, so restless, it cannot find the way to save itself. That is why the Perfect Master comes to the Universe." As he spoke, I didn't dare unfold my legs. My feet went numb.

Mahatma Fakiranand's first task was to weed out those who weren't ready. He questioned each of us individually and kicked out almost everyone. "Go hear more *satsang*." "Do service in the *ashram*. Come back later." Everyone else had attended *satsang* dozens of times. I was definitely not going to make the cut.

When it was my turn, I told Mahatma Fakiranand that my big brother lived in the *ashram*. When I said I was only fifteen, he replied, "That makes you the most pure." As a final test, he had me prostrate myself in front of Guru Maharaj Ji's photo. I lay flat on my belly, arms stretched in front of me like a racing dive. As the synthetic strands of shag carpet tickled my lips, he asked, "Would you cut your head off for Guru Maharaj Ji?"

Every cell in my body vibrated in affirmation. "Yes, I would cut my head off for Guru Maharaj Ji." I wanted to be blissed out like Paul and his friends.

After we swore our allegiance, Mahatma Fakiranand had us sit in the half-lotus position and close our eyes. He touched each of us on the third eye, in the middle of our forehead. This was the actual moment of receiving Knowledge, when he transmitted *prana*, divine energy, from Guru Maharaj Ji to us. When he pressed my third eye with his long, bony finger, I saw a flashing black-and-white checkerboard in front of my closed eyes—the divine light Paul had been talking about.

Mahatma Fakiranand taught us four sacred, secret meditation techniques so we could see Divine Light, hear Divine Music, taste

Divine Nectar, and hear the Holy Word of God. If we wanted to realize God, he told us, we had to meditate two hours every morning and two hours every night and attend *satsang* every evening. How the hell was I supposed to do that and still make tenth-grade honor roll?

When the Knowledge Session was over, I stepped out into a deep night sky. I had no idea receiving Knowledge would take so long. Someone gave me a ride to the train station, and I didn't get home till after ten. Mom was at the kitchen table, her face mottled, mascara tracks on her cheeks. My best friend had ratted me out.

Mom stared at me with bleary, anguished eyes. "Now I've lost everyone! First your father, then your brother, and now you!"

But her recriminations couldn't touch me. I'd received Knowledge and didn't have to get caught up in her drama anymore. "You're not losing us, Mom. You're only suffering because of your attachment to the material world." I sprinted upstairs to my room. It was time to meditate.

She shouted at my retreating back. "You have no idea what my life is like!"

And I didn't have to.

Three years later, I moved into Guru Maharaj Ji's City of Love and Light in San Antonio, Texas. One hundred and twenty of us—including Paul—lived on three floors of the Gunter Hotel. We took vows of poverty, chastity, and obedience, meditated for an hour every morning and night, signed over our paychecks, and got two dollars spending money a week. I was assigned to the kitchen crew.

One morning, after scraping four industrial-sized trays of warm granola into storage tubs, I sat down with a shot of wheatgrass juice and composed the following letter:

> *Dear Mom,*
>
> *I just want you to know that Guru Maharaj Ji is my true father, and Mata Ji—his mother—is my true mother. You and Dad are just my worldly parents.*

> *Thanks for everything you've given me. You gave me life, and I couldn't practice Knowledge without a precious human body. But I want to be sure you understand that you're not really my mother. I am a child of God.*

I put it in an envelope, slapped on an eight-cent stamp, and mailed it that very afternoon.

—∾—

When I look back at my years as a devotee of Guru Maharaj Ji, I see a young girl in an upside-down world, looking for absolute answers. A daughter desperate to escape a controlling mother. An incest survivor growing up in the "Why Don't We Do It in the Road?" generation who needed a safe place to live where sex wasn't a constant casual proposition. Genuine spiritual hunger was also part of the equation. The fact that my unconventional choice made Mom apoplectic only made it sweeter, though I'd never have admitted it at the time.

I left the *ashram* at twenty-one. I'd been happy there, but the rules and constraints that had once protected me started to chafe. Lots of *premies* left the *ashram* when I did. They still loved Guru Maharaj Ji but wanted greater freedom. They aspired to practice Knowledge *and* have relationships. But it was more than that for me. In Maharaj Ji's world, thinking for yourself, what we called "being in your mind," was frowned upon. Wanting to do more than menial work was discouraged. And there was something inside of me that needed to flower. I just wasn't cut out to be a follower.

When I left the *ashram*, the spiritual "family" I'd passionately embraced ostracized me. It was a jarring and devastating loss.

Later, I tried to explain my feelings in a letter to Paul:

> *I've been feeling guilty that I haven't been in touch, like I'm your last ally from your past and I'm betraying you. I love you but cannot relate to what means everything to you: the guru. I've deprogrammed myself*

> *to the point where seeing you still in the premie trip makes me very grateful I escaped.*

Initially, Paul was part of the exodus from the ashram, too, but his experiment with worldly freedom was short-lived. Six months after he left, he returned to the fold and remained devoted to Guru Maharaj Ji for years to come. It felt like Paul was another beloved thing I had lost. Our diverging paths led me to judge him harshly and view him with disdain. Two years later, I wrote to him:

> *You write to me, but in effect you've cut me out of your life, because the only way I can enter your world is through your perspective. Do you really think that those of us not practicing Knowledge are walking in darkness? I'm angry that my one and only brother is inaccessible to me. I've shared things with you I've never even come close to sharing with anyone else, and I resent strongly that we'll probably never manifest that closeness again.*

It wasn't until he reached his thirties that Paul left the *ashram*, went to acupuncture school, married Ingrid, a former *premie*, and had a daughter, my niece, Sonya. But by then, the closeness we had once shared had been lost.

CHAPTER 10

ANXIETY

2,140 Days

In the months leading up to Mom's move, there was always a new crisis. The more anxious she became, the more I retreated into List mode: fake, flat, and reassuring. I focused on the endless tasks that had to be completed before her arrival. Then I called my brother. "Can you help Mom at her end?"

"It's not the best time for me, but yeah, I can fly to New Jersey next week."

Paul hired movers, closed out Mom's affairs, did everything he could to expedite the sale of her condo. He was as resourceful and dogged as I was; when he showed up, things got done. Doing was a family trait.

Despite my efficiency, I was falling apart. It started in small ways: stopping for a ginger cookie on my way home from class, then a brownie later, snapping at the kids, reaching for a joint. The kids gravitated toward Karyn. I spent evenings at the dining room table, head buried in my laptop, exuding my *How dare you bother me?* vibe. I barely acknowledged Bryan, Karyn's adult son, when he dropped by to visit. When Karyn tried to tell me about her latest breakthrough in her yoga practice, I stared right through her. She spent more time out in the yurt, practicing headstands. When it was time for bed, I turned my back on her, and she turned her back on me. I lived in my "doing" bubble.

—m—

After her condo sold, Mom's panicked calls increased. Each time, I talked her down off the ledge. I had to; she'd already signed the papers. But it was more than that. I'd promised myself I wouldn't become one of those daughters flying across the country every month to tend to an aging parent.

When Mom finally told her friends that she was moving, they gave her a series of going-away parties. The folk-dance club. The theater troupe. The storytelling group. Her friends from Shakespeare class. The psychodramatists. Her old friends. Her new friends. Her travel buddies. Her former colleagues from the Neptune Township Child Study Team.

One night, she called, sobbing. "I can't leave New Jersey. But I have to. People have given me all these going-away parties. I can't change my mind now. What would they think of me?"

The next day, she bought a one-way plane ticket to California.

When her flight confirmation hit my inbox, a ribbon of anxiety unfurled in my chest. The next morning, adrenaline shocked me awake at 3:00 a.m. I slipped four tablets of a homeopathic sleep aid under my tongue. Nothing. Twenty minutes later, I reached for the Ativan, left-over from chemo, and broke off half. Thirty minutes later, I took the other half. And then a whole. Nothing. I flipped the covers off. Flipped them on. I tried to slow my breathing, inhaling for the count of four, exhaling for the count of six. But nothing could touch my anxiety. Still, I didn't wake Karyn. She had to face 125 high school students in the morning. She was about to retire, and her last year teaching was hard enough already.

That's what I told myself, but the real reason I didn't wake Karyn was that I'd forgotten who she was to me. I'd forgotten I had a spouse who loved me.

CHAPTER 11

PRIDE

Laura 23, Abe 61, San Francisco

The day I told my father I was a lesbian, he congratulated me. That June, and every June after that, until he was too sick to do it anymore, he marched with me in the San Francisco Gay Pride Parade. The first year we marched together, 1980, it was me and Dad and his partner, Ophelia.

Dad had a metal shopping cart that he'd "liberated" from Safeway. It sat in the back corner of his space at Project Artaud, the artists' live-work community he'd helped to found. That first Gay Pride day, he got up early, bought a bunch of brightly colored helium-filled balloons, and tied them around the top edge of the cart. He set his giant conga drum inside, and the three of us took turns pushing the cart from Sixteenth and Alabama all the way to Market Street to join the parade, clacking the wheels over asphalt and lifting them over trolley tracks. The bright balloons ricocheted off each other in the early-summer breeze like popcorn popping in a pan.

As we approached Market Street, the crowds grew: men in flouncy pink dresses and size-thirteen stilettos; Dykes on Bikes, femme girlfriends riding on the back of their Harleys; leathermen in chaps and studs, asses bare; Cheer San Francisco, tossing their lightest members up in the air and catching them inches above the sidewalk; submissives wearing studded dog collars, whip marks striping their backs. We pushed Dad's cart through it all.

Cymbals crashed, and the drumming of Sistah Boom filled the air. A truck blared "I Will Survive" as twenty bodies gyrated on a flatbed. A lone man quoted scripture on a downtown corner, drowned out by the clickety-clack of high heels, the clanging of cable-car bells, the jingle of tambourines. Escalators on Market Street disgorged gay teachers, gay police officers, gay nurses, gay accountants, gay prostitutes, gay athletes, gay social workers, gay secretaries, gay plumbers, taxi drivers, and judges. Everyone was out, and celebration was in the air. Gay Pride was on.

Ophelia, Dad, and I pushed the cart to the staging area for our contingent—Parents and Friends of Lesbians and Gays. PFLAG was a tiny group back then, but we were more powerful than the loudest disco truck and the largest marching band. Thousands of people stood on either side of Market Street, watching the parade, and when we walked by, Dad beating his big drum, they wept. Gay people flee to San Francisco after being beaten, harassed, kicked out of their homes. They arrive by the tens of thousands to the gay mecca by the Bay to create new lives, carrying the same primal wound—rejection by their families. Six rows deep, filling the sidewalks on both sides, they cheered for us and cried, a mile-long standing ovation for Dad and me and the other members of our tiny band, marching proudly down the street. Roaring applause followed us all the way to the Embarcadero. And at the end of the parade, after the speeches and ice cream, we heaved Dad's shopping cart all the way back through the city, over trolley tracks, discarded flyers, sequins, and glitter—until next year.

Four months after I came out to my father, I came out to my mother. We were in Miami Beach for a huge family party celebrating my grandfather's ninetieth birthday—four years before I remembered his abuse. I'd flown in from California; Mom from New Jersey. It was one of the rare times we'd be together in person.

Over a tray of tiny hot dogs speared with cellophane-flagged toothpicks, I approached her. “Can we take a walk?”

She spoke through a mouthful of hot dog. “Now? You want to go for a walk now? In the middle of the party?”

“There’s something I need to tell you.”

“What’s the matter?”

I looked around at the relatives all around us. “Let’s take a walk.”

Mom’s voice rose. “Oh my God. What is it?”

“It won’t take long.” I headed through the backyard toward the railroad tracks. She followed.

Shit. Why did I think my grandfather’s birthday party was the right time to come out to my mother? Because it had to be done in person, and this was my only opportunity. Because I wanted her to stop asking me whether I had a boyfriend. Because I couldn’t stand having my whole life feel like a lie.

As Mom stepped over the rails to follow me, fear wafted off her tightly coiled body. What was she thinking? Abortion? Cancer? *Just say it, Laura.*

“Mom, I’m a lesbian.” *Oh my God, I said it.*

Disgust and rage fought for supremacy in her eyes. “You’ve confirmed my worst fear about you.”

I gave her my best death glare. Then I clammed up, just like always, but she was too far into her anguished monologue to notice. “You’ll never have children! You’re going to live a lonely life in a dingy bar!” She carted out every stereotype about being a dyke. She spat out the words, “Now I’ll never have grandchildren.”

I pivoted on the crooked wooden tie. Broken glass and debris littered the space between us. “This isn’t about you!”

“Maybe it’s just a stage. Maybe you haven’t met the right man. You can still have a normal life.” Mom reached across the rail for my hand, and I yanked it away. She looked stricken, as if I’d slapped her. *Good!*

“You think I’m prejudiced, but I’m not. I don’t think there’s anything wrong with homosexuals. I lived in Greenwich Village. Your father and I had homosexual friends. He was a communist, for God’s sake. I’m very open-minded. People can do whatever they want behind closed doors. I just don’t want you leading an unhappy, miserable life.”

Then she exploded. “How dare you do this to me, today of all days. It’s my father’s ninetieth birthday!”

We stared at each other over the dirty tracks. Then we went back to the party, and neither of us said a word. She helped the little kids put on skits about my grandfather’s life. We ate bagels and cake and sang “Happy Birthday” to him. He would only live for another year.

I couldn’t wait for that charade of a party to end.

CHAPTER 12

PERFECT LANDING

2,124 Days

At De Anza Mobile Home Park, I found an older unit that Mom could afford. She wired the money, and the manager handed me the key. De Anza was an age-fifty-five-plus community, though most of the residents were Mom's age, eighty and above. There were social activities, a clubhouse, bridge games, tai chi, a hot tub, and a swimming pool. A meandering road through the park led to a gazebo overlooking the Pacific. A creek ran through the place, complete with a resident swan. Mom's unit was old but serviceable. Empty, the place looked dingy, but once Karyn and I filled it with Mom's colorful art from around the world, it would be transformed. The space was just right for one person who loved to entertain: two bedrooms, a living room, two bathrooms, a washer and dryer, and a kitchen with a lime-green island. I had the place painted and the carpets deep cleaned. Most of the stains came out; her couch and bed would cover the rest.

Checking things off The List kept me too busy to feel. The moving van and Mom's car arrived the week before she did, just the way I'd planned it. That weekend, Karyn and I set up Mom's things. We uncrated the bed frame and the carved wooden headboard Mom had bought in Mexico. We made up the bed, strategically arranging the orange and turquoise throw pillows in diamonds on the white expanse. Her small TV went on top of her heavy wooden dresser. I ordered cable. The remote found its place on the bedside table, tucked next to a brightly colored Mexican table lamp.

We set up her couch and chairs, glass coffee table, and big TV. I carefully opened the giant box of masks, which she'd collected on her travels. Karyn and I spent an hour mounting them on the wall, positioning them perfectly.

Mom loved her masks—the ones on the wall and the ones she wore every day. I wore my share of masks, too. Most of them, I hoped, were invisible.

Karyn and I transformed the tiny open area beside the kitchen into an office. We pushed the heavy wooden desk against the wall to make room for Mom's old recliner, where she loved to nap, read the *New York Times*, and do the crossword puzzle. I'd ordered a *Times* subscription to start the day before her arrival. We stacked the boxes of artwork against the living room wall and shoved the rest of her cartons into the spare bedroom. Everything for the kitchen we stashed along one wall; I wanted to set that up with Mom.

The place looked great, but was I ready?

2,109 DAYS

The night before Mom's flight was due to arrive, I walked through Safeway in a trance, buying her favorite foods, toilet paper, and dish soap. I brought over an old radio, tuned it to NPR. Folded the *New York Times* open to the crossword puzzle, set it on her chair, and placed a blue ballpoint pen—Mom's favorite writing implement—beside it.

At midnight, when I finally climbed into bed, Karyn set down her book and turned to face me. "How are you doing?"

"We got it all done. I think we're ready."

"I asked, 'How are *you* doing?'"

"Fine, I'm just fine." My whole body was buzzing, and I couldn't imagine how I was ever going to sleep.

"But how are you *feeling*, Laura?"

I couldn't dig deeper than my press release. "Mom and I are in a great place now. We've worked really hard for this moment."

"Laura, you're talking to *me*."

I looked at her warm face peering at me from her pillow—and actually saw her for the first time in days. A wall cracked open inside me. "I'm scared. I don't know if I can do this—if I can really take care of her."

Karyn stretched a welcoming arm across the pillows. I snuggled in. Her body felt warm, and she smelled like home. I let her slow breathing steady mine.

2,108 DAYS

By five o'clock the next morning, I had a pot of homemade chicken soup simmering on the stove. Slipping back into bed, I savored Karyn's warm embrace. Three hours later, I dropped the kids at school, drove over to Mom's place to put half a pot of soup in the fridge, and stuck a Post-it note with a heart on the lid.

I was seated with my students by 9:00 a.m. I'm sure they read their work to me, and I'm sure I responded, but I was teaching on autopilot, hovering just outside my body.

At noon, I headed to the airport with a bag of pistachios, Mom's favorite. I tried to read a novel at the gate, but my eyes slid over the words. I got up and paced, scanning each new group of arrivals.

When she finally strode through the gate, Mom wore blue silky slacks, patent leather flats, and a boxy light turquoise jacket adorned with colorful batik animals. Dyed-blond hair framed her face. She carried a shiny blue pocketbook in one hand and a copy of the *New York Times Magazine* section in the other.

"Laurie, it's so good to see you!" She grabbed me in a tight bear hug. Stiffly, I placed my arms around her, counted one Mississippi, two Mississippi, three Mississippi, and let go.

My loving preparations had just collided with my long-practiced fears.

"Laurie, I can't believe I did it. I'm actually here."

"Welcome to California, Mom. We've got everything set up for you."

Before we headed to the car, I excused myself, went to the bathroom, locked myself in a stall, and texted Karyn. "Mom has landed. ETA 4:30."

She texted back. "I'll bring the kids. Should I get takeout?"

"Yes, please. How about Chinese?"

—∞—

On the drive back to Santa Cruz, we chatted as Mom cracked pistachios with her teeth. I told her about the black belts the kids were earning in Korean martial arts, and my fantasy of leading a writers' tour to Bali. I gave her the latest news on Bryan, whom she was belatedly acknowledging as my stepson. "And Karyn's really going for it as a yoga teacher. I'm so proud of her." As we got closer to town, we moved on to the news: the latest on Obama's transition team. Mom was a lifelong Democrat and a proud poll worker. For us, politics was always a safe topic of conversation.

As I pulled into her driveway, the siding on her mobile home suddenly looked shabby. I hoped she wouldn't notice. *Please, let this be enough for her.*

I unlocked the front door and let Mom walk in first. Her eyes took in the couch and the lamps, the fresh paint, and her masks showcased on the wall. I held my breath. She started to cry.

She hates it. I should have known I'd never make her happy.

"Oh, Laurie . . ." *Shit. Here it comes.*

She turned to me. "Darling, I can't believe what you've done for me!" A warm smile radiated from her face.

My next breath went deeper. I snapped back into my body. The worry in my belly disappeared. "Karyn and I did it. Together."

"I *love* my daughter-in-law." When Mom said those words, I wanted to skip. I felt like a little girl bringing home straight As.

"Come see the rest of it."

Mom took her time, savoring every detail. She oohed and aahed over the food in the fridge. Loved the Post-it heart. Laughed when she saw the crossword puzzle and the waiting pen. Smiled at her old familiar desk, the pillows set just so, her beloved headboard and lamps. "Darling, I can't believe you did all this for me."

"It's like I've been telling you. We wanted you to come."

—∞—

Karyn and the kids arrived with dinner. We ate on paper plates, then got to work. Karyn planted a winter garden in the flower boxes out front. Eli, a high school sophomore with a technological bent, had Mom's new router connected in minutes. Soon her AOL account was up and running, and emails that had accumulated during her long day of travel were pouring in—friends from New Jersey checking in. Lizzy, soon to be twelve, was into toiletries—she organized the bathroom. Mom and I put away her clothes. She told Eli where she wanted her artwork; he hammered in the hooks and hung the pictures, while the rest of us shouted, "A little higher on the right." Eli gave Mom a beautiful origami rose he'd folded from one of his special sheets of handmade paper. I helped Mom unpack the kitchen. She put everything in the same spots I would have chosen.

By the time we broke down the boxes, it was after 9:30 p.m. We left Mom in bed with the TV on, exhausted but grateful. "Thank you, darling. Thank you, all of you. I never could have done it without you."

By the time we got home, Tiger, Lizzy's cat, was meowing frantically for his supper. Karyn didn't have her lesson plans ready for the next day, and neither did I. Stacks of dirty laundry teetered in the bathroom, Eli was going to be up till 1:00 a.m. doing AP Chemistry homework, and Lizzy had an English essay due that would take at least an hour. But Mom's walls were brilliant with art, and her flower boxes were planted. She was watching *Charlie Rose*, and her answering machine was ready for all the new friends she was about to make.

CHAPTER 13
WHIPLASH

2,107 Days

The next morning, I was jarred awake by a call at 5:00 a.m. I ripped off my CPAP mask and reached for the phone. Why hadn't I turned off the ringer? *I guess I won't be turning it off for a long time to come.*

Mom's voice burned in my ear. "Laurie, I'm calling the airlines right now. I have to go back to New Jersey!" So much for Grateful Mom.

Karyn opened one eye and looked at me, a concerned expression on her face. "It's just Mom," I mouthed. I slipped out of bed and carried Mom into the living room. She was deep into her rant.

"It's not just that. The garbage trucks have been beeping for hours. And this place doesn't smell right."

I grabbed The List from the dining room table. At the top, circled, were the words "8:15 Pick up Mom: Bank."

"Mom, it's five in the morning. You just woke me up. You woke Karyn up."

"Well, it's eight o'clock in New Jersey. I've been up for hours. I waited as long as I could." Her harsh voice tore a hole in the morning.

I ran my fingers over the edge of the deep purple couch cushion. The zipper was exposed, the pillow facing the wrong way. I flipped it around, so the zipper wouldn't show. I rubbed sleep from my eyes and sighed. "Mom, what's the matter?"

"What do you mean, what's the matter? I've left behind everyone I care about. I'll never see my sisters again. I'll never see Ruth. I'll never see Bea. How could I abandon them like that? I'm a terrible sister."

As Mom's emotions flared, mine flattened. I withdrew and put on my "Good Daughter" mask. Modulating my voice, I spoke to Mom in smooth, soothing tones. "You just arrived. It's going to take time. It's natural to have doubts. Why don't you turn on NPR? Make yourself an English muffin?"

"How can I make myself an English muffin? There's no toaster in this place!"

Good Daughter placated the raging tiger. "We'll buy you a new toaster." *Breathe in, breathe out. She's scared, that's all.* "Why don't you get dressed, take a walk down to the ocean? I'll pick you up after I drop the kids at school. I'm taking you to the bank this morning."

Mom's panic deflated as fast as it had come. "Thanks, darling. I forgot. You're so good to me."

Whiplash again.

CHAPTER 14

DINNER PARTY

Laura 15, Temme 43, New Jersey

When I was in tenth grade, Mom asked me to help her prepare a dinner party for some women from work I didn't know. I said yes. I loved cooking with Mom. We'd been doing it ever since I was a little girl, me perched on a step stool, licking the beaters and learning to crack the eggs. I loved the smell of cookies baking in the oven, onions and garlic frying in a pan. Mom taught me how to make meat loaf and spaghetti sauce from scratch, and by the time I was a teenager, I'd become the family baker. We pirouetted through the kitchen together, fluid, like dancers.

Our menu that day featured beef stroganoff and French onion soup. I cooked the filling for a lemon meringue pie; Mom made the graham cracker crust. While I trimmed green beans, she tossed salad. Together, we added leaves to the dining room table. I steadied the chair while she climbed up to reach the fancy white dishes with silver edges. I ironed her best blue tablecloth and matching cloth napkins. As a centerpiece, she set out the papier-mâché candleholders I'd made in art class. "Laurie, they look so pretty!"

Mom artfully arranged mixed nuts, Boursin cheese, and Triscuits on the coffee table. I wiped the ashtrays with a damp paper towel.

An hour before her guests were due to arrive, Mom went upstairs to "put on her face" and change. "Laurie," she called down, "put on something nice." I chose my peasant blouse with blue embroidery on the yoke. Mom said it brought out the color of my eyes.

As she chatted up her guests in the living room, I poured soup into matching bowls, laid slabs of Swiss on top, and slid them under the flames of the broiler. Two minutes later, I pulled them out, perfectly gooey and brown, just as Mom rushed into the kitchen. "Those look terrific!" As she praised me, her eyes scanned me head to toe. She tucked my long blond hair behind my ears, spat on her thumb, and wiped something off my cheek. I winced.

Mom carried out the first steaming bowl of soup, and I carried out the second. She beamed at her guests. "This is my darling daughter, Laurie. She made these candlesticks."

I blushed and looked down, scurried back to the kitchen. Thankfully, she hadn't forced me to join them, to make small talk with a roomful of adults I didn't know. I happily ate in the kitchen as laughter filled the dining room.

Through the doorway, I heard Mom roll out a story from her vast repertoire in a breathy, excited voice. I'd heard her tell it exactly the same way a hundred times. But now she had a brand-new audience, laughing in all the right places.

When it was time for dessert, Mom came in to get the pie. "Laurie," she whispered, "they *love* everything!" I followed her out with dessert plates and forks. As I headed back toward the kitchen, she called out, "Laurie?" When I didn't turn around, she spoke louder. "Come here." It wasn't a request, but I was probably the only one in the room who could tell.

I shoved my hands into my apron pocket, slowly turned, and faced her.

"Come on over," she said. "I won't bite." She smiled broadly, but I could feel her reeling me in. I shuffled closer but kept my distance. She reached out and grabbed my wrist, pulling me until I was standing right beside her. She surveyed her friends. "Do you know what Laurie did?" *Oh no. Not again.* I started to pull away, but her fingers tightened around my wrist.

"Laurie won first place at the speech arts festival!" The women around the table started to cluck. They beamed at Mom. She glowed, drinking in their approval. "Laurie won for dramatic interpretation."

I'd asked her not to do this. I'd asked her not to a hundred times.

Mom grinned at her friends. "We all know where she gets her talent from!"

I tried to pull away again, but her grip tightened.

"Laurie, why don't you do your monologue?" It sounded like a question, but the pressure on my wrist told me otherwise. "I'm sure they'd all love it."

I muttered, "I don't want to."

She turned to her guests. "Wouldn't you love to see Laurie perform?"

There were murmurs of encouragement around the table. "Oh, that would be wonderful."

"If you're half as talented as your mother . . ."

All those eyes staring at me, lipsticked mouths open in anticipation. I stared out the window at the big hedge that boxed in our yard. Then I glanced at Mom, hoping for a reprieve. The smile never left her face, but her eyes bore into mine.

I was hovering somewhere outside my body.

The best thing to do was to just get it over with. I'd practiced my speech so many times, the words came out easily. I hit the right inflections and paused in the right places, but my voice echoed through a hollow tunnel.

The next thing I knew, they were clapping.

"That was wonderful!"

"You're right, Temme—she's a chip off the old block."

Mom beamed, soaking in their praise. "Of course, I was her coach."

I gave her my best evil eye and stormed into the kitchen.

"Laurie, come back here!" Mom called. "Come out and take a bow."

No. I took my apron off and threw it on the ground. I'd never stood up to her like that before. *I won't.*

Through the open doorway, Mom apologized for my poor behavior. "I don't know what's gotten into her. Teenagers. They think only of themselves."

An hour later, as we cleaned the kitchen, Mom recounted the high points of the evening. I remained silent, jamming dishes into the dishwasher while she scrubbed the pots and pans. I didn't look up. I didn't smile at her jokes. My back remained stiff. I was done performing. I whispered under my breath, "Why did you do that?"

"What, darling?"

I wanted to say never mind, forget it, but the truth was burning inside me. "Why did you make me do that?"

"I don't know what you're talking about."

"My monologue."

"What about it? You were terrific."

I spoke a little louder. "Mom, you made me perform."

"That's crazy. I did no such thing."

"You squeezed my arm."

"Laurie, I barely touched you. You're imagining things."

"I am not." I rubbed the sore place on my wrist. "You made me do it."

"Nonsense." Mom's mouth thinned, and her voice radiated certainty. "You *wanted* to perform for those people. Laurie, you're as big a ham as I am."

I knew it. I never should have said anything.

Mom took a step closer until all I could see was her face. "All I did was give you a little encouragement. You wanted to do it."

My head started spinning. Was she right? Everyone needs encouragement.

"Actually, Laurie, you're the one who embarrassed me. Miss Big Shot gets up in front of a whole auditorium but won't take a bow in her own house? Why did you hide in the kitchen like that? That was very selfish of you."

I looked down at the apron, still wadded up on the floor.

Mom squeezed the sponge dry and dropped it in the sink. "Look; it's late. You were a big help today. Let's put this behind us. I forgive you."

That night in bed, I went over the evening again. How I felt in the dining room. Her request. Their applause. That strange floaty feeling.

The pressure of her thumb on my wrist. But everything had gone fuzzy. None of it made sense.

—∞—

I grew up certain that I was crazy—that Mom was right, and I was wrong. Underneath the idyllic exterior, a broad wash of confusion covered the canvas of my life. I had no language for it; I knew nothing of boundaries or autonomy. All I knew was that I felt like Mom owned me and that I had to get away. Something new was taking root inside me—the start of who I was meant to be, and I could no longer afford to grant her rummage rights to the tender, unformed parts of me.

My mother was too formidable to confront directly—that would come later—so as a young girl, I adopted a different strategy. I chose the bluntest instrument at my disposal, the only one I had access to at the time: I went silent. I answered in monosyllables. I never let her near me.

Lots of teenagers do that. I know; Karyn and I have raised three of them. But what I did with my mother was more than normal adolescent withdrawal, more than a thirteen-year-old rolling her eyes at her mother's stupidity. My need to shut out my mother wasn't developmental; it was primal—I had to pry myself away from her to become me.

And so, I hardened. I no longer saw the mother who sang me lullabies, let me cheat at Scrabble, curled up next to me on the old brown couch watching *The Six Wives of Henry VIII* on *Masterpiece Theatre.* I no longer saw the woman who stood outside my Isolette and pulled me into the world with her fierce love, protecting the daughter who survived.

I saw a poisonous spider wrapping me in her web.

AFTER MOM'S DEATH

MEMORY

"A memory is a complicated thing, a relative to truth, but not its twin."

—Barbara Kingsolver

I'm deep into the turquoise boxes, thinking a lot about how selective memory can be. Reflecting on the stories I've shaped, held on to, and repeated—grooves I've created in my brain that say, *This is the story of my life. Here's what my relationship with my mother looked like. Here's the terrible thing she said to me. Here's the terrible thing I said back to her. Here's how she fucked up as a mother. Here's how I fucked up as a daughter. Here's how she betrayed me. How she tried to control me, mold me, colonize me.*

For decades, I insisted, "My mother and I didn't speak for seven years." But the musty evidence I'm reading shows otherwise. There was never a seven-year period when we didn't speak. There were years we struggled; years I dreaded every contact with her; years she must have dreaded my next searing revelation. But throughout those bitter years, we never stopped writing letters. There was always that written thread between us.

We both saved those letters.

I'm reading them now, opening them carefully, so the brittle pages do not tear. Whiffs of mildew rise as I force myself to remain in the chair. I bargain with myself: I can take a break in ten minutes. An hour from now, I can take a walk, eat half a bar of chocolate. It takes everything I have not to dissociate. Sometimes I pass out in dreamless slumber. My head is spinning. My heart's cracked open. My back hurts from sitting. But I'm compelled to continue. Something I need to understand—that I've struggled to understand for so long—is in those letters.

They're filled with anger and disappointment. But they also document loyalty and love. Reading them, I cringe. Sometimes, I laugh out loud. Cry. Because the letters make it clear that we never gave up on each other. Our relationship was stretched to the breaking point—but never broke completely. That's what I'm discovering, and it's making me ask, *What else has been missing in the stories I've tended and curated all these years?*

There's definitely truth in the stories I've told, but it's only part of the truth. Our history was never that bleak.

For decades, I remembered only the nasty, accusatory letters Mom sent, but forgot the loving motherly advice that arrived in between. In a card sent during the height of our estrangement, in May 1990, she wrote:

> *My fantasy is that we would not have to work so hard on our relationship—that the expression of feelings could flow freely without fearing the price of "saying the wrong thing." But alas, that is not where we are! There just isn't enough deep-seated trust.*
>
> *Our relationship, as it presently exists, is one of the major tragedies of my life, perhaps yours as well . . . How it hurts when I see a mother and daughter*

sharing a happy moment . . . After all these years, I still don't have the answer, but I hate our relationship as it is . . . and the sad reality is that there is little chance that things can improve, unless we tackle it again . . . One suggestion is to try to overcome the geographical distance—to structure more regular visits, to create some pleasurable history for us, to try to make up for twenty lost years. We share interests that we can enjoy together. We can now both afford more visits, and I believe we can't afford not to. At this moment, between my tears, I want to have shed my last over you and our unending struggle. Time keeps getting shorter.

I await your reply.

I have no memory of this letter or of my mother risking this kind of honesty during those awful years between us.

A truth teller can only tell as much of the truth as she can face at a given time.

I wonder if I'm up to the task before me: to tell this story—not just my story, the one slanted through my "daughter of the narcissist" lens, but *our* story, the one revealed in the actual tangible evidence we left behind. There is so much I am hungry for and afraid to admit.

CHAPTER 15

THE BANK

2,107 Days

Her first morning in town, Mom and I pulled into the bank parking lot at 8:45 a.m. With *Morning Edition* in the background, we composed a shopping list of things she needed for her new home. At 8:55, we stood outside the locked glass doors of the lobby, waiting to be let in. Mom checked her watch repeatedly, her mouth a thin line.

"Mom, they open at nine."

When the teller unlocked the doors at 9:01, she glared at him. "It's about time." I smiled apologetically at the underpaid bank clerk.

Moments later, we were sitting with a bank officer, and Mom was filling out the forms to establish a checking account, a savings account, and a trust account, adding me as cosigner. I'd done this, years earlier, with my father when his health began to fail, but this was a tough one for Mom. My mother had been financially independent for forty years—and proud of it, ever since her divorce. But we both knew someday I'd be managing her affairs.

When the banker handed us the papers to sign, Mom laughed nervously and looked at me. "I hope I can trust you with my money." I did my best to look honest and reliable. My eyes said, *I want to do this for you.* She hesitated, but only for a moment. Her eyes looked into mine and said, *I trust you.*

We pulled out our pens and signed.

Once Mom established her bank accounts, it was time to buy everything she needed for her new place. That week, when I wasn't teaching or driving the kids, I took Mom on a giant shopping spree. At eighty-one, she could still shop me under the table. I couldn't believe her stamina. But underneath that core physical strength, I was shocked by her fragility. She was fearful. Her emotions raged in sudden storms. When she snapped at me, Good Daughter donned her mask, and I withdrew into my hard, smooth shell. Mom's volatility wasn't new to me; it had just been better hidden. Now she walked around raw.

And I walked around shaken.

CHAPTER 16

DIRTY OLD MAN

Laura 14, Temme 43, New York City

The summer of 1971, my breasts grew overnight, and I didn't know what to do with them. I covered them with baggy shirts, but they rose like mountains anyway. When I walked down the street, cars slowed, and men whistled. I was propositioned all the time.

Two years earlier, I was certain I'd be flat-chested forever. I'd begged Mom to get me one of the white frilly AA bras that the other undeveloped girls wore. But she didn't believe in training bras. "You've got nothing there to put in them. You're flat as a pancake."

Then suddenly, in two months, my breasts ballooned past DDD. I hunched my shoulders in a vain attempt to hide my chest. My blond hair, which had always been straight, transformed into a wavy curtain. I parted it in the middle and let it drape straight down to cover my blackheads and the hard, tan polka dots of Clearasil that peppered my face.

Midway through the summer, Mom and I drove to New York to see Bubby and Poppa. It was just the two of us. Dad was living at Project Artaud, painting giant murals, and Paul was away at the University of Colorado, driving an old hearse. Mom and I arrived at BPNY alone.

At fourteen, I still had no conscious memory of my grandfather's abuse. But other things about him made me drag my heels that day. I was dreading a ritual that had long been practiced in my family. As all the girls—Mom, her sisters, Bea and Ruth, and all the girl cousins before me—reached adolescence, Poppa insisted that they lift their shirts and bare their budding breasts for his inspection. It was a rite of passage. A family tradition.

After Poppa unlocked the two deadbolts and the chain, we entered the dark apartment. There were the familiar sepia photos from the Old Country, a Yiddish newspaper strewn on a chair, the sizzling smell of *latkes*. Poppa took in my new chest and chuckled with delight. "Are they growing yet?"

I shrank away from my body until I could no longer feel the sticky summer heat on my skin. Just a cool, empty place inside.

Mom looked at me expectantly. Poppa waited for me to comply. "Let me see. Just a little peek." He said it lightly. Wasn't this all just an amusing little joke?

I fingered the hem of my white peasant shirt. The embroidery on top was turquoise, green, and gold. They were looking at me. Waiting. Poppa's eyes gleamed with anticipation.

"No." The word ignited from somewhere deep inside me.

Mom's face hardened. "Laurie, what's the big deal? Do you have to be so unpleasant? We all did it."

I pulled the bottom of my shirt down over my jeans. The words tumbled out of an unfamiliar place. "I don't want to."

Mom's eyes flared with anger, and her shoulders squared. "Don't be so uptight, Laurie. It will only take a minute." She looked at me appraisingly, as she had so many times before. "You have a lovely figure. You have nothing to be ashamed of."

That's where the memory ends. The only thing I know for sure is that I didn't lift up my shirt, and that I was the only girl in the family ever to refuse.

Sometimes when I think back to this moment, I imagine it happening at another time of year, with our whole family crammed into that tiny apartment, at a *seder* maybe. In that version, I see my teenage self, standing up to all of them, every one of my aunts and cousins, all the women and girls, the ones from the past and the ones from the future, all the Ross women, generations of them, shouting, "Why are you making such a big deal about this? We all did it." A whole chorus of shirt lifters, clamoring for me to bare my chest. Just one look. Give the dirty old man one look. But I didn't listen to any of them—not the ones who were there, not the ones in my head. A kernel of resistance rose up inside me. I said no. It would be years before I'd remember what had happened with Poppa when I was small, but someone fierce woke up inside me that day. She soon dropped back into slumber, but she was there.

CHAPTER 17

LITANY

2,047 Days

Two months after her move, Mom lived at the top of my speed dials. Fielding her rants became part of my daily routine. People in Santa Cruz were rude; people in New Jersey were cultured and smart. The ocean in Santa Cruz was too cold. The Atlantic Ocean was better. Even the waves didn't look right.

Each day, she rolled out a new litany of complaints. NPR wasn't on the radio anymore. Online bridge wasn't working. She'd lost her car keys, and that "bastard at the locksmith's shop" had stolen them.

"Mom, I'm sure the locksmith didn't steal your keys. Why would he want your keys? He *makes* keys."

"That bastard wants $150 to give me a new key! I'm not paying $150. It's highway robbery. They just want to take advantage of an old woman."

"Mom, you lost your keys. You lost both sets of keys. That's what it costs to rekey a car."

"He's ripping me off. This is all his fault."

"It's not his fault. He's trying to help you."

She roared, "He's a crook. Why are you taking his side?" Then she hung up on me.

I yanked the headset out of my ear and headed to the bakery for a pear-ginger scone.

2,020 DAYS

Mom called, sobbing. "The next time I see my sister, I'm going to be standing over her grave." Then she snarled, "None of this would be happening if I'd stayed in New Jersey where I belong. Why did you make me move out here, anyway?"

Make you move out here? You're the one who called *me* to say you were coming.

"I have no friends. I'm all alone."

My jaw tightened. So, we don't count at all? Your grandchildren don't count? Your daughter-in-law doesn't count? I don't count? You moved out here to be with us. Now you have no one?

I wanted to hang up on her, but Good Daughter intervened with her smooth, placid voice, papering over everything. "Mom, it's going to be okay."

"No, it isn't. I hate California. I wish I'd never left New Jersey."

Where the hell was Paul?

2,000 DAYS

Every day, I struggled to cope. I talked to a friend, binge-watched *Grey's Anatomy,* danced to Motown in the car, vented on the page. I got acupuncture and massages and a medical marijuana registration card. I saw every half-decent movie that came out that winter, even some really bad ones, slipping out on afternoons when I was supposed to be doing something else—The List be damned. In the early mornings, I sat for ten minutes, reviving my abandoned meditation practice. I said *metta*—a Buddhist lovingkindness prayer—for me and Mom, Karyn, Paul, and the kids, for Bryan and his family, and for all beings everywhere. And every night, I complained to Karyn, who loved her mother-in-law and always helped me find my way back to kindness.

CHAPTER 18

BUBBY

Laura 16, Temme 45, Forest Hills, Queens

The last time I saw my grandmother, Bubby was living out her final months in a nursing home in Queens, near my aunt Ruth and uncle Howard, two hours from our home in New Jersey. One Saturday, Mom was going to visit Bubby and asked me to come along. At that stage in my life, my answer to anything my mother suggested was an automatic no, but she insisted. I'd never been inside a nursing home before.

The smell of ammonia and pee smacked us the moment we walked through the door. Old wrinkled people lined the halls. Some were bent over; others were tied to their wheelchairs. Snot streamed onto one man's chest. A woman's hands lay bent and useless in her lap. A man in a baggy stained shirt stared into space. A woman wailed, "Help!"

I shrank as far inside my skin as I could go.

Bubby looked tiny in her narrow bed. Thick plastic hearing aids filled her ears. She couldn't see well enough to know we were standing right in front of her. Mom leaned over and spoke loudly, right into her ear. "Ma, it's me, Temme."

Bubby's face remained blank. "Bea? Bea?" Bubby thought Mom was one of my aunts.

Mom spoke louder. "No, Ma. Bea was here last week. It's me, Temme."

Bubby took Mom's hand in her smooth, shiny claw. "Ruth?" Ruth was Mom's younger sister. She lived nearby and visited every day. Bubby still didn't know us.

Mom raised her voice again. "No, Ma. Ruth was here yesterday. Today, it's my turn. It's Temme."

Bubby stared at Mom for a long time. The moment she recognized her, she began pleading. "Temka, please take me home. I had a home. I can cook. I can sew. Please, take me home."

Mom grabbed my arm and yanked me to stand beside her. "Ma, Laurie's here." Mom pushed me forward. "Say hello to your grandmother."

I stared at Bubby. How could anyone be that old? I mumbled, "Hi, Bubby. It's me, Laura."

Mom urged me forward again. "Talk louder."

I straightened my wire rims and bent over, stringy blond hair falling across my face. This time, I spoke directly into Bubby's ear. She smelled like mothballs and hand lotion. When she recognized my voice, she smiled for the first time. "It's so good to see you, *darlingka*. You've gotten so big. I'm so glad you came." But then her face went blank again. Her cheeks sagged, like a cake collapsing in the oven. "Bea, I want to go home."

Mom leaned down and shouted in her ear. "Ma, it's not Bea. It's Temme!"

"Temka, they're trying to kill me. They're trying to poison me. I want to be with my family. Please take me home."

For the next half hour, as old people moaned in the hallway, Bubby begged us to take her home. The smell of urine and bleach made me gag. I tugged at Mom's sleeve, trying to get her to go, but she shrugged me away.

Finally, Mom said, "We're going now, Ma."

As we walked out, my grandmother's voice trailed behind us. "Don't leave me. I had a home. I have a family. They're trying to kill me. Please take me home."

Mom fast walked to the car, and I had to run to keep up. Before she started the engine, she turned to me, her face fierce. Her words seared into me. "I never want to end up like that. Don't you *ever* put me in a nursing home. If I ever need a walker or a wheelchair, just take me out back and shoot me. Promise me, Laurie, that you won't let that happen to me."

CHAPTER 19

CENTER STAGE

1,865 Days

Eight months after Mom's arrival, Karyn and I were taking a walk when I suddenly said, "Something feels off, but I just can't put my finger on it."

A minute later it hit me: Mom hadn't called in three days.

Little by little, she'd started reaching out. She joined the temple. Started attending lectures. Seeing movies. Making friends. She even joined a meditation class.

The old Temme was coming back—the one with a full dance card and three calendars.

Pretty soon, Mom was bragging about her popularity, rooting around in her pocketbook, and pulling out the hard, blue plastic handicapped placard she carried with her everywhere. "My friends all want to take me with them, and it's all because of this." She waved it in the air and cackled with pleasure. It was impossible not to laugh with her.

One day, she called to announce, "Laurie, this is one of the happiest periods of my life."

"What happened, Mom? A month ago, you were miserable."

"I finally realized I wasn't ever moving back to New Jersey. My life is here now, and I decided to make the best of it."

As Mom's life improved, so did mine. I started sleeping through the night. Karyn and I went on dates again. I was able to do some long-term planning for my business. I launched my first writers' trip to Bali. I took Eli on a college-viewing trip and set my pot stash aside.

A year after her move, my mother had more friends than I did, and I'd been living in Santa Cruz for thirty years. When I dropped by to see her, she was never home. I had to book time to spend with her, just like the old days.

Once again, she was living her life on center stage.

LAURA 7, TEMME 36, NEW JERSEY

As a little girl, I knew my mother was special. As soon as I could read, I got to lie on the big bed with her, helping her learn her lines. Mom was the star at the Center Drama Workshop in Long Branch, New Jersey. Twice a year, she played a leading role: the Girl in *The Tenth Man*, Cora in *The Dark at the Top of the Stairs*, Linda Loman in *Death of a Salesman*, Mrs. Keller in *The Miracle Worker*.

While she studied blocking with her fellow actors, Dad quizzed us on spelling words and put us to bed. The weekend before each production, Dad built sets and painted them. I helped, pushing dripping rollers across flimsy canvas flats.

For a long time, I wasn't allowed to see Mom's plays. They started past my bedtime, and the themes were too adult. Mom didn't think I could sit still that long. But when my new big-girl teeth came in, I finally got to see her play Elizabeth Proctor in *The Crucible*.

Before she left for the theater that night, Mom laid out special clothes for me: a blue sailor dress, white tights, and shiny black Mary Janes. I sat in the front row, with Dad on one side and Paul on the other, in seats with our names on them. While I waited for the curtain to go up, I swung my legs, reading about Mom in the program, shiny shoes dangling above the floor. She was famous.

"Dad," I whispered, "when's the play going to start?"

"Soon." He squeezed my hand in his big warm one.

When the curtain finally opened and the play began, Mom looked like Mom, but she was different. Her voice was big and loud, even when she was whispering. The play was about witches being burned at the stake and a good man who was treated like a bad man. They hanged him in the end. Mom was his wife, but she wasn't married to him in real life. She was married to Dad.

The parts I didn't understand didn't matter. All that mattered was seeing my mother up there, bigger than life—glowing, everyone staring at her, transfixed. I couldn't believe that Elizabeth Proctor was really my mother, who tucked me in and sang me lullabies.

When the play was over, the actors held hands and bowed. The whole audience stood up and cheered. Dad put me on his shoulders. I was so proud. Mom stepped in front, and the room ignited in applause. People yelled, "Bravo!" and she bowed again, looking so grand up there, happy in a way I had never seen before.

It would be years before I understood just how hungry my mother was for that kind of admiration.

CHAPTER 20

REMEMBERING

Laura 27, Temme 56, Santa Cruz

The first time I fell in love hard it was with Gwen, a dancer my age who lived in Santa Cruz. It was the summer of 1984.

Even Mom was happy for me. In the four years since I'd come out to her, she'd gotten over her horror at my being a lesbian. When we talked on the phone, Mom didn't ignore Gwen. She asked how she was. She asked how we were.

And we were doing great—licking lemon chicken off each other's fingers as we planned our future: the trips we'd take, the home we'd create, the kids we were going to have. We fantasized our lives right up until the end—two old ladies rocking companionably on the porch, grandchildren playing in the yard. For the first time in my life, I believed I wasn't destined to be alone. Gwen was definitely the One.

I was living in San Francisco at the time, so we alternated weekends, one at her house, one at mine. I was planning a move back to Santa Cruz; we'd be living together soon. It was only a matter of time.

—∞—

One sunny Sunday morning, Gwen and I were lying in her bed, curved together like spoons, her reassuring weight warming my back. I was half-asleep, half-awake. Her musky breath touched my neck, soft and familiar. Her fingertips reached out to touch me.

I turned to face her, to study the green-gold eyes I loved. To wonder at this miracle woman who had crashed through my defenses. Gwen had disarmed me. Before, I'd been a loner, too busy achieving, living in my head, afraid of love, a terror I couldn't name keeping me distant. I'd dismissed other lovers when they got too close. Gwen was the one I dreamed of but never thought possible, whose soft presence still surprised and delighted me those slow weekend mornings. I was happier than I'd ever been. So, to answer her searching fingers, I reached up to stroke her face. She pressed her belly into mine, and I felt the sudden heat of passion flare.

Gwen kissed me, teasing and slow, waiting for me to answer, for me to rise. I kissed her back. My body pressed against her, skin tingling, nerves on fire. There was a gleam in her eyes. A thin sheen of sweat coated her skin. "I want you," she whispered, her voice husky. Her fingers slid up my thigh.

That's when I felt it. A spark of terror and then a wall. *Shit. Gone again.* I couldn't feel her kisses. I couldn't feel her touch. *No, no, no. Damn it. C'mon, Laura. You want to be here. You want to do this. This is the woman you love.* I tried to reel myself back into my body, but it was impossible. I was already gone, my mind floating free.

A door slammed next door. Kids' laughter poured out. Old grief surged through me. *What is wrong with me?* I slowed down my caresses, pulled my mouth away. "I'm sorry, honey."

Gwen stared at me. Angry tears filled her eyes. I had failed again. This wasn't the first time. Or the second. This was familiar territory, a vast chasm spreading between us, wider and wider the closer we got.

For months, Gwen had been patient. But now, she exploded. "What's wrong with you? Where the hell do you go?"

She loomed over me. I recoiled. Who was this angry stranger?

Hammering rang out. The neighborhood was waking up. But I was nowhere to be found.

Gwen's voice softened. Concern flooded her eyes. "Breathe, honey. Just breathe."

I tried to breathe as her questions bore inside me: *Why can't I make love with the woman I love? Why do I disappear?*

The newspaper thwacked Gwen's front door. The slam reverberated through my body. A terror I could not name seared through me. I shook, a rag doll coming undone. But there were no seams. I had no body. I'd never cried like this before.

Gwen stroked my forehead, peppered it with kisses. "Sweetheart, what is it?"

Something deep inside was breaking free, too awful and terrible to name. I knew I was about to say something, but I had no idea what it would be. I didn't recognize the words until they spilled from my lips. "I was molested." A tiny child's voice finally breaking free. As my words cut through the stillness of the sunny-morning air, I knew that they were true.

Gwen turned away from me, stared out the window at the children. My eyes traced the jagged crack on the ceiling.

In the days and weeks to come, new incest memories kept breaking through. Three months later, the "love of my life" left me. We couldn't face my tsunami of trauma and live up to the fantasy of who we'd hoped to be.

CHAPTER 21

ACCIDENT

1,700 Days

I knew we were headed down a slippery slope the day Mom called and asked, "Do you think I should have the convicts fix my car?"

It was a month after Mom's eighty-second birthday, just after Thanksgiving 2009. I was at Rotten Robbie, the cheapest gas in town, filling my tank after dropping the kids at school. Mom's voice echoed through the sleek plastic headset in my ear. "Hire the convicts? No, I don't think that's a good idea." I hefted the nozzle and set it back in its metal cradle. "Take your car to a regular body shop; have your insurance fix it. Do it right." I wanted to shout, *Are you kidding?* But rubbing Mom's poor judgment in her face was cruel.

It had all started a week earlier, the Tuesday before Thanksgiving, the big reunion for my side of the family. Karyn and I were hosting. We'd have a crowd of twenty squeezed around multiple tables, filling our house to capacity.

By Monday, our first guests had arrived. Preparations were in full swing. The refrigerator was crammed with food.

That night, fourteen of us gathered for dinner. Mom and Karyn each had two glasses of wine. At 8:00 p.m., before dessert, Mom stood up, interrupted the conversation, blurted, "I've got to go," and bolted out the door. Karyn and I looked at each other over the half-cleared table. She raised an eyebrow; I raised one back. Mom was famous for her sudden exits. She got bored when she wasn't getting enough attention. Something better was happening somewhere else. One minute, she was there; the next, she was out the door.

—∞—

The following day, I headed over to Mom's for a cooking party with my cousins, Miriam and Don. When we arrived, grocery bags in hand, Mom was pacing around her tiny kitchen, face pale, mascara smeared. Her clothes were rumpled, the same ones she'd had on the night before. Her eyes darted from one face to the other. "I had an accident," she blurted out. "I hit a parked car last night."

I froze. My first impulse was not to take her in my arms. "Are you okay? Was anyone hurt?"

"No one was hurt, but you should see the car."

The passenger side was scraped and battered. The front door wouldn't open. A foot-long piece of some other car's black plastic bumper was wedged into the door.

We walked back in silence. Mom stood at the head of the kitchen island. I tried to keep my voice from shaking. "What happened?"

Mom's voice flared in accusation. "The other car was sticking way out. It shouldn't have been parked like that."

"What happened to the other car?"

She threw up an arm. "I don't know. I didn't stop. I just drove away."

A hit-and-run? Oh, Mom.

"I'd had a couple glasses of wine. I didn't want to take a breathalyzer. I can't let them take my license away! So, I just drove home."

"Did you sleep?"

"I didn't sleep all night."

My fists clenched and I wanted to shake her, but I forced my voice to soften. "Why didn't you call me?"

She stuck her chin out, but it was quivering. "I don't know. I didn't think of it!"

What if she'd hit a pedestrian? A kid on a bike? As I ticked through the possibilities, I forced myself to walk over and put my arm around her. My stiff arm sat awkwardly on her shoulder. She sagged against me. "Mom, are you okay?"

She exploded, "Of course I'm not okay! You think I'd be okay after something like that?"

I shrank back but didn't take my arm away. It stayed there, a mannequin of an arm, the best I could offer.

I spoke in even tones. "Mom, sit down. We have to deal with this." This was a dance I knew well—calming the raging inferno.

Don took her hands in his. His voice firm, eyes loving. "Temme, you have to call the police. The person whose car you hit has probably called the police, and they may be looking for your car right now. You have to report this."

Just like that. Kind. Insistent. We flanked her on either side and led her to the couch.

"Let's practice." I put an imaginary phone up to my ear and pretended to be the dispatcher, answering the phone. "Hello, Santa Cruz police . . ."

Mom held an imaginary phone to her ear, too, but this role was way too real for her. "I can't tell them what really happened. I can't tell them I had *wine*!" She hissed out the truth, eyes like a cornered animal. "I don't even know where it happened."

You don't know where it happened? You were drinking. You drove away. Oh my God.

Mom sat up straight, a little soldier, her broad shoulders pulled back. "Well, it was somewhere between your house and here! It was dark." Her voice veered upward again, sharp as a knife. I retreated farther into my body. "Why aren't there any fucking streetlights in this town? That's just like Santa Cruz. It shouldn't be that dark!"

Mom couldn't imagine life without her car, but someone could have died. I *had* to deal with this. "I'll get the *challah* started. While it's rising, let's retrace your route in the daytime and see if we can find the place it happened."

She nodded, relieved I was taking control. She didn't have to call the police, not yet.

I pulled out yeast, raisins, walnuts, and dates. The food still had to get cooked. I threw the ingredients together, my mind racing.

Half an hour later, I drove Mom back to my house. I pointed out a few places where cars were parked perpendicular to the roadway, but nothing looked familiar. I had her practice calling the police, and by the time we arrived back at her place, she was primed. I put the phone on speaker and dialed. All of us gathered around, offering support. The smell of yeast filled the room.

"Hello, Santa Cruz police."

"I'd like to report an accident."

"What happened, ma'am?"

"Well, I was driving home from my daughter's last night, and I hit a parked car."

"When did this accident happen?"

"Last night."

"Ma'am, it's eleven o'clock in the morning."

"I'm aware of that, Officer. It was wrong of me. But it was dark, and I was scared, and I didn't want to get out of my car at night and knock on a strange door."

I couldn't believe how calm and rational she sounded. Her acting skills were kicking in. I wanted to grab the phone and shout, *She can't remember anything, and she was drinking! She's a menace on the road. Please take her license away.* I gripped the couch instead.

"Officer, I know I should have called, but I came home and went to bed. I called my daughter. She came over this morning, and now we're calling you."

"And where did this accident happen?"

"I'm not sure. It was dark, and I was scared. I'm sorry, Officer. I just can't remember."

The dispatcher said he'd send someone over. While we waited, we cooked. I made the batter for pumpkin bread. Miriam greased the pans. Mom made her famous mock chopped liver. I shaped the *challah* into a giant braided loaf, and Don dusted the poppy seeds on top. I set it aside for its final rise. The house was full of good smells when the officers arrived.

In their half-hour interview, they never once asked Mom if she'd been drinking. I wanted to slip them a note: *Don't you have an established protocol for older drivers who have accidents—like making them take a new road test?* They did not, at least not for privileged white women like my mother. They were not going to lift this burden from my shoulders.

The officers took the big black rubber bumper with them when they left. They said they'd send someone out to drive the route and ask questions.

We never heard from them again.

And so, the responsibility for Mom's driving—choosing between her independence and public safety—remained in my hands. I knew that giving up her license would devastate her, so I convinced myself that it would be okay to let her keep driving. She didn't drive much. If anything, she drove too slowly. What were the odds she'd do real damage? That she'd hurt someone? I weighed those questions against the desolation she'd feel if I took away her license. But the real truth is I lacked courage. I couldn't face her wrath. So, I abdicated my responsibility and hoped for the best.

And my nights of anxious worry increased.

CHAPTER 22

BASTARD

Laura 27, Abe 65, San Francisco

Two weeks after that horrible morning in Gwen's bed, I called my father. I was terrified to tell him what I was remembering, but we'd grown close, and I needed him to know. "Dad, I have something important to tell you, but I need to do it in person."

Thirty minutes later, I sat across from him on his huge Goodwill couch at Project Artaud. As he waited for me to speak, I avoided his eyes and stared out at his apartment. Hundreds of colored sample carpet squares, pieced together in a shaggy dirty checkerboard, blanketed the cement. Beyond them, his stolen shopping cart overflowed with art supplies. Maybe this was a terrible idea. But if I couldn't tell Dad, the easy parent, how would I ever tell Mom?

Finally, he couldn't take my silence anymore. "Laura, what is it?"

"Dad . . ." My voice broke.

The bass from a rehearsal down the hall reverberated through the thick walls like a heartbeat. "When I was a little girl . . ." My voice faltered. I'd never told him when I was a kid. How could I tell him now? But I pressed on. "Poppa sexually abused me."

Dad's eyes got hard, then soft. A kaleidoscope of emotions crossed his face: shock, sadness, despair, grief, anger. When he finally spoke, his voice sliced the air like a knife. "I always thought he was a bastard."

Dad was shocked, but he wasn't surprised.

He wrapped his arms around me, and I wept in his embrace. *Oh my God, he believes me. Someone in my family believes me.*

Maybe it wouldn't be as bad as I thought to tell Mom. But I wasn't ready yet.

CHAPTER 23
THE WALL

1,593 Days

A year after Mom magically transformed into Santa Cruz's Miss Senior Popularity, her friends began calling me, concerned. "I'm really worried about your mother." She'd make plans with them, then forget to show up. Her friends would come to fetch her and find her napping on the couch, TV blaring into the street. Or she'd snap at them for not showing up when she thought they should. In her mind, the fact that she'd missed the play was their fault. It wasn't long before all but her closest friends pulled away.

One morning, I called Mom after teaching a weeklong retreat out of town. Her need had been building up for days. Rather than address her growing loneliness, she complained about her computer. "I want to type my story, and I can't. The margins aren't working. I can't center the title on the page. And the printer is broken again."

"I'll be right over." I had a small window of free time, and despite her prickliness, I'd missed her. I drove over and walked straight to her computer. Created new margins, double-spaced the text, changed the font. Cleared the paper jam. "What else can I do?"

I knew this hour would never be enough. Her life wasn't something I could fix.

She burst into tears. "I'm going deaf. I can't even hear you."

I spoke louder. "Did you go to the new audiologist?"

"It was just a big racket to sell hearing aids. That guy is a crook."

As she paced between her desk and the kitchen, I had the impulse to comfort her, so I walked over and placed my hands on her rigid shoulders. It was like caressing a rock.

She snarled, "Take your hands off me. You're faking it."

I whipped my arms away. She was right. My hug, if you could call it that, *wasn't* genuine. It *was* forced. I rarely reached out to touch her; I thought about touching her. I shoved my hands deep into the pockets of my hoodie. "Mom, tell me more."

"I'm just so depressed. I don't fit in here! The phone never rings. I don't know what I'm putting out, but it must be poison. I go to the pool, and all the other women are in twos and threes, and I'm there all by myself. I try to go to the movie group, but I can't hear them. They're all young and think different than me."

"Mom, there's a myth about happy old people. What's there to be happy about? You're losing your hearing and your memory. Getting old sucks."

She snapped back. "There are lots of happy old people. I see them all around me."

I wanted to recoil but replied in the same artificial voice. "Why don't you call your doctor? Maybe she can help you."

"I don't feel like confiding in her."

"She's your doctor. She should know how low you're feeling." *And maybe she'll put you on antidepressants so I don't have to listen to your complaints every day.*

Empathy for Mom was not my strong suit.

As she continued her litany, I nodded in the appropriate places but was composing a grocery list in my head. I thought about Lizzy, thirteen and blossoming, bursting into life. I thought about Eli, taking the SAT test a mile away, as I stood there, not touching Mom. Not touching her in any way. She was untouchable.

Will I be like her when I get old?

I glanced at the clock. My class started in an hour. "I've got to go. Can I give you a hug goodbye?"

She collapsed against me. I awkwardly put my arms around her. I hated leaving her like that. No, really, who was I kidding? I couldn't wait to get out of there.

—∞—

Three decades earlier, I had erected an impenetrable wall between us—a fortress with narrow slits so I could watch her approach. I ensured that my defenses were prepared anytime she came near me. I always had an escape plan.

It's true; we later reconciled. And the fact that we were able to create a functional relationship *was* a miracle. But it wasn't an intimate miracle, because I never took down my wall. Oh, I taught myself to be kind to her, in a "fake it till you make it" sort of way, but I still held her at bay. My wall just got subtler. It wasn't permeable. It was hard and opaque, and there was no door. We only met in the antechamber, the common room where guests are received. Only my polished self was on display, my masked self, and only in the antechamber. Mom never saw my inner sanctum, and I never saw hers. I got as close as I could within the constraints I had established, but closed is closed, and a closed heart is a lonely one.

The price I paid to keep my mother out, at first with withdrawal, later with an armed fortress, and finally, with the polite rules of détente, was love. The pure, unfettered love I longed for. The pure, unfettered love she craved.

That day in her kitchen when I couldn't comfort her, I had to face it. My mother was still a stranger to me, with tentacles of need I was loath to touch. I wanted to be more than kind, to do more than merely what was right. I wanted to love my mother, just once, freely and with the relief of a lost, exhausted child, beyond words and beyond all pretense. I wanted to lay my head on a place that was safe, just once, before it was too late.

CHAPTER 24

DISCLOSURE

Laura 28, Temme 56, San Francisco

A month after I had my first incest memory, I finally found the courage to return my mother's many calls. After weeks of silence on my part, she'd left her first message: "Hi, sweetheart, it's Mom. I haven't heard from you. Let's talk." Two days later: "I'm worried about you. Call me." The day after that, she could no longer mask the anxiety in her voice. "Laurie, what's going on? You haven't called me back. Are you okay?"

Each time I checked my answering machine and heard her voice, pinpricks of panic careened through me. Her messages grew increasingly frantic; I started hitting the Skip button after the first syllable—the moment I recognized the sound of her voice. Mom left six messages the first week. I saved them all; I couldn't delete Mom.

The second week, she enlisted Paul: "Hey, little sister, what's going on? Why haven't you called Mom?" I didn't call him back either.

Two days later, Dad invited me out for a steak burrito at La Cumbre. "Your mother called. She's really worried. I told her you're okay, but you need to call her." *Wow, she must be really desperate if she's calling Dad.*

But I wasn't ready to tell Mom what I was remembering. More memories were breaking through, and I was barely functioning. I talked it over with my therapist. She didn't think I was ready either. So, I did what she suggested—called when I knew my mother would be at work and left a message. "I'm okay. I'm going through some things, and I'm not ready to talk to you about them. I'll call when I'm ready."

That night, Mom left a message on my answering machine. "Laurie, darling, I'm sorry you're going through such a hard time. I know what that's like. I've been there. I just want you to know I'm with you, one hundred percent. I have faith in you. Whatever it is, you're going to figure it out. I have your back and always will. I can wait. I'll be here when you're ready."

That brought me a week of peace. But then I came home to a new message. Mom's voice had an edge, and her words were slightly slurred. "I really need to talk to you. If you don't call back, I'm flying out to California."

I no longer had a choice.

The next day, I spent my lunch hour whispering into my phone at work, having an emergency strategy session with my therapist. That night, I got home before my roommates. It was six o'clock in California, nine o'clock in New Jersey. I holed up in my bedroom, pulled my Princess phone onto my lap. Slipped my forefinger into the round dial and called Mom's number, the number I grew up with, the one I knew by heart. As the phone rang, I imagined her in front of the TV, watching *Masterpiece Theatre*, wearing a silky robe, a glass of wine in one hand, a Parliament in the other. "It'll be okay. It'll be okay," I chanted as I waited for her to pick up. Please say, *Darling, I'm so sorry. You're going to get through this. Trust me. I'll be here every step of the way.*

I was sitting on the hard tufted mattress I'd splurged on at Futon Shop in San Francisco, pressed against the backboard of my plywood-and-cinder-block bed. Unanswered rings echoed in my ear. *Should I hang up? There's still time.* I imagined Mom showing up on my doorstep. *I have to tell her. She needs to know.* I let the phone ring.

Please. Please. Please.

She picked up on the sixth ring. "Laurie? Darling, is that you?" The moment I heard her voice, everything went loose and wobbly inside. "It's so good to finally talk to you." I wrapped my finger into the tight curl of the phone cord.

This is it. I have to just say it. But I can't.

"Laurie, Laurie, are you there?" Beneath her eager voice, I heard the strike of a match on a matchbook cover, a deep inhale. Sounds I'd known and hated for a lifetime. All those cigarette warning labels Paul and I tacked up on our parents' door. The pack I crumbled into the toilet when I was eight. The day I sat down next to her in the den on the flat brown couch, the one covered with a Mexican serape, picked up one of her cigarettes, and lit up. I was fourteen, and there was nothing she could say or do; I already knew how to inhale.

I imagined her sitting on that serape now, the blue ceramic ashtray I made her for Mother's Day heaped with spent Parliaments, lipstick ringing the filters. I heard her take another drag. *This is it.* "Mom, I have something to tell you." My voice, a miserable squeak. *Damn it. Why do I have to sound like such a pitiful child?*

Worry pierced tiny holes in the warmth of her voice. "What is it, darling? What's wrong?" She waited for me to speak.

I looked around my room, searching for something, anything, to anchor me, to remind me I was real. My gaze fell on an old door from Goodwill on top of two sawhorses. Dad had driven over from Project Artaud to help me drag them up from the corner of Masonic and Haight. *I have a desk.* My new Mac 128 and my dot matrix printer. *I have a computer.* Next to the desk, a plastic crate on its side, full of my favorite books. *I am a reader.* On the floor next to my bed, an anthology of lesbian love poems, inscribed with a loving note from Gwen. *I have a girlfriend.* My journal with a pen clipped on the front. *I am a writer.*

I should have written to Mom instead. *How can I possibly say the words out loud?* I grabbed my white teddy bear from under the sheets and hugged it to my chest. *It's now or never.*

"Mom . . ."

I can't say it. I just can't. I pictured my therapist's face. Gwen's steady countenance. Her voice: "Sweetheart, you can do this."

I tried again. "Mom, when I was a little girl . . ." But my voice stalled.

"Laurie, what is it, darling?" Her voice pulsed with warmth and encouragement. "You can tell me anything."

I dug my fingers into the white plush of my bear and forced the words out through tight lips. "When I was a little girl, I was molested."

It's out, and I can't take it back.

"What did you say?" Shock waves reverberated across the miles between us.

I let Mom's question hang in the air. Saying it once was bad enough.

She took a drag of her cigarette. Her voice was firmer this time. Insistent. "Laurie, what did you just say?"

A siren ripped down the street, heading to an emergency. *I have to answer. I always have to answer Mom.* I pulled my knees closer and mumbled my response. "I was molested."

She said nothing. A second siren, then a third, raced by. Somewhere, something terrible was happening. I fell into Mom's silence and kept falling. *I should never have told her.*

Mom crooned the ancient song of mothers comforting their children. "Oh my God," or "Oh, honey." Something like that, but I couldn't hear because of the rushing in my ears. I shut my eyes. Floated out of my body.

"Darling, I'm so sorry."

Did she just say she was sorry? *My God, she believes me! I don't have to face this alone.* I snapped back into my body, and the room came back into focus: My desk. My computer. My bed. My books. My weight on the bed. *I was right to tell her. It's all going to be okay. I can depend on Mom.*

The front door slammed—my housemates arriving from work. Soon the kitchen would be filled with their chatter. Mom's voice rolled toward me like a soft caress. "Laurie, are you okay?"

Pressure built up behind my eyes, and I struggled to control my voice. "I'm having a really hard time."

"Do you remember what the doctor told me about you when you were born?"

I knew what she was going to say, but I wanted to hear it again. "Tell me."

"He said if you lived, you'd be stronger than most babies. Vicki didn't make it, but you did. You were stronger. You *are* stronger. You're going to get through this."

Cabinets opened and closed in the kitchen on the far side of the wall. Cooking sounds: The thwack of a knife on wood. The sizzle of oil.

The smell of garlic in a pan. When I got off the phone, something warm and delicious would be waiting.

Mom sighed. "Darling, I know this is terribly hard for you. Take all the time you need to tell me."

When she said that, the lightning bolts in my chest disappeared. Blood streamed back into my hands and feet. The sirens faded into the distance. This was going much better than the scenarios I'd rehearsed with my therapist. I remembered her advice: "Don't say anything you don't want to say. Keep control of the conversation. This call is for you." *But I don't have to worry about that now. I told Mom, and she is showing up for me.* I couldn't wait to tell my therapist.

I stretched out my legs. Released my teddy bear back onto the bed. Took a deep breath. But I still hadn't told Mom the hardest part. *And I don't think I can.* The knot in my stomach returned. I wiped away a few small tears. "You really believe me?"

Her response was immediate. "Of course I believe you! Why wouldn't I? You were always an honest child."

The smell of curry made my stomach grumble. How could I get hungry at a time like this?

A long-distance buzz hummed through the wire. Mom had stopped talking, and that couldn't be good. Or could it? My fingers traced the matted fur on my bear's face. I was hovering right on the edge of my skin.

Say something, Mom. Please keep talking.

Mom inhaled. I could almost hear the smoke pooling around her head. When she spoke again, her voice was different. Narrower. A tight wire. I knew that tight wire. "When did this happen?"

I sucked myself deep into my body and put on my armor, but my armor was full of holes. *If only Vicki were here; I wouldn't be doing this alone.*

Mom's voice thinned. "Laurie, tell me when." It wasn't a question.

Please stop. Just call me sweetheart, and tell me I'm going to be okay. Say that again, please. I reached for my therapist's words: "You don't have to say anything you don't want to say," but her voice was fading. I couldn't remember her face. I was on the phone with Mom now, and I had to play by Mom's rules. I replied in a whisper. "It started when I was three."

"Three?"

"Yes."

"Three? Oh my God, Laurie. I'm so sorry, darling."

She's sorry. She knows how helpless I was. It wasn't my fault, right, Mom?

"Did you say three? Did I hear you right? Hold on a sec." I heard Mom get up. The phone clattered onto the tiny tiles of the coffee table. Then I heard nothing. A moment later, she picked up the extension in the kitchen—the yellow phone with the curly cord that stretched across the room. The hum of the refrigerator vibrated in my ear. Ice cubes clinked in a glass. A splash of liquid. The strike of a match. A long, slow inhale. Mom was trying to put it all together. Tumblers were falling in my brain, too—like *Where the fuck were you?* I clenched my jaw but said nothing. I'd said too much already.

A truck ground its gears out on the street, an ugly grating sound. When Mom spoke again, hysteria lapped at the edge of her voice. "When exactly did this happen?"

Shut up! I wanted to hang up, but I couldn't do that to Mom. I replied in a quiet voice. "It went on for a very long time." In other words, it wasn't a babysitter. It wasn't a random stranger.

Mom's next question started in a whisper and rose to a ragged shout. "Who? Who did this to you?"

No. Anything but that. But if I don't tell her, she'll think it was Dad. Of course she will. It's always the father. I can't let her think it's Dad.

Laughter rippled through the wall from the kitchen, a million miles away. "It wasn't Dad."

"Well, who was it? A neighbor? A teacher? A kid at school?" There was no softness in her voice now. "Tell me. Who was it?"

I forced my mouth to shape the awful, terrible words. "It was . . . Poppa."

"What did you say?"

I couldn't bear to say it again. I said nothing.

"Did you say . . . Poppa?"

I nodded. *Don't make me say it again.*

Mom's voice drilled deep into my ear. "My father?"

I replied in a whisper. "Yes."

"No!" Mom gasped. "It can't be." She sounded like she was being strangled.

I did this to her. I've made a terrible mistake. I take it back. It never happened.

When Mom could finally speak again, her voice was raw. "This is just such a shock." Then she went silent again. I forced myself to breathe into my belly. A calming breath. *Mom just needs time. I've had weeks to get used to this, and I'm not used to it at all—it's just as terrible now as it was when I first remembered. Worse. Mom will be back. She just needs a few minutes.* I fingered the turquoise ribbon around my bear's neck. Counted the seconds. One Mississippi. Two Mississippi. *Soon she'll tell me how brave I am.* I looked down at the book of poems Gwen gave me. My desk. My journal. Twenty Mississippi. Twenty-one Mississippi. *You'll be okay, darling.* She'll say it again.

Tightness gripped my belly. My throat. My chest. Thirty-five Mississippi. Ice clinked. Mom took another swallow. Another drag. *She just needs time.*

Fifty Mississippi. *She's just trying to find the right words, the perfect thing to say: Don't worry, darling. We'll get through this together.*

My roommates laughed in the kitchen.

She said I was an honest child. Of course she believes me.

Ninety-four Mississippi. *Say something, Mom, please.* I held my breath.

One hundred. My voice leaked out in a whisper. "Mom . . . Mom, are you still there?"

When she spoke again, steel bound her voice. "You were never alone with him."

This wasn't something I'd practiced. I had no idea what to say, so I told her the truth. "It was when we visited. After *Shabbos* dinner in the back room. He'd tell me the story about the skunk and the railroad car, and the light was . . ."

"You were never out of my sight."

My ears pounded. I couldn't see. *You don't give a shit about me. It's always about you!*

When I finally responded, it was in a tight, clipped voice. "You know, Mom, I've been reading a lot, and according to all the studies, men don't just start molesting children when they're seventy years old."

Mom's breath drew back, the ocean before a tsunami.

"If he did it to me, then he probably did it to . . ."

"HOW DARE YOU!" Mom's voice crashed over me. Something broke deep inside, a fender crumpling in a collision. "You were always selfish."

Yes, Mom, I've always been selfish. Of course she's right. She is always right.

"You're a goddamn liar!"

If you say so, Mom, it must be true. I am a liar. Liar, liar, pants on fire.

"You only look out for yourself."

I'm a bad, terrible daughter.

"How could you do this to me? First you blamed me for the divorce. Then you turned down that scholarship to Wellesley. A full scholarship! I wasn't made of money. How could you do that to me?"

I squeezed myself into a tighter ball.

"Then you ran off with that guru. That fat fuck! Then you decided you were a lesbian!" Mom spat out the word as if she could barely stand to say it.

I pressed the phone against my ear, drinking in every word: Mom's rage, my lullaby.

"I could handle all of that. All the shit you've put me through! It hasn't been easy having you as a daughter. But this . . . accusation! You couldn't have hurt me worse if you'd shot me!"

It's true. I'm an awful person. But I need you.

My heart pounded like a thin-skinned drum. *If only there was a light on the wall, like at Bubby and Poppa's, I could disappear.*

Please tell me I'm going to be okay. Just say it again.

Mom's words ripped through the miles. "You're ruining my life! I hope someday you have a daughter just like you!"

Then she hung up on me.

I clutched my knees and rocked, the receiver still plastered to my ear.

Click.

Dial tone.

Oh my God. What have I done?

The little girl I'd kept locked away for more than twenty years finally had her say. Now, I was going to pay.

—𝔪—

The night I told my mother about the incest was the night I got it—I was going to have to get through this without her. Flashbacks, terror, and shame already had me reeling. Now, I had a new trauma to deal with: my mother had chosen her dead father over me, her living daughter.

In the months that followed, a recurring image haunted me. I was standing outside a large sealed glass room, like one of those "you can smoke in here" lounges in airports. The walls were thick, clear, and smooth, with no doors or windows. I could see in, but there was no way I could get in. Inside were all kinds of people: doctors and hairdressers, farmworkers and teachers, accountants and elevator operators, moms and dads, little kids, teenagers, old men and women. People getting up in the morning, brewing coffee, making lunches, going to work, heading to school, eating dinner, making love. They were laughing, crying, talking, and hugging. They were all sizes, races, and nationalities, and they all had one thing in common: they were living happy, interconnected lives. They belonged to couples, families, and communities. And I was always on the outside, longing to get in—certain I'd remain stuck outside forever. Outside was where I belonged, where I was meant to be. A speck of dust floating through the universe, untethered.

That year, I lived from therapy session to therapy session, struggling to survive, never knowing when I'd have another flashback: Poppa unbuckling his belt, reaching under my nightie, putting a peppermint Life Saver on my tongue when he was done.

Years later, Ellen Bass and I would coin the phrase "The Emergency Stage" to describe this devastating phase of the healing process, but when I was going through it, it wasn't a chapter title; it was my own desperate, miserable, life. I could think of nothing but incest. I was certain the pain would never end.

People promised me that healing was possible, that the only way out was through. If I was going to find my way out of the nightmare I was in, I was going to have to do it without my mother. I couldn't bear her denial, rage, and fear providing color commentary on the hell that was my life. So, I strengthened the wall between us.

The silence was particularly painful on special days: Mother's Day. Her birthday. My birthday. Thanksgiving. Passover. The night Best Picture was announced. I made plans for those days: dinner with my chosen family, a hike, three movies in a row, a feminist *seder*, an extra therapy session, Thanksgiving with friends. But loss stalked me at those events.

Some gut punches I couldn't plan for. Seeing a mother and daughter laughing together on the street could trigger a crippling tailspin.

I cobbled together a chosen family of friends, including Dad and the few relatives who believed me. Paul was not included. He was not a reliable ally; he flipped between supporting me and placating Mom. I wished Paul could have been there for me at the worst time in my life, but the truth was I hadn't trusted him for a long time. I relied on my friends who loved and believed me.

But Mom's absence loomed over them all.

AFTER MOM'S DEATH

BEEKEEPER

Once I opened the door to reading about my history with my mother, I spent weeks with my nose buried in ancient journals and stacks of decades-old correspondence. Day after day, I went to my office, plunked myself down on my mother's blue recliner, and devoured the past. Memories rose up, along with the mildew.

I had saved everything. Between journal entries, my old notebooks were filled with letters, typed and handwritten, attached with rusty paper clips: letters from my mother, my father, my brother, and my friends—some friends I still treasure decades later and others whose names I no longer remember. Who was Theresa, the passionate Italian playwright, anyway?

I kept copies of every letter I wrote my mother—sent and unsent. First drafts full of honest rage, so different from the carefully edited versions that she eventually received. And I saved all the letters she sent to me. At the height of our estrangement, this exchange between us was typical.

Here, I'm twenty-eight and pouring out my heart to Mom.

After reading your letter asking me to make a "nice" family visit to the East Coast, I was filled with rage. I fear the power of my anger to destroy, to eradicate the future hope of any bridge. Afraid if I say what's in my heart, our break will become irreconcilable. I haven't wanted to face that, but in truth, I feel I have little in the way of family to visit. Family is supposed to be there, through thick and thin. You taught me that. Your friends will always leave and change, but your family will always be there. Well, it's my friends who have pulled me through this agonizing time. You, and most of the rest of "my family," have cast me out because I will no longer be silent about the wounds I endured as a small child.

Whenever I've come to you in crisis, every goddamn time, you've reacted the same: "You've confirmed my worst fear about you," or "You've wasted another year." This to a frightened twenty-one-year-old just out of four years in a monastery. Or how about this one? "You're doing this to destroy me." Well, I'm not. I'm not living my life to destroy you. I'm doing it to survive. It's my life now. You can't have it.

Do you think I like hardening in rage? Don't you think I want a "nice family" to visit? I want reconciliation, but not your way. I can't sweep the last year away like it never happened, so we can go back to trading chopped-liver recipes over the phone.

I miss that, Mom. Miss calling you up after the Oscars to talk old-movie history, cooking holiday dinners and playing Scrabble, sitting in front of your fireplace, smoking our biennial joint. I miss it all. But your denial is in the way. I don't know how to make room for both: for the irreconcilable to sit with the caring.

You asked me to tell you about my life. What should I say? That I got laid off from my job, and now I'm seeking funding to work on my incest book full-time? That I spend my days interviewing women survivors of sexual abuse out of a need for inspiration that healing is possible? What can I write to you about? The weather in San Francisco? The fact that I have no love life because my sexuality was decimated by your father's touch? How can I tell you about my life? You don't want to hear any of it!

Writing this hurts. It is an actual physical pain, a longing for something out of reach. I don't know how to reconcile such rage with the depth of love I feel. For half a year, I tried silence, setting boundaries so I could separate and focus on my own need to heal. Is there a next step? For me, there is only the terrible rage and the awful love. And I don't know what to do with either of them.

A few weeks later, I received this response from her:

I read your letter amid mixed feelings of anger, hurt, and compassion and decided to send no reply. I deserve at this time in my life not to have to defend myself against such rabid attacks. Whatever I say will only end up as further ammunition of all the evil I inflicted upon you. But silence is not my way, especially when I feel your terrible pain. I pray you will be able to work through your suffering. Assuming you were a victim of child molestation, are you going to hang on to it forever, make this the cause of your life, and destroy your potential for happiness?

Yes, I also hear your ambivalence, the love for family. You are wrong about one thing—you do have

a family. You certainly have a mother, but I no longer wish to play the masochist who happily accepts the abuse you seem to need to heap on me. When you are ready for the relationship we deserve together, I shall be ready. Nothing is ever perfect.

Laura, you will soon be twenty-nine. I remember your birth so clearly, your childhood. My memories are happy ones. I hope you can make this a good year for yourself.

As I study our correspondence, one dynamic stands out: I was reaching out to my mother and pushing her away at the same time. I never stopped yearning for her, even as I held her at bay. Like a beekeeper who wears protective gear to reduce the number of stings, I protected myself as I extended my hand.

CHAPTER 25

GENESIS

Laura 28, Temme 57, Santa Cruz

During the terrible time when I was inundated by incest memories and Mom and I were at war, I was trying to figure what to do with my career. A year earlier, in 1983, I'd moved back to California after two years working as a reporter and talk-show host for Rainbird Community Broadcasting in Ketchikan, Alaska. I was working three part-time media jobs in the Bay Area, but none was the right fit. I was uncertain about my next step. So, I threw a party.

I invited a dozen people—friends and folks I'd worked with before. I cooked them a meal, but before we ate, I made a presentation, complete with flip charts about the kinds of things I liked to do (being on the radio, writing, interviewing people) and the kinds of things I never wanted to do (work in a corporation, wear a suit to work, obey lots of stupid petty rules). Then I had them fill out a four-page questionnaire about me: what they saw as my strengths and weaknesses, my talents, the careers they might imagine for me. I kept the participants on task; we also ate and had fun together.

If nothing else, that party demonstrated my strongest talents at the time: communication, organization, initiative, and *chutzpah*. Mom would have been proud of me, but unfortunately, we weren't speaking at the time. She knew nothing about this party.

One of the people I invited to the "What Should Laura Do with Her Life?" party was Ellen Bass. I'd participated in her writing circles when I was twenty-three and new to Santa Cruz. In the intervening years, we'd become friends. Ellen had just published *I Never Told Anyone: Writings by Women Survivors of Child Sexual Abuse,* the first book where women shared stories of having been sexually abused. I knew about the book and the impact it was having, and Ellen knew I'd been having incest memories. What I didn't know, and learned at that party, was that Ellen's publisher, Harper & Row, wanted her to write a sequel, a book about healing. When she told me she'd said no, I asked, "Would you consider writing it if you had me as a collaborator?"

Ellen knew I had the writing chops. "Laura, if I was going to write it with anyone, I'd write it with you, but I know what it takes to write a book, and you don't." Ellen had a partner, a family, a young daughter, and she was leading groups and writing poems. She had no time for another book on incest. She told me no.

I was young, single, and child-free, consumed in my own healing process. The idea of writing a book about healing grabbed me, so I waged a strategic campaign to convince Ellen to agree. "How about if I do all the legwork for the first year, and then you jump in, once your obligations are over?" "What if I do all the interviews?" "How about if I do all the parts you don't want to do?" I was friendly, determined, and relentless.

Six weeks later, a yellow envelope arrived in the mail. The return address was from Ellen. Tearing it open, I pulled out a card with embossed pastel balloons imprinted on the front. Inside, a single word in cursive:

And that's how *The Courage to Heal,* the book Mom hated, the one that tore us even farther apart, was born.

CHAPTER 26

PRECIPICE

1,539 Days

In early May 2010, I flew home after teaching a writing retreat overseas. After sixteen hours in airplanes, a six-hour layover, and four hours of sleep, I couldn't wait to get home. Karyn was cooking a reunion dinner: one of her famous stir-fries, with a pear-apple crisp made out of fruit from our trees. The kids were baking popovers. Eli couldn't wait to show me the nine-tailed origami fox he had designed and folded. Lizzy had an essay due the next day that she wanted me to edit; she'd texted me on my layover. Editing her eighth-grade essays was one place that was still sweet between us.

My eyes burned with fatigue. I'd be slammed back into teaching the next day, but this was going to be our celebratory night. From the airport, I faced a long, windy drive home, but I could taste that stir-fry. I couldn't wait to hug my family, take a long, hot bath, and sleep with Karyn in my own bed.

While waiting for my bags, I pushed Mom on speed dial—the perfect time to check in. I pressed the phone against my ear to block out the slam of suitcases. "I'm back. How's it going?"

"Good. How was your trip?"

I walked away from the carousel, looking for a quieter spot. There was something in her voice—what was it? "My trip was great. I loved it. How are you doing?"

"I'm hanging in. Watching a little 'teedleveedle.'" Mom's nickname for TV. "Oh, and my leg hurts."

As suitcases cascaded down the chute, I imagined Karyn at our yellow kitchen table, chopping fresh chard from the garden. "What's the matter? Did you pull a muscle?"

"I tripped over the dishwasher door and fell. Why the hell do they make dishwashers like that?"

My first suitcase thudded to a stop. It was big and black like all the others, but thank you, Karyn, for the pink polka-dot luggage tag.

Mom buzzed like a hornet in my ear. "That dishwasher is a death trap. I'm going to write to the company. It's a terrible design. I don't know why that fucking door was open!" *Right. You live alone, and you don't know why it was open?*

Mom had saved up all her frustration, waiting for me to get home. She never complained to Paul. Whenever they talked, everything was always hunky-dory. He'd describe the latest meditation CD he was making her, and she'd swear life was great.

After the unclaimed bags circled a third time, the motor shut down, and the conveyor belt stopped. Eight of us stood waiting, praying to the Great Baggage God in the sky.

At home, the kids would be pulling out their favorite popover recipe. I had to get home.

"Really, Laurie, my leg. It's no big deal. I fell. I cut it. But it's okay. I took care of it."

"That's great, Mom."

The carousel jerked back into life, and my second bag teetered on top. *Hallelujah.* I smiled, imagining the brilliant red bougainvillea and birds-of-paradise at our front door, the porch light glowing in welcome.

"Mom, my bags are here. I've got to go. But I got you a present." A new mask to add to her collection. "Can I stop by tomorrow after class?"

"Laurie, darling, I know you're dying to see Karyn and the kids, but do you think you could stop by this evening and take a quick look at my leg?"

"Sure, Mom."

Shit.

As I dragged my bags to the car, I did the math in my head. Once I hit Santa Cruz, ten minutes to Mom's place. A fifteen-minute visit, half an hour tops. Twenty minutes to get home. An hour altogether, max. I texted Karyn: "Mom hurt her leg. Got to go see her. Can we start a little later?"

—᯾—

When I pulled up at Mom's, NPR news was blaring out onto the street. I walked in, strode to the radio, turned the volume down.

Mom was lying in her big recliner, pen in hand, the *New York Times* crossword creased neatly on her lap. I folded back the crocheted blanket and rolled up her stretch pants. Ouch. The wound gaped open like a dying fish. When I touched it, Mom flinched. Her leg was hot and swollen. "How long has it been like this?"

"I don't know. What are you asking me for?" *Because it's your fucking leg.*

"This is serious. Why didn't you go to the doctor?"

"I don't know. I didn't feel like it. It's such a hassle."

"You should have had this looked at."

She stuck out her chin. "What's the big deal? I tripped. I fell. I got up. I knew you were coming home soon."

"Why didn't you tell Paul?" Why hadn't she called Karyn?

"Your brother lives in Arizona. Why would I bother him with a little thing like this?" Right. Accidents with dishwashers were far too mundane for their conversations. It wasn't part of their soul contract.

I took another look at the angry wound. It was puffy and red. "It's infected."

"It's just a little cut."

"This is serious."

She snapped at me. "Stop attacking me."

"I'm not attacking you. I'm concerned about you." And now I had no choice. "I'm taking you to the doctor." I texted Karyn and the kids: "Mom's leg looks bad. Heading to the walk-in clinic. Start without me."

Lizzy texted me back. "Too bad, Mom."

I texted back: "Save me a popover."

Mom wasn't triaged until 8:00 p.m. The nurse said the wait could be up to an hour. I imagined my empty place at the table, my popover deflating into a tacky brown disc.

I pulled out the cards I always keep at the bottom of my purse and dealt us a hand of 500 rummy. We played on the waiting room chairs, placing our melds on an empty seat between us. As cards passed between us, my body relaxed. We'd been playing this game for half a century. I jotted our scores on a battered envelope and beat her three games in a row. Just as she started winning, they called out her name.

A nurse took Mom's vitals, then left the room. I sneaked a look at my phone: 8:30. Maybe I could still make dessert: ice cream melting on steaming apple cobbler.

Twenty minutes later, the doctor came in, took a look at the wound, and proclaimed that Mom would be fine. They bandaged her and asked where to fax the prescription. I checked my phone. It was after 9:00 p.m. The only open pharmacy was all the way across town. *Shit.*

Mom waited in the car while I stood in line. When it was finally my turn, her antibiotics weren't ready.

Lizzy texted me a shot of the three of them, smiling at the table, playing Rummikub. The message underneath said, "Mom, what about my essay?"

I texted back: "Sorry, sweetie. Grandma needs me. Send it to my phone?"

The instant reply: "You know you can't edit on your phone."

She was right. I texted back: "I'll be home as soon as I can."

Damn Mom. She'd kept it a big, fat secret until I got home.

When I finally slid into the car, clutching the white pharmacy bag, Mom snarled, "What took you so long?"

I spoke through gritted teeth. "It wasn't ready."

"I'm cold, Laurie. I didn't bring a jacket." *Bad daughter.* Why hadn't I thought of that? Because neither of us thought this would take all night. I slipped off my sweatshirt and wrapped it around her. Goose bumps stippled my skin. I rummaged through my purse, found a stale almond-butter bar, broke off half, offered the rest to her.

It was after 11:00 p.m. when I finally tucked her in. When I pulled up at home, the house was dark. I couldn't see the bougainvillea. Eli had gone to his girlfriend's house to spend the night. Karyn was asleep, a murder mystery sliding off her chest. I knocked on Lizzy's door and peeked in. Engrossed in a call, she gave me one of her "Mom, this is private" stares. I mouthed the words, "Your essay?" She ripped half a sheet of notebook paper out of her binder and scrawled: "Too late. I already turned it in."

I sat down to the plate of stir-fry Karyn had left out for me and ate my dinner alone. As I thought about all I'd missed, a familiar empty place opened up inside, as if I didn't have a life full of blessings. I drifted back to the fire escape where I'd cast my mind as a little girl, sucking on a thinning Life Saver. I rinsed my dish, went out to the back porch where Lizzy couldn't smell it, and lit a joint. As the red-hot tip glowed, I stared out into the night.

The next morning, as I made breakfast for the kids, Karyn emerged from our bedroom and hugged me. "Sorry we couldn't save you a popover."

"The life span of a popover around here is two minutes. How about a rain check? Tonight?"

As NPR reported on the inferno that had engulfed the Deepwater Horizon oil rig, I told Karyn about Mom's leg. Soon, I was rushing the kids out the door and racing to class. I had a headache and could barely pay attention. A ragged, distracted writing teacher who can't listen? I had to do better.

That afternoon, I cooked a pot of lentil soup. Called two prospective students and went over the week's to-dos with my virtual assistant, a woman from Ohio whom I'd never met. After dinner, the four of us watched *Sherlock*, the kids groaning each time I hit Pause to ask, "What just happened?" Benedict Cumberbatch talked so fast that I couldn't decipher anything he said.

"God, Mom," Lizzy said. "Why don't you just listen?"

Home sweet home.

After the kids disappeared into their rooms, Karyn and I sat on the couch, rubbed each other's feet, and caught up. Mom's accident faded away.

Two days later, Mom called. "Laurie, I don't feel so good."

I rushed right over.

The moment I walked in, hot, stale air assaulted me. The smell of unwashed clothes filled the room; the place had been shut up tight. Mom slumped on the couch.

Oh shit. Where have I been?

Was she wearing the same outfit she'd had on three days before? Yes, she was. Two of her neighbors walked by outside, chatting about a film. I knew things were bad when Mom didn't notice them; she never missed an opportunity to feel left out.

I sat down beside her. Her face was pale. Her hair stringy. Breath sour. Sweat glistened on her face. "Mom, get up." I reached under her shoulders. Her body was clammy, her forehead burning. I tried to hoist her.

"Stop it; you're hurting me!" Her eyes darted like moths near a flame. "I'm too dizzy. I can't get up!"

"I'm calling an ambulance. I'm taking you to the emergency room."

Her dull eyes shot into focus. "I am not going to the hospital! It's the worst place for old people to be. For an aspirin—thirty dollars! It's all a giant racket."

"Mom, you have to—look at you!"

"It's my life and I'm not going, and you can't make me!"

Shit. Shit. Shit.

I brought her some water. "Drink this. I'm going to call your doctor and describe your symptoms. How about that?"

She nodded grudgingly. I slipped into the bathroom so she couldn't hear me. Five minutes later, I returned. "A visiting nurse just happens to be nearby. She'll be right over."

I grabbed the cards from the coffee table, flicked off the rubber band. I was dealing our second hand of 500 rummy when the nurse arrived. She checked Mom's vitals, looked at her wound, asked a few questions. Mom minimized everything.

"Temme, can you excuse us a moment?" The nurse signaled me to follow her outside. The moment the door closed behind us, she called an ambulance, then turned to me. "Pack her a bag. This is serious."

"How serious?"

"Let's just say it's good I was in the neighborhood."

It took me three minutes to pack Mom's duffel: silk paisley nightgown; medical power of attorney; Medicare card; small radio; the *New York Times*; pink case for her dentures; Efferdent; a change of clothes; her beloved handicapped placard.

When I returned, the nurse was holding Mom's hand, speaking in warm tones. "It's just a precaution, Temme. You have to go. An ambulance is on the way."

Mom's eyes sought mine, searching for something to hold on to. I barely managed to meet her gaze, frightened of the need I saw there.

Strapped to the gurney, Mom looked tiny. As I followed the ambulance in my car, I called Karyn and asked her to pick up the kids. Left a message for Paul: "Taking Mom to the ER. Call me." At the hospital, I insisted on staying with Mom for every step. The IV. The blood draws. The heart monitor. When they placed the catheter, she screamed in panic and pain. I took her hand. Stroked her mottled skin. "It's okay. I'm here."

Multiple teams came in, asking the same questions, taking the same history, always asking for her birthday—a sore point with my mother, who prided herself on looking much younger than her age.

Mom's potassium levels were sky high. Her breathing shallow.

At six o'clock, I scanned my phone. Karyn had left three messages. Bryan had called to express his concern. Eli and Lizzy had texted, but there was nothing from Paul. Why not? He always checked his messages. I called him again. "It's me. It's urgent. Call me."

Four hours after we arrived, Mom got her diagnosis: acute renal failure. They pumped her full of drugs, and she slept. There was talk of dialysis, but they'd have to wait and see. The kidney doctor, a no-nonsense woman from Russia, stood beside me as we both looked down at Mom. "If you hadn't brought her in today, she would have died."

At 9:00 p.m., Karyn encouraged me to drive home and get something to eat. From Paul, still nothing. *I've got your back.* Yeah, right.

The ICU nurse promised to call me if there was the slightest change. Karyn greeted me at the front door.

"Is she going to be okay?"

"I don't know."

"Are you hungry?"

"I don't know. Has Paul called?"

"No. Where is he?"

"I have no idea. He hasn't responded to my calls. I'm going to try email."

Karyn led me into the kitchen, cooked me poached eggs and toast, and listened.

She was just as worried as I was.

Before heading back to the ICU, I drew myself a bath and lit a candle. Eased myself into the water, stared out the window at the waning moon. The mellow tones of the bass chime in the garden echoed across the shimmy of leaves. A dog barked. A coyote yipped in the distance. I stretched my legs out into the steaming water.

My mother almost died today. I tried it on. Mom had been the most powerful presence in my life—in good times and bad—for five decades. I'd become who I was in opposition to her. Who would I be without her?

—∞—

As I jogged back down the hall to Mom's room at Dominican Hospital, her distinctive snore rang out, pealing like the finest of bells. I slipped into her room, carrying a pillow, my laptop, and my phone. A book of short stories by Roald Dahl, good for reading aloud. I hoped Mom would be able to listen.

I made a nest in the visitor's chair. Opened my computer. At the top of my inbox was Paul's vacation autoresponder. The subject line: "Off the grid in Montana." Montana. Who was in Montana? Oh yeah. Paul's latest spiritual teacher. Her specialty was deep psychic release, and he went to her retreats several times a year. I couldn't remember her name and had no idea where the retreat might be. His email said he'd be off the grid for *five* more days.

What if Mom died?

—∞—

The white blanket barely rose and fell with her breath. How had she gotten so small? Could she really be the same woman I'd loved as a girl? Hated as a teenager? Characterized as a monster? Tamed into a sometimes-friend? Mom and I had done better than anyone witnessing our relationship had expected. Better than *we* expected. I'd invited her to move to California, and she had come. When we signed those papers years before, it had all been theoretical. Become her medical power of attorney? Sure. Now it was real. Paul was thousands of miles away. Her life was in my hands.

Mom's blood pressure cuff hissed and tightened. She stirred. Gasped. Stopped breathing. Snored again. Mom had sleep apnea, just like I did, but she'd never master a CPAP machine. She could barely send an email. Besides, she was convinced that the whole sleep medicine thing was just another scam.

At 4:00 a.m., I tried to read but couldn't focus. I watched Mom instead. The red light of the oximeter cast a pink glow on her cheeks. A bruised purple flower bloomed on her wrist where the IV pierced her tender skin. White hair arced across the pillow. Her face was relaxed, the face of a child.

How many times had she watched me sleep?

Slowly, the hospital came to life around us. A breakfast cart clattered down the hall. Someone called out, "Happy Mother's Day," as doctors made their rounds. Mom's eyes fluttered open, telegraphing confusion, panic, and fear. As soon as she saw me, her whole body relaxed. Her eyes locked onto mine, and I didn't turn away.

Her face was wide open. Her eyes said, *I could have died yesterday*, and *I might die tomorrow.* And I was thinking the same.

The old stories no longer mattered. I pulled the visitor's chair as close as I could get.

Something was changing between us. We were entering a new world: two human beings, perched on the edge. We sat on the ledge between worlds in silence, legs dangling over the precipice. I sensed Vicki across the veil, rooting for us.

"Mom, this is why you moved here."

"I know." The blood pressure cuff squeezed her arm, like bellows stoking a flame.

"This is why you left New Jersey. So I could be here with you now."

"Yes, I know."

I still needed to get closer. "Scoot over," I told her, and Mom scooted. I slid into the bed.

PART II

"Out beyond ideas of wrongdoing and rightdoing, there is a field. I'll meet you there."

—Rumi

CHAPTER 27

SWEATER

Laura 34, San Francisco

I was at the height of my success when I decided I didn't want to travel around the country talking about incest anymore. I'd written four books about sexual abuse and was tired of being on the road. Telling my story onstage no longer felt right because it had become just that—a story. I had talked about the healing process for so long that my anguish and terror had been smoothed down to a few polished, glossy stones. The story of how I'd suffered and healed had begun to feel too much like a performance: no longer raw, vulnerable, or alive. I no longer wanted my life reduced to "He touched me; therefore, I am."

Every day, people told me how brave I was, but I knew that they were wrong. What I was doing had become safe. I didn't need to lead with my pain anymore. I'd done my work. I'd been in therapy for years. I was living in a skin that felt too small. I'd earned the right to slough off that skin, to give the new tender cells underneath a chance to breathe. I wanted to fly or fall based on my own merits, not because of what I'd suffered as a child. I wanted to build a new life, and not just recover from the life I'd had.

I kept thinking about two sisters I'd interviewed for *The Courage to Heal*. Their abuse had been extreme; their healing, inspirational. They talked about getting to a place where they felt like they were wearing sweaters that were too small—they were hot, tight, and uncomfortable, and they wanted to take them off, but it was all they knew. And the idea of living without those sweaters was terrifying.

My sweater was chafing like crazy. I'd spent years meeting people at the place of their deepest anguish. It had been a profound honor, but now I wanted to meet people for different reasons: because we shared a love of words, because we loved to cook or walk on the beach, babies in our arms. I was starting to have dreams again, everyday dreams. I wanted a spouse and children of my own. After years of feeling too damaged, I was starting to believe I was capable of loving and being loved. But I was never going to find a partner traveling city to city, telling my incest story.

And so, I left the road.

I met Karyn at a women's body-surfing clinic on the beach, shortly after moving back to Santa Cruz. A high school reading teacher who was developing a passion for yoga, Karyn was a single mother with an eleven-year-old son, Bryan. Karyn and I knew of each other but had never talked before. That conversation in wetsuits led to our first real date: going to see the Dalai Lama at the Vajrapani Institute, a small Buddhist center an hour away. Fifteen minutes into our drive, I asked Karyn straight out, "Are you open to having more children?" I was thirty-four years old; my baby clock was ticking, and I'd made myself a promise: I was not dating anyone else who didn't want kids.

"Yes," she replied with a smile. "I've always wanted a little brother or sister for Bryan."

That's how we began.

CHAPTER 28

RAINSTORM

Laura 35, Temme 64, East Coast

A year later, I flew to New Jersey to visit my mother. Our relationship was still volatile. Huge swaths of life could not be discussed, but we were cautiously trying to reconnect.

During my weeklong stay, we drove to a big family gathering somewhere in upstate New York—or maybe it was New England. I don't recall the occasion, probably someone's wedding or bar mitzvah or perhaps a fiftieth anniversary celebration. I hated going to those big family parties. Who wants to be the invisible lesbian at a fancy Jewish dinner party? Not that I had to worry about it. Ever since *The Courage to Heal,* I'd been disinvited to everything. This was the exception. I'd been offered an olive branch—invited because I was visiting Mom.

It was just the two of us, driving in her Saturn for hours. I was riding shotgun. Rain thundered on the roof. The wipers ricocheted back and forth. Mom chain-smoked in time to the fast squeak of rubber on glass.

There was something hypnotic about driving in the rain, something warm and cozy about the two of us, not looking at each other, not facing each other, staring out into the gray. Plowing along the edge of the industrial area, smokestacks on the skyline, big trucks splashing greasy water on Mom's sturdy, economical little car.

Mom drove the speed limit. Eighteen-wheelers honked, passing on our left. She pushed in the cigarette lighter, and it popped out with a click. As she pressed the red-hot center against a Parliament, the paper hissed, catching fire. She started talking about my father. Mom rarely discussed him—they'd been divorced twenty years—but she was in an expansive mood. "Your father and I had twenty-three good years together. We both wanted kids. We did family well. We were compatible. We agreed on the practical things. Education. Politics. Money—we were both cheap." Mom laughed, so I laughed, too. "But your father wasn't very romantic. And sex? It was never really a big part of our marriage. Your father wanted it, and I didn't."

What? Did she just say what I think she said? I couldn't believe it. Was that the real reason Dad left? Not so he could be free? Because they weren't having *sex*? My habitual storyline about my parents' divorce was suddenly unraveling. I stared out the streaked glass at the vehicle in front of us. I could barely make out the license plate, but it looked like Connecticut.

Mom took a deep drag, and the cigarette paper sizzled again. "To tell you the truth, I prefer being admired." *Did she really just admit that?* Mom was actually talking to me about her sex life. Me—her wayward daughter. Her wayward lesbian daughter. I leaned closer.

Smoke pooled against the glass and filled the front seat. My eyes burned. "You know, Laurie, I think the whole sex thing is kind of gross and distasteful. I don't like getting messy."

Really? I'm so sorry. "Is that how sex feels to you?"

She checked her blind spot, prepared to change lanes. The turn signal clicked like a Geiger counter. "I never really liked sex."

And this might be my only chance to find out why. I swiveled to face her. "Why not?"

Rain pelted the roof as she began her story. She spoke about her mother, growing up as a little girl in Russia—or was it Poland? We never knew—the border was always changing. Mom had never talked to me about the Old Country before, but now she spoke directly into the thundering storm. "When my mother was little, she was the youngest of ten children, and as the youngest, she slept with her parents because there weren't enough beds. One night her mother—your great-grandmother—was very sick, and her husband—your great-grandfather—wanted to have sex with her anyway. 'I'm too sick,' she cried, but he forced himself on her."

Mom stared out into the downpour, a look on her face I had never seen before. Haunted. As if I weren't there. She crushed her half-smoked cigarette in the ashtray, snapping it in two. "He raped her. And in the morning, when my mother woke up, her mother was dead beside her. Dead and cold in the bed."

"Oh my God, Mom." I shuddered. Stared into the darkening sky, trying to wrap my mind around her words. Around this legacy. More than strength and courage had been passed down to me by my Russian ancestors. Sexual violation wasn't new in our family. I'd suspected it, but no one had ever admitted it before.

Mom had a faraway look in her eyes. Where was this conversation going?

"On my wedding night with your father, I was a virgin. I didn't know anything about sex. I didn't know what was going to happen. I was completely unprepared. The morning of the wedding, my mother pinned the veil on my head, kissed me on the forehead, and whispered, 'Just lie back and endure it.'"

No way. Bubby said that? "That's terrible."

A huge semi passed on our left, splatting the windshield. I flinched, momentarily blinded. My mother was talking to me about sex *and* violation. Getting closer to the one thing I'd always wanted her to say. Maybe all these stories were priming the pump. Was she gathering the courage to finally admit it?

I shrank back into my seat. *If she forgets I'm here, maybe she'll keep talking.* And she did. She told me about the lovers she took when she traveled, how free she felt away from home. About the rich Arab man in the $3,000 suit who had wined and dined her in style. When he found out she was a Jew, he'd turned on her, sneering. "We will drive you into the sea."

Mom had never shared these parts of her life with me before. An unfamiliar feeling filled my body. Not shock or disgust or repulsion—things I might have felt as a teenager. As a twenty-seven-year-old. Or even as recently as the week before. No, this was something new, different, a feeling wholly unexpected: I felt honored.

Traffic bunched up, then spread out again. The gas gauge drooped, heading toward empty. An ambulance streaked by, siren wailing. I sent out a prayer for the recipient, hoping it wasn't a child. Then I turned back to her. "Why didn't you ever remarry? You were forty-two when Dad left, the most beautiful woman around. Why didn't any of your admirers stick?"

Mom took a deep drag and released the smoke from her lungs. "I don't like it when men get real. I don't like it when they fart and burp. I like my fantasies better."

Yes, that fit. The only surprise was Mom admitting it. I thought back to all the times I'd seen her on the stage. Living inside someone else's skin. Her face gleaming under the lights. The thunderous applause. Her despair when each play ended. Mom had always loved being admired from afar.

"I don't know if I ever told you this, Laurie, but every Saturday afternoon, when I was a teenager, I'd get lost in the movies. Back then, they were double features, with a newsreel and some comics—all for ten cents. I remember coming out of the theater where I'd been transfixed into another world, a magical world, and when I walked home, I would not wear my glasses." Mom's voice broke. "I did not want to see the reality of my life. That's why I've always lived in fantasy."

I let that confession settle for a moment. "And that's why you've always loved movies."

She nodded, put on a thick southern accent. "'I have always relied on the kindness of strangers.'"

I laughed as rain battered the roof. We had watched *A Streetcar Named Desire* more times than I could count. I replied with another of our favorite lines from Blanche DuBois, Mom's alter ego and favorite character: "'Sometimes—there's God—so quickly!'"

She laughed, delighted. Then she grew serious again. "The truth is, Laurie, I never thought any of the men were good enough."

I blurted out, "God, Mom, do you really think you're the greatest catch in the world?" *I can't believe I said that.* But Mom just laughed.

As the tires clacked on the wet road, tumblers clicked in my head. Before Karyn, I'd been the queen of serial monogamy. All those lovers

I'd rejected—perfectly good women—weren't good enough for me. That was a legacy from my mother? I wanted to tell Mom, but I never confided in her. Yet now she was confiding in me, heading straight toward the place I'd always wanted her to go. "Mom, you and me—we're the same. Six months after I met Karyn, I broke up with her. I thought she wasn't good enough."

"I didn't know that."

"Thank God I came to my senses."

"I'm glad you did. Karyn's a good woman."

Rain drummed the roof as I let her words soak in: *Karyn's a good woman.* My mother just blessed my lesbian partnership. *Could it be that she actually wants the best for me? For me and Karyn together?*

I leaned closer. I wanted to risk more, but something in her face stopped me. Loneliness. Raw, unfettered loneliness. A road map of regret etched across her features. When she spoke again, her voice was grave. "Laurie, don't make my mistakes."

"I won't, Mom." What I couldn't yet say was *I'm so sorry.*

As she regained her composure, I took in the magnitude of what had just occurred: I'd had a real conversation with my mother. I'd made myself vulnerable to my old enemy, and I wasn't annihilated. In fact, she revealed herself to me.

Maybe it was the downpour. Maybe it was the steady swish of the wipers. Maybe it was the two of us sitting side by side, staring straight ahead. Years later, with my own teenagers, I learned that our best chance for conversation was always in the car. Maybe my mother knew that, too. Whatever it was, for those few hours on our way to the event I can't recall, we stepped out of our roles: oppressive, domineering, emotional mother and withholding, cold, selfish daughter. We became two girlfriends gabbing about our lives. Well, mostly, she was gabbing. Except for my one confession about breaking up with Karyn, I wasn't ready to share my life with her. Only the highly redacted version. But Mom was feeling no such reservations.

When we stopped for gas, I bought two packs of licorice—red for me, black for her. Back on the road, we chomped our Twizzlers with delight. Mom changed lanes, took a big bite, and the sharp tang of anise filled the car. "I shouldn't tell you this, but my friend told me about a friend of hers who says her life was saved by your book. My friend thought I'd be happy about it, that I'd be proud of you." She hissed when she said it, but then her voice softened. "And I was proud of you. I am proud of you, Laurie, but I still hate what you did."

When she said that, something cracked open inside me. I sat still, willing her to go on. And she did, her voice a harsh soliloquy. "I remember this one time I went into my father's room in the morning. And his penis was erect, and I remember thinking how ugly it was."

Oh my God. This is it.

"You know, Laurie, I've always told the story about Poppa's ninetieth birthday party, about the skits we did for him: 'Morris Ross, this is your life.' We did a skit about him being a bootlegger. And one about his time in the navy. But I always forgot to tell the part about him making all the girls show him their breasts when they started to develop. Years later, when I realized that . . . I started crying really hard. And I still don't know why."

I held my breath. The day Mom insisted that I lift up my shirt, I'd made my stand alone. Now finally, it would be the two of us.

Rain slicked down the windows, enclosing us in a bubble. In the stillest, simplest voice I could find, I said the words I'd longed to say but had never risked before. "Mom, I've always wondered if it happened to you, too. If that's why all of this has been so hard for you."

She said nothing, but I could feel her recoil. She shoved in the cigarette lighter. Waited for the click. I waited, too, my body on alert. Her hand reached out—not to me—to bring fire to her lips. She lit her cigarette, took a long drag, and spiraled deep into herself.

The conversation was over.

I stared out into the rain.

CHAPTER 29

PERSISTENCE

Laura 36, Temme 64, Santa Cruz

I found out I was pregnant while sitting on the cracked wooden seat of an outhouse in Utah. As I stared at the blue line on the white plastic wand, a fat brown spider dangled down the cobwebbed wall. I lowered the lid on the smelly sea of shit, flung open the door, and raced down the path to our campsite. I shouted to Karyn, "It's blue! We're having a baby!" Then I turned to Bryan, who at fourteen was not at all keen on knowing anything about my body. "Bryan, you're going to have a little brother or sister."

I'd dreamed of this moment for years, then undreamed it. In the early years of remembering the incest, I was certain that I was too damaged to become a mother. How could I possibly be a fit parent? If I had a baby, wouldn't I just repeat the abuse I'd suffered as a child? I felt terrified. Sunk before I even began. But years of therapy and Karyn's steady love had brought me to this moment.

It was 1992, the year that newspapers and magazines across the country were attacking the burgeoning incest survivors' movement, enhancing the claims of the newly formed False Memory Syndrome Foundation, FMSF. They were coming after us, Ellen Bass and me, because we were the coauthors of *The Courage to Heal,* the book that had most visibly inspired survivors' empowerment. They pointed their sharp, accusing fingers at us, insisting that we were destroying their families by implanting "false memories" in their vulnerable daughters. And they didn't just accuse us—they sued us.

While I slogged through weeks of nausea, reading pregnancy books, obsessed with every twinge, feeling the quickening—that first amazing fish-flop of new life in my belly—the attacks against us grew. Women on the street began smiling at me, clucking in approval for the first time in my adult life; with my visible pregnancy, I was passing as a heterosexual woman. As the word "mother" came to be no longer about *her,* but now intimately familiar to *me,* Ellen went on the road to defend us.

As authors of *The Courage to Heal,* we were invited to be interviewed by every media outlet in the country. Or so it seemed. The reporters always promised that *of course* they wanted to represent our side of the story; *of course* they were on the side of survivors; *of course* their article or radio show or TV episode would promote healing. They *believed* in us and our message; they *believed* the women we'd interviewed, the women we'd written for, so we said yes. Well, actually, it was Ellen who said yes, because I was pregnant and cocooning, protecting my heart and the tiny Eli seed growing inside me. "I'll take care of this, Laura," Ellen promised in a moment of generosity that I'm sure she lived to regret, though she was far too polite to ever say so. Ellen is a woman who always keeps her promises.

As my belly swelled, I craved liver, a food I normally detest. Karyn bought it organic twice a week, cooked it extra well done, smothered with browned onions and ultracrispy bacon, not a pucker of white fat remaining. While I happily devoured platefuls of it, Ellen got on airplane after airplane and flew off to appear on *Donahue* and *Good Morning America* and dozens of other shows. A driver would meet her at the airport, with her name—Ellen Bass—held high on a cardboard sign, then drive her to the studio for makeup (depending on their budget) and, and from there, to the set. The hot lights beat down on her—Ellen in her flowered polyester dress, the men claiming to be falsely accused, an occasional angry wife, usually flanked by a so-called memory expert, touting bogus theories. They all lined up against her, even the smooth moderators, the ones who'd been so welcoming in the green room. Once the cameras rolled, they attacked relentlessly. But Ellen never caved. She persisted.

Sometimes, she'd call me from her hotel room to report on the horrible things they'd said to her. She'd tell me how she remained steady, looking straight into the blinking red light above the camera, ignoring the men and talking only to the survivors she knew were watching at home on TV. "You aren't alone," she said to the blinking red light. "Healing is possible," she told the women. "It wasn't your fault." And "I believe you."

As my cravings changed from liver to skirt steak, the panel on my maternity stretch jeans expanded, and I made friends with other mothers-to-be. We met and stretched and dreamed about motherhood. I loved being pregnant. I grew my baby and stayed home. Ellen was our warrior.

A group of incest survivors started a defense fund on our behalf. This was in the days before internet usage was widespread, so they put up signs in public bathrooms and laundromat bulletin boards, cafés, and independent bookstores. They placed small ads in the back of the grassroots newsletters proliferating for survivors in those days, raising money to fight the lawsuits steamrolling over us. Every few days, I'd drive to the Santa Cruz post office to pick up yet another huge sack of mail. Sitting at my desk, I sliced open hundreds of letters. Inside were dollar bills—a single wrinkled one, a fiver, sometimes a twenty. And love notes—"Hang in there. You're fighting for all of us."

The mail just kept coming. And so did the money, more than $70,000 in small bills, enough to cover half the fees for our attorney. Our publisher, Harper & Row, paid the other half. Months later, the lawsuits against us were dropped on first amendment grounds. We had won.

But the whole time those donations were rolling in, Ellen never stopped speaking into those cameras, always to the women at home, while the men did everything that they could to destroy her, to destroy us. But they couldn't. We may have been on the front lines, but there was a whole wedge of angry, determined, empowered women behind us.

I never told my mother about any of this. She had no idea it was happening.

AFTER MOM'S DEATH

DOORWAY

As I continue to dig through our old correspondence, I've been weeping over a letter Mom wrote to me in November 1992, during the second trimester of my pregnancy with Eli, a time when I was refusing to see her.

> *Dear Laura,*
> *Lately, I've been preoccupied by thoughts of you for many reasons, primarily your pregnancy and my preparing to move out of our family house after thirty years.*
>
> *First things first, I would love to have a photo of you as a pregnant woman since I probably won't see you in that condition.*
>
> *It might be of interest how I'm handling this event with my friends. "Laurie is expecting a baby—something she has wanted for a long time—she is thrilled. She has conceived by artificial insemination and is in a happy, supportive relationship with a woman I have met and like. I believe she will be an excellent mother.*

I am so happy for her." This is not only to my closest friends, but also to casual acquaintances.

In preparation for moving, I came across four boxes of letters in the attic. I became lost in reading them, yours first. There is now a box labelled "Laurie" starting with 1978. One dated 1979 said, "I hope you will save my letters since I may be a famous writer one day—ha! ha!" Indeed, I did. Indeed, you did.

In regard to your letters, where do I begin? For starters, you were a damn good writer, going way back—expressive, colorful, funny. Repeatedly you state your desire to be a writer and for the last five years or so—a mother.

The shocking realization was the closeness we achieved in our correspondence. With all the guardedness of recent years, I was beginning to believe you never loved me. But your letters are full of warmth, love, confidences about your lovers, advice-seeking about your career and pleasure in our correspondence—a real mother/daughter bond. It was a happy revelation that brought tears as well as a longing to recapture that in our relationship. Even after that painful period in 1984, there was some real communication. Then the flow of letters trickled down to occasional cute cards on ceremonial occasions. No doubt, the same occurred on my end—each of us distrustful of putting our feelings on paper.

I want it to be otherwise. This wonderful event in your life could be the catalyst to bring us together as mother, daughter, and grandchild. I want to give your child the warmth and attention of a loving grandmother. I want to be there for you in the challenges of motherhood. My thoughts go back to you as a vulnerable, tiny, premature baby valiantly fighting for life, and I feel overwhelmed with love and respect for your struggle.

Let us open that door.

P.S. My fantasy is that you and I could go through these letters together—to share the saga of a mother and daughter—the pain and the love—and have "the courage to heal."

I just love that Mom had the *chutzpah* to use those words, "the courage to heal." And I'm sad that we never sat down and read the letters together. She asked me to, but I blew her off repeatedly. I didn't want to reopen old wounds. I was too busy. I didn't think it mattered.

But I'm grateful that our correspondence survived. It's my turn to read them, to learn from them, and to grieve our lost opportunity to share them together.

CHAPTER 30

NEW LIFE

Laura 36, Temme 65, Santa Cruz

When I called Mom to tell her that I was pregnant, she was thrilled. With a grandchild on the way, she assumed I'd welcome her back into my life. But I didn't. She never saw me pregnant. She didn't get to bring me chicken soup when I was on bed rest. I didn't invite her to my baby shower. I kept her at arm's length the whole time I was pregnant—more than arm's length; I kept her three thousand miles away.

When I think about how I would feel if Eli or Lizzy were having a baby and barred my participation, I'd be devastated. I'm sure Mom was, but our relationship was still so volatile that I didn't feel safe around her. So, she never saw my belly grow.

When Eli was born in March 1993, I felt too raw for Mom to come. Karyn urged me to invite her, but I wasn't ready. I wish that hadn't been the case, but my reluctance accurately reflected our relationship at the time. And where *I* was: a brand-new mother trying to figure out how to feed my baby. Eli would only nurse on one side, and I had to pump the other side six times a day. That breast grew larger than a watermelon. I was so green, I couldn't figure out how to take a shower and be a mother at the same time. I was buried in an avalanche of hormones, and tears were definitely flowing with the milk. I wasn't willing to be that vulnerable around my mother, so I made her wait.

She complained and raged—to her friends, not to me—but she waited. Maybe because the stakes were so high, she respected my boundaries for the very first time.

I sent photos. Mailed birth announcements. And made her wait three long months to come. When I finally invited her to Eli's baby-naming ceremony, we were both on our best behavior, and things went well. There were no disasters. No conflagrations. She got to hold Eli in her arms. We took lots of pictures for her to show her friends. That visit was a turning point. Baby Eli gave us something to talk about besides the unresolved issues between us.

It felt right that Mom was there. I'd watched her with my niece, Sonya, and knew she'd be a committed, loyal grandmother. I wanted that for Eli, and she wanted the same, and that, more than anything, motivated us both to work harder at our relationship.

CHAPTER 31

RECONCILIATION

Laura 39, Temme 67, Santa Cruz

Eli was a toddler and Lizzy was still a dream when Mom called me one September afternoon. She was retired, and for many years, she'd spent her winters in San Miguel de Allende, along with the other snowbirds. She loved the social whirl of San Miguel: drinking margaritas and going out to lunch with her sophisticated, artsy, world-traveling friends. Mom thrived in Mexico. Each winter, she studied Spanish, attended poetry readings, art openings, and cooking classes. Dabbled in art. Acted in plays. She had adventures: admirers of the male persuasion. The aura of romance sizzled on those cobblestone streets. For Mom, San Miguel was magic.

But that day on the phone, she announced she wasn't going back. "I've decided to try something new. Next winter, I'm going to rent an apartment in Santa Cruz and spend two months in California."

"You want to come *here*?" Eli was at my feet, playing with string, slowly tying my feet to the dull chrome leg of our kitchen table.

"Don't worry, Laurie. I'm not going to stay with you. You know how busy I am. You'll hardly see me. I'll have my own life, but we'll be able to see more of each other. I'll get to know your family. I'll get to know Eli. Be a real grandmother to him."

Oh, right. This was about Eli—Mom getting her hands on her precious grandson. It wasn't about our reconciliation at all. "I don't know, Mom."

"Laurie, remember Eli's baby naming? It went so well." As Eli wrapped my ankle tight with string, I recalled that summer day. All the people we cared about crowded into our living room. Paul and Sonya. Dad and Mom—getting along. Dad's partner, Ophelia, and Mom chatting amiably about their respective social work careers. Bryan, at fifteen, sprouting the hint of a mustache and playing with his new baby brother. Mom read a beautiful prayer she'd written for the occasion. She hugged Karyn, congratulating her and fully acknowledging her as Eli's other parent. Paul took a beautiful picture of us that day: three generations—grandmother, daughter, and grandson. And Mom sang Eli "Hush Little Baby" as she rocked him to sleep.

"Yeah, I remember." What was harder to admit was the longing I felt for us to be able to look at each other without suspicion or fear.

"Laurie, we'll never reconcile if we only see each other once a year. If we don't create new experiences, all we'll ever have is the past."

"I don't know, Mom."

Eli reached up and tapped my other knee. I cut him a new piece of string. Peals of laughter rose as he wrapped my second calf to metal.

"Don't worry, darling. You won't have to take care of me."

I wanted to say yes, but resentment simmered inside me. Mom hadn't *asked* if she could come; she'd *informed* me. If I'd told her not to, I could have stopped her, but I was just ambivalent enough to say, "Okay, we can try it."

Mom wasn't happy with my tepid response, but that winter, she came. She searched for an apartment and moved in all by herself. I didn't lift a finger to help her.

—ʊʊ—

The next few winters, Mom sublet a place in Santa Cruz. We went through the motions of rebuilding our relationship: sharing holidays, taking Eli to the park, playing 500 rummy, going to the movies, but we were always walking on eggshells. There were triggers everywhere, and no room for mistakes. And we made lots of mistakes. Like kindling waiting to be lit, all it took was one misspoken word: a comment from Mom about my body, a positive remark from me about the Palestinians, the fact that she bought artichokes full of pesticides. Didn't she care about farmworkers?

Mom didn't hold back. "Your house is filthy. Look at those windowsills. Where did you grow up—in a barn?" "It's criminal to raise kids without TV. They'll never fit in." "Why do you let Eli scream like that? He's spoiled rotten."

I had plenty of judgments about her, too. I just didn't say them out loud. She drank too much. She smoked too much. She talked too much. Her stories never ended. I didn't like the way she chewed her food. Mine was a private, secret war. Silent condemnation ticked inside me, but I never lit the fuse. Containment, flatness, control—that was my strategy.

For each successful interaction we had, there was a concurrent failure. But after a few years of persistence on both our parts, intentionally accruing positive shared experiences like beads on a string, things slowly began to change. And they didn't change the way I thought they would. I'd always assumed that reconciliation required a major reckoning about all the terrible things that had ever happened. But reweaving our relationship was more about the little things.

—∾—

During her fourth winter stay, when Eli was six and Lizzy newly three, Mom rented a place without a washer and dryer. I invited her to drop off her dirty clothes and offered to wash them. It gave her an excuse to drop by unannounced. She was out of underwear. She needed socks. Her nightgown was dirty.

As I wrote in my backyard studio, Mom's clothes swished inside our washer. I loved taking a break to lift them, wet and heavy, and heave them into the dryer, knowing a little piece of her was tumbling around in the dry heat while I worked nearby.

As I stacked her linens, pants, shirts, and bras, I imagined all the clothes she'd folded for me: tiny cotton diapers, stretchy infant playsuits, sparkly leotards with matching tights, the beautiful red dress she sewed for me in second grade, blue jeans and T-shirts—my uniform in high school. I imagined her much younger, pregnant, standing over a small white dresser, folding and refolding my baby clothes, caressing each little sleeve, wondering who I might be. Never dreaming that Vicki and I were two.

I pictured Mom's face, soft and open, a young mother, savoring the creamy nap of cotton. Maybe she pressed my tiny jammies up to her cheek, thinking of me. Forty-three years later, I pressed her top sheet against my face, thinking of her.

When people ask, "How did you two reconcile?" I tell them, "The most important thing is that we both really wanted to." It was a practice. Choice by choice. Interaction by interaction. We broke old habits and established new ones. When Mom berated a waitperson, I held my tongue. When I nursed Lizzy in public, she averted her eyes but said nothing. We focused on doing things we enjoyed together. And each winter, our family piled into Mom's place to watch the Oscars. We had to—at our house, we had no TV.

By the time Mom had clocked seven years of winter visits, our progress became exponential. We reached critical mass. After a dustup one day, she stormed off in a huff, slamming the door, and I realized I wasn't worried. I knew our fight wasn't permanent. I knew she'd be back. I knew *we'd* be back. I could feel it in that place inside that always knows the truth: our reconciliation was no longer a work in progress. It was a work of art. It didn't mean we wouldn't fight. It meant we could fight.

The next day, I dropped by her place. As she dealt out our first hand of 500 rummy, her eyes filled with tears. "You know, Laurie, I no longer worry that you're going to keep me from my grandchildren."

My throat thickened. "Eli and Lizzy are lucky to have you."

CHAPTER 32

DOWN THERE

Laura 47, Temme 76, Santa Cruz

In February 2004, a few weeks after she arrived for her ninth winter, Mom called. "Laurie, have you got a minute? I'd like to run something by you."

"What's up?" I was making my favorite one-pot meal, lemon-apple chicken. I reached for two lemons, rolled them on the counter to loosen the pulp, jabbed them with a knife, and stuffed them whole into the bird.

"I'm thinking of trying out for *The Vagina Monologues*."

"That's great, Mom. You should try out."

"It's been years since I've been in a play. The last time I tried out, I didn't get the part."

I remembered that disappointment. Mom had called from New Jersey, crushed.

"If you don't try out, you definitely won't get cast." I cut onions in chunks, followed by carrots, parsnips, apples, and yams. I placed them around the chicken and tossed in a generous handful of prunes.

"I don't know if I can learn lines anymore. My memory isn't as good as it used to be."

I sliced two more lemons and placed them artfully over the bird. "I'll help you, Mom. It will be like old times." I slid the pan into the oven.

"Maybe my acting days are over." Mom voiced her doubts repeatedly, but I could tell she really wanted to try out.

"There's a perfect role for you, written for a woman in her seventies." I knew the play well; I'd acted in it myself a few years before. "I've still got my script. I'll drop it by tomorrow."

—∾—

Mom found the role embarrassing. Like the character she would portray, she wasn't comfortable talking about "down there." The morning of the audition, she was still wavering, but late that night, she called, elated. "You'll never guess what happened! I read for the part, and everyone, including the director, gave me a standing ovation!"

The director had no idea of the gift she'd given my mother. Parts for older women were rare, and Mom's confidence had been badly shaken. This role would boost her flagging self-esteem. But the director had given me a gift as well. I hadn't seen Mom act in almost thirty years, not since I left home at seventeen. Unexpected tears startled me. I lowered my voice to mask them. "Why don't you come over for dinner tomorrow? We can work on your lines."

—∾—

The next night, we all piled into the living room. I built a fire in the woodstove. Karyn and I lay together on our purple fainting couch. Eli read *Eragon*, and Lizzy quietly yipped on the floor, pretending to be a dog.

Mom handed me the script and started at the top. "Down there? I haven't been down there since 1953. No, it had nothing to do with Eisenhower. No, no, it's a cellar down there. It's very damp, clammy."

Mom hesitated. I prompted her. "You don't want . . ."

She started again. "You don't want to go down there. Trust me. You'd get sick." She stopped, searching for the line.

I cued her again. "Suffocating. Very nauseating."

Her progress was slow, but she steadily remembered more. After an hour, I said, "Okay, take it from the top."

Suddenly, Lizzy piped up. In her sweetest just-turned-eight voice, she said, "Down there? I haven't been down there since 1953. And no, it had nothing to do with Eisenhower."

We all burst out laughing and couldn't stop. Lizzy grabbed the script from my hand and read the scene from the top. She used Mom's inflections, an old lady's Brooklyn accent. Our little puppy had been listening all along.

"I'll help you, Grandma!" She prompted Mom perfectly, reading lines from a play she couldn't possibly understand.

Karyn and I shared a long look of parental pride. Then I turned to Mom, my voice thick. "I'm so glad you got the part."

CHAPTER 33

LESSON PLAN

Laura 47, Temme 76, Santa Cruz

The following Saturday, I was teaching a one-day Introduction to Writing Practice workshop at the local community college. On a whim, I invited Mom to attend. Usually, I kept work and Mom separate. I worried she might throw me off my rhythm, but we were doing well. It was only a one-day class. Six hours. No big deal.

"Laurie, I'd love to come!"

Mom insisted on paying and registering like any other student. She bought a brand-new notebook and tucked her favorite crossword puzzle pen into her bag. I told her to pack a sack lunch, and we drove out together.

I opened the session by establishing class ground rules. "If you didn't write it, don't share it." "Just because someone chooses to read to the group doesn't mean they want to discuss their story later. Writers need to control how and when they share their writing. In today's class, we're not going to comment on each other's work. The only response you're going to give is 'Thank you.' Nothing more." I scanned the room. People were listening intently. "We're not going to praise each other either. Believe it or not, praise can shut a writer down as quickly as criticism."

I made eye contact with each student, including Mom. "Can you raise your hand to let me know you agree to these ground rules?" Everyone raised a hand.

"One last thing. If someone breaks the rules, please let me know."

Five minutes later, the scratching of pens filled the air. Pretty soon, people were reading their work out loud, each person's share giving courage to the next. Mom jumped right in with a story about her mother's beautiful singing voice. I smiled. I'd only known Bubby as an old woman; I'd never heard her sing. Then the next person read. And the next. Soon, people were laughing. Crying. Connecting. Finding the truth. Sharing the truth. The workshop was rolling.

During lunch, two students came up to me. "That woman over there," the first one said, pointing at Mom, "gushed about how great my story was. I thought you'd want to know." Ten minutes later, a second student told me that Mom had given her advice about how to improve her story. Neither of them knew "that woman" was my mother.

Mom was eating a turkey sandwich when I slid into the chair beside her. I lowered my voice to a whisper. "You broke the rules. You're not supposed to talk to people about their writing."

Mom took a big bite of sandwich and looked at me as if I were crazy. As she spoke, half-eaten food rolled around in her mouth. "Why would someone complain about a perfectly good compliment? She was a good writer. I told her she was talented. I didn't say anything wrong. I was very complimentary." I looked away, wondering what had possessed me to invite my mother to class.

"Mom, you agreed. We don't give feedback in this class."

She took another bite, a big one. "What kind of stupid rule is that?"

My stomach tightened. "It's my rule. My class. I always teach this way."

"Well, it's ridiculous."

Shit. I'd driven her here. I couldn't teach if I was pissed at her. I slowed my breath. Forced my voice to be conciliatory. "It's just three more hours. Can you please just obey the rules this afternoon?"

"Ach, Laurie, you're making a mountain out of a molehill. All I said was something nice." She took the last bite of her sandwich, and

I headed back to my desk before she started to chew. I sat down to review my notes for the afternoon. And then I started to laugh. I had to. She was incorrigible.

CHAPTER 34

THE DEAL

Seven Years Earlier

Laura 40, Temme 69, Santa Cruz

"Mom, I'd like to write a book about us. About our reconciliation."

It was the last day of my mother's second winter visit, and Lizzy was just starting to crawl. I'd invited Mom to meet me for a final lunch at her favorite restaurant—just the two of us. Ristorante Avanti was packed.

I'd been needing to have—and avoiding—this conversation for weeks. I was not going to write another book exposing our history without Mom's permission. Proceeding without it would derail the gains we'd achieved. I wasn't willing to take that risk.

As the waiter dropped off a basket of crusty sourdough, I leaned toward Mom and continued my pitch. "After all the progress we've made healing our relationship, I got interested in the topic of reconciliation. How people make peace with each other. How they don't."

Mom picked at a cuticle while I made my case. I scanned her face, trying to decipher her reaction, but I couldn't read her. I ripped off a piece of bread, slowly dragged the crust through the glistening olive oil. I was asking a lot, and I knew it. It sucked having a writer in the family, especially one like me, writing about the most intimate parts of my life, and by extension, hers. I filled the silence with false bravado. "At least I'm done writing about sexual abuse. You should be happy about that."

Her lips thinned, but she permitted a small, careful smile. "Thank God for small miracles." We both gave a short burst of edgy laughter.

After the waiter took our orders, I tore off a second chunk of bread. I could never eat enough—I was a nursing mother. I chose my words carefully. "This could be my next big thing." I'd discussed it with my editor. She'd floated it to her boss, and they'd given me a green light. There'd be a substantial advance, enough to pay our bills for half a year. But first, I had to get Mom to agree. I tore the bread in half with my teeth.

"I don't know, Laurie." She ran her fingers over the tablecloth, tracing the fold. "Your first book—it almost killed me."

I was not getting into a discussion of *The Courage to Heal* with my mother. Our growing rapprochement relied on keeping our irreconcilable differences compartmentalized in the past.

Now, I needed her blessing. This was the book I wanted to write. I had a family. A four-year-old. A new baby. Bryan was in college, and I was helping to pay for it.

I spoke with enthusiasm, modulating my voice with just a touch of firmness. "This book will be completely different. It will celebrate what we've accomplished. Besides, it won't just be about us. We'll just be a little thread in the book. I'm going to interview lots of other people."

Mom loved the limelight, but like me, she liked to hide her flaws even more. She sipped her ice water. "I just don't know, Laurie."

My jaw tightened. "Mom, what you and I have accomplished together is remarkable. People could learn from us. This book could help a lot of people."

"Yes, I'm sure it could . . ." But her voice trailed off. I could tell she was itching for a cigarette, but she didn't realize I knew she still smoked. She'd been trying to quit for thirty years.

Two pieces of blackberry pie arrived at the table to our left, a lit candle rising from the center of each. Two women, early thirties. They were identical: same face, same body, different hairdos. I tried not to stare. Mom was looking, too. Both of us thinking the same: *What if she had lived?* Vicki was a loss we shared.

As the women at the next table sang "Happy Birthday" for two, I swallowed hard. An ancient emptiness rose up inside me. I tried to hide that yearning from Mom, but she looked at the twins, and then back at me. Her eyes softened. "Okay, darling, tell me about your book."

Over grilled salmon, I described my plans. How I'd interview Vietnam veterans who went back to Vietnam, people who'd used restorative justice, family members who had succeeded and failed in their attempts to make peace with each other. "And of course, I'll tell our story. That's the motivation for it all."

Mom asked a few questions but remained noncommittal. As I checked my watch, voices in Spanish rose and fell in the kitchen. I had a three-and-a-half-hour respite between Lizzy's feedings. We'd been out three hours already; my breasts were getting full.

I brushed the crumbs from Mom's side of the table into my waiting palm. "We've had a great visit. Karyn and I are so glad that you are a part of our lives, that you're getting to know the kids and they're getting to know you. You're a terrific grandmother."

She teared up. "Laurie, I love my winters in Santa Cruz. After everything we've been through, you've welcomed me here. I wouldn't want anything to get in the way of that."

The waiter dropped the bill on the table, right between us. I reached over and pulled it to my side. She reached for the check. "Let me take that."

"I invited you. It's my treat." I slipped my credit card into the folio.

Mom picked at her cuticle again. It was red and raw. "I really want to help you out, darling."

But something was still standing in her way. "Then what's the real problem, Mom?"

She hesitated. "I just don't know if I can trust you."

Heat rushed to my face. The woman who had betrayed *me* was calling me the betrayer. But if I confronted her, this conversation would be over. I had to keep the boundaries firm: *That was then. This is now.* I plastered on what I hoped would be a reassuring smile. "Mom, I'm older now. This time, I want to interview you. So you can tell our story your way. It won't just be my story. It will be *our* story."

Mom gazed at the twins across the room, laughing and opening gifts. "I'd really like that." Her eyes lingered on the women a little too long. "I want to do this for you, Laurie . . ."

But she turned her head and withdrew her hands from the table.

I needed this book contract for my family. Once I signed it, we both knew there'd be no turning back. I pressed on. "This time, you'll get to read it first. I promise I won't publish anything you're not comfortable with. The last thing I want is for my book on reconciliation to mess things up between us." I looked her in the eye. "I care more about you than I do about this book." Hot tears pressed up, surprising me.

Our waiter returned the folio, and I scrawled in the tip. When I looked down, a milk stain was spreading across my shirt. I leaned forward in my chair and placed my hands on the table. "Mom?"

When she finally returned my gaze, her eyes were certain. "Okay, Laurie. Go ahead. I'm going to trust you." Her voice didn't waver.

"You won't be sorry. I promise." I held her eyes, and she held mine.

As I reached for my hoodie, my body sagged in relief. Now I could pay my half of the mortgage. Eli's tuition at preschool. Bryan's room and board. Now I could go home and nurse my baby. I tossed my napkin onto the table and zipped up my sweatshirt over the growing stain.

CHAPTER 35

INTERVIEW

Laura 41, Temme 70, Santa Cruz

It wasn't until the following winter that we finally scheduled our interview. The book had a name now: *I Thought We'd Never Speak Again: The Road from Estrangement to Reconciliation.* The first draft was almost complete. Hers would be the final interview. It was March 1998, a quiet winter afternoon.

I made sure we'd be alone.

We carried steaming mugs of tea into the living room. Evidence of the kids was everywhere—a stack of board books teetering in the corner, Russian nesting dolls rolling in pieces on the hearth. A stack of brightly colored origami paper and a dozen failed attempts at Eli's first paper crane. Karyn's turquoise yoga mat, waiting rolled in the corner.

Karyn was picking up the kids on her way home from work: Lizzy from toddler care. Eli from preschool. They'd be bursting through the door in less than three hours.

Mom sank deep into one end of the brown flowered sofa. The cushions sagged from years of kids jumping where they weren't supposed to. I sank deep into the other. Between us was my old Sony cassette recorder from my years working in radio, a gift from Mom for my twenty-sixth birthday—top of the line. Now, the machine was a dinosaur, but I still used it for interviews. Snug in its black leather case, it sat waiting. A mic on a stand pointed Mom's way. A box of waiting tissues at her feet.

I slipped a cassette into the machine and faced her. Knotted fingers pressed deep into her lap. I could feel her mind churning: *Why did I agree to this? What has Laurie gotten me into now?*

I waited. A crow cawed on the power lines. Then another. They were dropping walnuts on the asphalt to crack them. Mom looked up, doubt furrowing her brow.

I arranged my face in a neutral position and ignored the tightness in my chest. One Mississippi. Two Mississippi. *Mom won't bail on me. Or will she?*

I unfolded my notes. *If I act like it's going to happen, it will.* I gentled my voice. "Mom. I'm good at this."

Resolve and uncertainty battled in her eyes.

I paused, wondering just how hard to push. "Remember, this is your chance to tell our story your way."

When I said that, her eyes settled. She sat up on the couch and nodded. *Hallelujah.*

I turned on the recorder and broke the silence with my professional voice: clear, well enunciated, and softened with kindness—not the kindness of a daughter toward her mother, but rather, the practiced kindness of an interviewer toward a subject ready to bare her soul. As a talk-show host and author, I'd spent years persuading people to share the rawest parts of their lives with me. But I had never done an interview like this.

"We're here today to hear your side of our estrangement and reconciliation story. For the sake of this interview, I'm going to ask you to respond to my questions as if I'm not the person you're talking about. I'd like you to talk about me in the third person, instead of directly to me. It will really help. Do you think you can do that?"

Mom mulled over my request. Looked out the window. Our neighbor, pruning roses, saw her and waved. "I'll try."

I glanced at my notes. I needed a moment to quiet the scared girl thumping in my chest. I was a professional. I carefully modulated my voice. "Can you start by telling me what you think caused the rift with your daughter initially?"

Mom began tentatively, but as she spoke, her voice grew firmer. "For a very long time, starting when you were a teenager . . ."

"When *she* was a teenager."

She paused, accepted my correction. "When she was a teenager. I felt my daughter hated me, and I really couldn't figure out why. I always saw myself as a loving mother. It was extremely painful for me because I was at a very vulnerable time in my life. I was trying to find my way on my own after my husband left me. I was worried about my son, who was away at college experimenting with drugs. And the only person I was living with was this daughter who was angry at me all the time. There was nothing I could do to please Laurie." Her eyes brimmed with tears. "I tried everything in my power to support you after Dad left."

"To support *her.* Remember, Mom, I'm not me." I had to keep control of this interview. I couldn't let it turn into therapy. "But you're doing great."

Mom paused, then picked up the thread. "I hoped her anger was just teenage rebellion, her reaction to me as the custodial parent who tried to set limits. But she just kept drifting farther away from me—living her life in total opposition to how I hoped she would live. At sixteen, my daughter turned down a full scholarship to Wellesley College. She became involved with a charlatan, a thirteen-year-old guru. She moved far away from me. But the worst part wasn't what she was doing; it was how much she distanced herself from me. As the years went by, we had less and less in common. There was less we could talk about, less that might bring us together."

Mom's version, a well-burnished tale. My jaw clenched at all of her omissions, but this was her turn to tell the story her way.

"Things kept going from bad to worse. I just about accepted one decision of hers when I'd be confronted with another disappointment and then another." Frustration edged her words, and her voice grew thick. "Then came the final blow. She called to tell me that my father had sexually abused her. When in my shock, I reacted to that—granted, not in the best way—she got mad and wouldn't talk to me. My daughter wrote a very popular book in which I felt personally attacked and humiliated. It put me in a position of being torn between my caring about her and my love for my original family, and it almost destroyed me."

Well, it almost destroyed me, too! You abandoned me when I needed you the most. But I pushed the voice of that wounded girl away. *Later. I'll listen to you later.* I started floating out of my body, so I pressed my bare feet against the floor, felt the cool wood rise up to meet me. I checked the recorder. Let Mom's words wash over me. She was reliving every bit of the pain, her grief as intense as it had been decades before.

"After that blow, my daughter and I both made efforts to come together, but our lives had diverged so much, it was hard. There were so many things we couldn't talk about. At one point, I flew across the country to go to therapy with her, and I felt like she and the therapist ganged up on me. They expected me to grovel and say, 'I'm sorry. Everything I did was wrong,' but I couldn't do that. Instead of making things better, therapy only made things worse."

Her voice filled with tears. My throat did, too. That therapy session had been horrible for both of us. And now she was back in that room, feeling ambushed all over again. "Laurie and I tried to speak a few other times, but we could never make any progress. Finally, we both came to the conclusion that these efforts to get validation from each other weren't going to work, so we decided to leave the unresolved stuff sitting there. We've never been able to talk about the force that drove us apart the most—the accusation of sexual abuse. I've had to accept that my relationship with my daughter cannot include her memories of my father."

She'd gotten right down to the bone. I couldn't let her stay there alone. I sloughed off my role and took her hand. It felt unfamiliar—and warm.

I gave her a moment to compose herself. Took back my hand. Donned the cloak of interviewer again. My voice gentle, I pressed on. "What finally allowed you to move forward despite the fact that I said your father abused me and you didn't believe me?" I was so engrossed in her story that I'd forgotten the third-person routine. This was new territory, something we'd never risked before.

Mom looked up, a question burning in her eyes. "I don't know if I should tell you this. I'm not sure you'll be able to handle it."

"Go ahead." I leaned forward. Held my breath.

"Well, I just couldn't believe your accusations. I've searched my memory and concluded that my father could never have done that to you. Then I read a lot of literature from the False Memory Syndrome Foundation."

I froze.

The False Memory Syndrome Foundation? Oh my God.

"Jesus, Mom, you went to them?"

"They described the typical incest survivor with false memories, and you fit the profile one thousand percent. That was the real turning point for me. Instead of seeing you as my tormentor, I started seeing you as someone under the influence of people who had convinced you those memories were true. That helped me stop feeling I had to protect myself and my family against you."

I felt dizzy. I didn't know what to say. Whether to laugh or cry. "Really? The False Memory Syndrome Foundation helped you make peace with me?"

"Yes, it did. So, I decided to go to one of their meetings."

I stared at her. The wall heater whooshed out a sudden wave of heat. "What happened?"

Mom looked at me, a practiced smile brightening her beleaguered face. She was a great storyteller. She had me in her thrall, and she knew it. Leaning forward, with her actress voice, she spilled the rest of the story. "I drove down to the meeting—I think it was in Philadelphia. Someone got up and started attacking you and your book, and I immediately wanted to get up and punch the guy. No one there knew I was your mother, but I wanted to shout, 'How dare you say that about my daughter?' In that moment, I realized I felt much more loyal to you than I did to them. I picked up my pocketbook and left."

I laughed out loud, trying to envision it—Mom showing up, hoping for validation, then rejecting the very people she'd hoped would save her. I could see her storming out, clutching her patent leather pocketbook. The click of her heels on linoleum. The slam of the door.

—∞—

With Mom's revelation, all pretense of conducting an interview was over. We sat quietly, relishing the space she'd just created with her honesty. That's when I felt an unexpected bubble of truth rising up from my core. I spoke my next words without premeditation, revealing an allegiance hidden so deep inside that I had no idea what I was about to say. "Mom, I'd like to take care of you when you're old. I think you should move to California."

I was just as shocked to say it as she was to hear it, yet the best part of me was smiling. The part in charge of my evolution as a human being, the part committed to pushing past my fears and limits, the part that was whole and had never been wounded—that part was cheering.

For once, Mom was speechless. Did she cry? I don't remember. I know I didn't. I was far too controlled to cry. But we both needed a moment of privacy to take in the magnitude of what I had just said. We looked away from each other, unable to meet each other's gaze. Then we looked back. And really looked at each other. I stepped out from behind the wall I had always erected between us, and for the first time in decades, let her see me.

My body reverberated with the impact of my words. It wasn't that I wanted to take them back. It was more like: What have I done? Can the rest of me possibly step up and fulfill the promise my soul just uttered?

Mom shifted her body away and stared out at the crows, uncertainty shadowing her face. Her brow furrowed. Her hands curled in her lap like a question mark.

Mom had always been able to read me perfectly, but this time I was the one reading her. As she sat there, not looking at me, I knew just what she was thinking: *Can I really trust Laurie with the rest of my life? Or will she betray me again?*

CHAPTER 36

FEEDBACK

Laura 43, Temme 72, Santa Cruz

Two years after our interview, I completed the final draft of *I Thought We'd Never Speak Again*. I had one last set of revisions to go. As I'd told my mother initially, the book was primarily based on other people's stories, but the parts about us were raw and significant. Now it was time for me to fulfill my end of the bargain: letting her read and respond to what I'd written.

I was terrified to give her the book.

My revisions were due in April and finalizing the material about my mother was one of my last tasks. Each visit we had that winter, I thought about bringing her the manuscript, but panicked every time. I needed her approval but couldn't ask for it. Mom's copy of the book sat untouched on my desk.

Finally, a month before she was returning to New Jersey, I invited her out to lunch. As we made small talk, she seemed to sense something was wrong but waited for me to bring it up. But as we finished our salads, she blurted out, "Laurie, what's the matter?" Concern colored her face.

I hesitated. I knew what was in my backpack, and she didn't. *Maybe I should just tell her I have a headache. Then I can keep my bag zipped and return the book to its safe spot on my desk.*

But a little voice inside me insisted, *You promised.*

As I zipped open the bulging bag, I said, "It's the book, Mom." I pulled out the thick manuscript with its smooth green card-stock cover and set it on the table. It filled the space between us. Bound with a thick plastic spiral, *I Thought We'd Never Speak Again* dwarfed our watery iced teas and empty salad plates. I let my hand linger on the binding. Mom kept hers in her lap. She stared at it. I stared at it. I swallowed hard. My heart thrashed in my chest, a bird in a too-small cage: *What if she hates it?*

She pulled the book over to her side of the table. "Well, I guess this is it."

The busboy appeared to collect our dirty dishes, ignoring the huge manuscript now in front of Mom. We smiled politely, waiting for his departure.

"So, Laurie, what do you want me to do with it?"

"Write your comments on the pages. I want your reactions, how you really feel." Then I paused. Forced myself to meet her eyes. My voice wavered. "I want you to tell me if there's anything you can't live with."

That was my criterion for making changes: something Mom couldn't live with. I prayed for a short list. I didn't know what I'd do if it was long.

"I can do that."

"I'm on a deadline. You have three weeks to read it. Three weeks *max*. If you can get it back sooner, that would be great."

Mom nodded in agreement. "I can do that."

Our waitress approached with our entrées, paused at eavesdropping distance, and waited. Mom lifted the book, placed it on the chair farthest away from me, and set her pocketbook on top.

It was hers now.

—ω—

That night, the streak of "wide awake" in my belly just wouldn't quit. Ever since I'd handed her the book, part of me felt missing. But it wouldn't be for long. She'd dive in straightaway, find the book so compelling that she'd get through it the first few days—a week, max. Mom was a voracious reader, and this book was about her. She'd probably cracked the spine the moment she got into her car. I imagined her reading late into the night, the light of her Mexican table lamp glowing down on the double-spaced pages. Maybe she was up reading it now. That's probably why I couldn't sleep—that psychic tie between us. She was riveted. I'd get it back in plenty of time to integrate her changes.

—∾—

A week went by. We watched the Oscars together. Mom said nothing. I said nothing. I knew she was reading it. She knew she was reading it, but neither of us said a word. This was taking longer than I thought, but the book was brand-new to her. I'd been living with my words for a long time—I could practically recite all four hundred pages by heart. Of course she needed time.

By day ten, my equanimity had crumbled. I was afraid to broach the subject but could think of nothing else. What chapter was she on? Was she talking it over with her friends? Her therapist? Did she think I'd been fair? Would she be able to tolerate my version of her worst mistakes as a mother? And lurking beneath it all, What would she ask me to change?

It wasn't like I could pull the book. It was going to press and had to stay pretty much the way it was. Yet within those constraints, I didn't want the book I'd written, inspired by us, to tear us apart again. I trusted that Mom would say yes to as much as she could. But if she hated everything and made me cut her out, I'd be gutting the heart of the book.

Late at night, I went through the manuscript with a fine-toothed comb, imagining how she might react to every line. She might have a real problem with the passages where I had described the ugly scenes that had led to our estrangement. I'd definitely taken a risk there, but how could I tell our story without describing how bad things had been? Our interview—she'd probably love that part. And how could she not love the sentence where I said she was the bravest person I'd ever met? *But if she says,* I hate to do this, darling, but I've changed my mind, *what will I do then?*

Each time Mom stopped by, I checked out the bag she was carrying. But it was always a normal-sized pocketbook, nothing large enough to hide a fat green book.

As the days ticked by, Mom started looking different to me—her skin tauter, her edges sharper. The woman before me was not the mother I'd made peace with. Temme Davis, the mother of my adolescence and young adulthood, blazed up, looming over me. I eyed her with ancient suspicion. I felt young and afraid.

Maybe I wasn't as far along on the path to reconciliation as I'd thought.

Ten days before my mother's flight back to New Jersey, I stared at my phone. Would she leave without responding? I didn't think she'd do that—but maybe this was her revenge for *The Courage to Heal.* Her silence was driving me mad, but I was too lost in my trance of disempowerment to break it. Grown-up Laura was nowhere to be found.

In the final days before her flight, Mom picked Lizzy up at preschool. Clapped at Eli's school play. She remained pleasant but inscrutable. All those decades of acting were paying off. But I had no such training.

Two days before Mom's departure, I chose a time when I knew she'd be out and left a message. "Can you come over tomorrow at one o'clock?" I hesitated. "We can have some tea . . . and talk about things." I cursed myself as soon as I hung up. What was I so afraid of? The answer was obvious: the ogre I'd created in my head. That I had *always* created in my head.

She emailed back that evening. "See you tomorrow."

When Mom arrived the next day, there was no big green book in her hands. She was carrying an oversized bag, but I'd seen her carry it before. Did it look heavier than usual? I couldn't tell.

I led her to the back deck, made two big mugs of fresh peppermint tea, just the way Karyn taught me, bruising the leaves first and then adding boiling water. Mint grew wild, all over our yard.

We sat perched at a small round red table that had just enough space for two folding chairs. As we sipped our tea, we discussed Karyn's yoga for back care training, my writing classes, the last movie Mom had seen with her friends, Lizzy's obsession with Dorothy and *The Wizard of Oz.* I showed off the blue-and-white-checked pinafore Karyn was sewing for her and Eli's latest origami model. Soon, only wet leaves remained at the bottom of our cups. I was out of my body, hovering just over my head.

A blue jay landed in our birdbath and splashed its feathers. We both smiled at its obvious pleasure.

Silence fell between us as a plane roared overhead. Mom reached into the oversized bag at her feet, pulled out the manuscript, and set it on the table. *Oh my God, there it is.*

The book looked worn and well read—its cover creased and coffee stained, the plastic binding askew. *My God, she's actually read it.* Dozens of yellow Post-its jutted from the pages. *She probably hated it—every tag a slam. But maybe she loved it.* Two years of work were about to crash and burn. I thought about our mortgage. Bryan's tuition. Our bills. I struggled not to rise out of my body, not to float off into the sky.

A faint whiff of jasmine brought me back. A hummingbird darted in a brilliant flash of green. The clip-clip of our neighbor's shears, pruning her roses, amplified. I tried not to stare at the book; I looked at the backyard instead. It was almost time to take the kids out on the railroad tracks to pick blackberries.

Stop it, Laura. Come back. You need to be here.

Mom fingered the ragged card stock. "Laurie, I'm going to be honest. There were a number of parts of the book that were hard for me to read, but there are only two things I'm going to ask you to change."

Despite the cool spring day, a line of sweat sprouted down my back.

"You know that story near the end about my seventieth birthday party? Where you and Paul flew to New Jersey with all my grandkids?"

"Yeah. Did you like that part?"

"That was one of the best days of my life. The way you two surprised me. When you all walked in like that, Eli in that lion costume and Lizzy in your arms, Paul and Sonya piling in behind—it was one of the greatest moments of my life. And, Laurie, you captured it so well. The way you wrote it made me cry. But . . ." And here she dropped into a stage whisper. "I don't want people to know how old I am. Can you just say it was a special birthday?"

I waited. Where was this headed?

She said nothing more. It couldn't be that simple. Then it hit me. It *was* that simple. I gave her a reassuring smile. "Sure, Mom. I can change that. Happy to."

"Thank you, darling."

My whole body relaxed. That would be an easy fix.

But then a second silence stretched between us. My throat tightened again. *It can't have taken three weeks for Mom to tell me that. Number two must be harder. Much harder.*

"There is one other thing . . ." Mom's voice trailed off, and she looked away. She stared at her hands, twisted in her lap. Her words slipped out quietly. "I'd like you to say more good things about me." She glanced up at me, a quick glance, enough for me to see the truth in her eyes. *I want people to know I'm a good person. That I was a good mother. That I loved you.*

Oh my God, she shouldn't have to ask for this. Tears of regret filled my eyes.

Mom leaned forward, framed by flowers, and I could suddenly see how small she really was. Her face, her body—everything looked softer. I thought about her resilience, her generosity, her humor, her strength. I thought about the woman who'd rebuilt her life when my father walked out on her. Temme Davis had pursued her passions, traveled the world, and triumphed on the stage. She'd said yes to this book and now was asking for something in return—for me, who'd judged her for so long, to remember the good.

"I'd love to do that for you, Mom."

Relief flooded her face.

"It will be easy. There are so many good things to say."

—∞—

Here's one. It happened in New Jersey, when Mom was still living in my childhood home. I was visiting from far away. I imagine myself in my early twenties. Maybe it was after I left the *ashram* at twenty-one, when I had no idea what the rest of my life might be. Perhaps it was after I came out to her, when I was on my high horse, spouting feminist philosophy, and she was certain I'd live out my life as a lonely lesbian in a seedy bar.

The night before, Mom and I had agreed to call a truce on whatever conflagration was consuming us, and to walk to the beach the next morning. After breakfast, we put on our windbreakers, laced up our sneakers, and headed out the front door toward the Atlantic.

The moment we stepped out onto the crooked sidewalk, the sky opened, as if God had decided that very day to start the flood. Sunny one moment; a downpour, the next. I gasped. She gasped. We were drenched in seconds, rain soaking our clothes, dripping from our noses, saturating our skin. Our socks and shoes, soggy white cotton in rubber soles. Mom yelled out, "It's raining cats and dogs." I nodded but could barely hear her. The rain was too loud.

We looked at each other, each expecting the other to run back into the shelter of the house. Mom shouted through the rain, "Let's go anyway." I gaped at her. Did my mother really want to get drenched with me in the rain? As she looked at me expectantly, a huge adventurous grin spread across her face. I'd never seen that look before. Her hair was stringy and wet, her cheeks painted with rivulets of rain, her dare unmistakable. I wanted to know this woman.

"Yes," I shouted, grinning back. She put her arm in mine, and it felt like it belonged there, and, together, we turned away from the known world and the walls of my childhood home and ran out onto the soggy streets, our glasses streaked so much, we couldn't see. Laughing, delighted, we strode out into the deluge.

PRESS KIT

Promotional letter from Temme Davis included in the *I Thought We'd Never Speak Again* press kit:

> I Thought We'd Never Speak Again *has profound meaning to me because, as Laura's mother, I am the one she thought she'd never speak to again. We became estranged over a difficult family issue that seemed to be permanently irreconcilable, complicated by our living on opposite sides of the country. This period in my life, without my daughter, was excruciatingly painful for me.*
>
> *Miraculously, motivated by a deep mother-daughter bond, we each took small tentative steps to break the impasse, and we did. I wanted my daughter in my life again, to be a grandmother to her children, and she wanted the same. That seemed to both of us a priority over the differences that separated us. It took time and the courage to push back the fears that we would be hurt again. Reconciliation required that we be in the present and focus on what we wanted now.*

As I grow older, it feels more and more important to let go of old differences that interfere with my happiness. I need closeness with family.

Laura's book tells many stories of people like us. The scenarios might be different, but the underlying theme concerns people and groups who are split apart and want it to be different, hoping to renew their relationships. When Laura first told me about her plans to write the book, I was naturally apprehensive, even though she assured me that I would have an opportunity to edit the manuscript. What was she going to say for the whole world to read? As I pored through I Thought We'd Never Speak Again, *the tears began to flow. Some passages were difficult for me, but I could sense Laura's desire to spare me any undue pain yet use our story to show how reconciliation is possible.*

In allowing this book to be published, I had to accept the fact that I was not "perfect," just human like everyone else. I ended up believing that we could be "imperfect" models for other people struggling with troubled relationships.

Discounting a mother's pride in her daughter's skill as a writer of clear, touching prose, I believe this book offers inspiration to people who need help reconciling differences. So many of us need to bring more love and understanding into our lives.

—Temme Davis, March 2001

PART III

"We habitually overestimate the domain we can control."

—Tara Brach

CHAPTER 37

PILLS

1,470 Days

It was back during her years as a Santa Cruz snowbird that my mother and I started having conversations about her old age and death, a subject she brought up regularly. "Laurie, I'm seventy-five years old, and I've reached the acceptable age for death. If I died now, no one would consider it a tragedy." She made it perfectly clear that she didn't want any extraordinary measures taken when her time came. "I've lived a good life. The way I look at it, I want to quit while I'm ahead."

Now she was in her eighties. After the dishwasher accident, and her close call with kidney failure in the ICU, Mom recovered, but after that, her life was never the same. She'd entered the endless cycle of medical interventions that plague the lives of the elderly. She'd become a cog in a wheel, a number on a chart, a birth date on a computer screen. She'd gone from being a healthy senior, physically strong with a poor memory, to an elderly patient with a different doctor for each part of her body.

She spent more time with her doctors than she did with her friends.

Mom couldn't possibly go to these appointments alone; she couldn't remember the symptoms she had to report or what the doctors said in return. So, I squeezed them into my life, a life already overflowing with busyness and blessings.

At the end of each appointment, Mom was often given a new medication. Half the time, she reacted badly to it and had to see a new doctor to get a second drug to deal with the side effects of the first. She became diabetic. Her blood pressure rose. She had a cough that never went away. Her skin discolored—big dark blotches from the Coumadin. It was hard to know what constituted a real ailment and what was a reaction to all the drugs.

She was anxious and teary and called me six times a day.

—~—

Late one night, after a three-medical-appointment week, I slipped into a hot bath, desperate to disappear into a novel. I sank deep into the steamy water and got lost in the story, until my reverie was interrupted by the chirp of my phone. Paul's image flashed across my screen. I let it ring once, twice. Why did he have to call so late? I sighed. Maybe he had something important to tell me. Good Daughter picked up the phone.

He barely greeted me before launching into his agenda. "I want to talk to you about Mom's medications." Shit. *I never should have picked up.* This wasn't the first time we'd had this conversation. "Mom's gotten much worse these past few months, and I think it's her medications. They're worse than the diseases they're supposed to treat. If she wasn't ingesting all these poisons, she'd have a chance to get better."

"I don't like them either, Paul. But she could have a stroke at any time."

"Natural remedies could do a much better job than the toxic stuff she's on. I've been doing the research. If we could just get her off the Coumadin, she'd be able to take them . . ."

"Paul, I just said she could have a stroke. Are you really willing to take that risk?"

"I'm not saying we should take her off everything."

I sat up against the smooth white porcelain. "And who's going to manage all this?"

"I knew you'd say that. I've found this great holistic clinic in Santa Cruz . . ."

I cranked open the window so the night air could cool my face. "Paul, I'm the one here every day. You're the one who *promises* to show up."

"I'm showing up right now. I've put a lot of time into this. I've found an acupuncturist in your area who will treat Mom."

"Do you know how many doctors I've already taken her to this week?"

Paul's voice remained steady. He was like a dog with a bone. "I really appreciate everything you do, Laura. But I don't think she needs to be declining so fast."

"Look, if you'd invited her to Phoenix in the first place, you could be giving her all the acupuncture and herbs you want."

"I'm putting the herbs in the mail tomorrow. They're easy to use."

I jabbed the red button to disconnect. There was no pleasure in my bath now. I stood up and grabbed a towel.

Back then, I didn't have the bandwidth to grapple with—or even recognize—the deeper questions I was facing: Could I ever see my brother as more than just an impediment to my plans? Would we ever recapture the closeness we'd had when we were young? Could I take care of my mother for the rest of her life if our underlying mother-daughter conflict remained unresolved? Would she and I ever surpass the functional but limited relationship we'd been so proud of, the one based on rigid boundaries and intractable rules? Could I love her without them?

CHAPTER 38

THE LIST

1,406 Days

As Lizzy entered tenth grade, Eli was finalizing his list of colleges. At the top was MIT. He'd dreamed of it ever since he was a thirteen-year-old paper folder, when he'd learned that the best origamists in the country were there.

One afternoon, maxed out from teaching, chauffeuring kids, and editing Eli's college essays, I got a call that Mom had passed out in a parking lot, sitting in her car with the engine running. Her horn was blaring, and she'd been nonresponsive. When she "woke up" in the hospital, she insisted she'd just been taking a nap.

I disappeared into the black hole of another Mom emergency. That night, I missed Lizzy's dance recital. When I finally got home in the wee hours of the morning, I started a brand-new list:

REASONS MOM CAN'T LIVE ALONE

1. She passed out in the car.
2. I found her front door wide open.

3. Front right burner left on for the SECOND time with a dish towel just inches away.
4. Random pills on the counter AGAIN.

I rewrote this list and tweaked it every day, because every day Mom was out in the world unattended was a day of havoc for me.

My favorite fantasy at the time went like this: I'd drop by Mom's new assisted-living facility, play a few hands of 500 rummy while watching *Jeopardy!*, slip home for a peaceful dinner with my family, and savor the silence of a phone that didn't ring. But whenever I broached the subject of getting help, Mom was adamant: "I am perfectly capable of living alone." So, I cursed under my breath, and we made do. *I* made do, never knowing from day to day when my life would be derailed.

1,203 DAYS

Seven months later, while Eli was off on a college visit, and I was preparing to teach out of town, I took Mom in for a checkup. The moment she sat on the exam table, she passed out. Soon, she was speeding to the hospital in an ambulance. The doctors adjusted her meds and released her. As she got into my car, her face looked pale, her eyes faraway.

"Mom, why don't you come home and spend the night with us?"

Early the next morning, I woke to the sound of rustling in the living room. I quietly got up and stood in the doorway. Mom was lying flat on her back on our big fainting couch, struggling to get up. At home, she had to go to the bathroom at night on her own. I needed to see what she could and couldn't do. So, instead of helping, I silently watched. My eyes widened in alarm.

Mom inched down the vast pillow of the couch, sliding on her back, until she could reach her cane. She lay there in her turquoise-and-gold silky nightgown, spent and panting. Lifting her head, she pressed down on the cushion, then onto her cane, to propel herself upright. She stood, leaning heavily on the cane, her spindly legs wobbling. Weaving back and forth, she headed toward the bathroom. I tried to shake the dread from my eyes.

I stepped into the room, plastered on a smile.

"Oh, Laurie. You're up!"

"Morning."

"Morning, darling." She looked toward the bathroom. "I'd like to take a shower."

"Let me help you turn it on." Our faucet regularly confounded even our most savvy guests. I followed Mom into the bathroom, where she teetered, one hand gripping the sink. I pulled back the shower curtain and ran the hot water, sticking my hand under the stream to make sure it was the right temperature. How many times had she done this for me?

Mom struggled and failed to get the nightgown over her head. I reached over, and in one motion, perfected from years of getting small shirts over oversized toddler heads, pulled her nightgown off and let it drop into a shimmering pile on the floor. I hadn't seen her naked in years. And I didn't want to.

Mom's body was a solid rectangle, shoulders squared off and fixed in place. Her belly, the source of so many disparaging comments, pooched out freely. Had it been fifty years I'd been listening to her talk about losing a few pounds?

Mom's white hair was flattened in back, and several strands rose straight in the air. The emergency call monitor in its white plastic case rested on her chest. I asked, "Can you wear that thing in the shower?"

She brought her short, boxy body up to the rim of the tub. "That's the place they say you need it most."

I pulled back the plastic curtain. "How's this temperature?"

"I'd like it hotter." We spoke the minimum words necessary. Neither of us wanted to be standing there together.

I adjusted the knob and asked again, "How's this?"

"Good." She leaned against me and struggled to lift one leg over the lip of the tub. "What should I hold on to?" Paul had installed grab bars in Mom's bathroom during his last visit. At our house, we didn't have any.

"You can hold on to me." She grasped my shoulders, lifted her other foot over the side and into the shower. Water splashed onto the floor.

"Where's the shampoo?"

I handed her Lizzy's green apple shampoo. The moment she pulled the curtain closed, I walked out and grabbed my laptop, carried it back, and perched on the toilet. I needed to disappear into the digital world. A paragraph into my first email, she yelled, "I'm done." Her voice blistered with impatience. "How the hell do you turn it off?"

I slapped my laptop shut, turned off the shower, and wrapped a towel around her, covering her as quickly as possible. I helped her out of the tub.

"Can you dry off my hair?" I towel-dried her hair, white strands spiking in all directions. "Help me get dressed." Her voice edged toward hysteria. She wanted this over as much as I did.

I reached for her underwear—the same horrible panty girdle she'd been wearing all my life. I stood behind her and lifted the synthetic panels over her belly. I did not look as I tugged. I just tugged, then wadded up the leg of her maroon stretch pants. She lifted her foot to step in. Her feet were peeling, and her toenails hooked over her toes. I fetched her shirt and cane, and she slowly made her way to the kitchen, where she fell heavily into a chair. It was the only way she could sit down anymore.

I had an eighteen-hour day ahead of me, and there was no way I could rush her. That alone was stressful enough—the vise grip familiar to anyone who cares for a family member and works outside the home. What I felt that morning was more than being squeezed for time, more than the sudden awareness that my mother had grown old. As I buttered toast and scrambled eggs for breakfast, I realized that our buffer was gone. For two decades, the success of our relationship had been contingent on keeping a reliable distance between us. I knew how to maneuver in that vigilant state of equilibrium, and so did Mom. But now the protection of that careful cushion was gone. If I was to fulfill my promise to my mother, I'd be entering territory I never intended to explore.

We both would be.

1,189 DAYS

Two weeks later, after a great week with Eli—he'd gotten the financial aid he needed to attend MIT—and a terrible week with Mom, I made a perfect cup of chai and sat down at the kitchen table to hone my "Reasons Mom Can't Live Alone" list. I'd just settled in when Karyn came to tell me that she was heading out to the yurt to meet a private yoga student. As she leaned over, she noticed the headline on my list.

"Are you serious, Laura?"

"About what?"

She pointed to my list. "This—a list of all the things Temme's doing wrong?"

"What's wrong with it?"

"I can't believe you. Why aren't you writing a list of her strengths?"

"They're not driving me nuts."

"You're always looking for the negative."

"She's my responsibility. It's not safe for her to live alone."

"Laura, you should be building her up, not tearing her down."

"That's not what I'm doing."

"Looks like it to me."

"That's not fair."

Karyn pulled out a chair and sat down beside me. "Laura, you've spent years bad-mouthing Temme."

Heat rose in my cheeks. "You're exaggerating."

"Really? Who's the one making the list of her mistakes?" Karyn's lips tightened. "I hope you never make a list like that about me."

I looked away and softened my tone. "You don't spend as much time with her as I do."

"I spend a lot of time with her." She was right. Karyn always treated Mom with kindness, tended her garden, visited while I was away.

"You *are* a great daughter-in-law, but she's always on her best behavior with you. You're not her daughter."

Karyn sighed. "No, I'm not. But sometimes I think I'm the only person who's on her side."

Her words seared through me. I swallowed hard.

Karyn glanced at her watch. As she rose, I reached for her hand. "Am I really that bad?"

Her eyes softened. "You care about her. You really do. But you have to stop anticipating how bad things are *going* to get. You're pushing her into a future that hasn't arrived yet." Her words reverberated, but I wasn't ready to admit it.

Karyn hugged me and stood. "You're doing a great job, Laura. But think about it."

—∞—

That afternoon, I walked to the beach and let Karyn's words take root. She was right. I *did* spend my visits building a case against Mom. I stockpiled the fact that she offered to write me the same check repeatedly as proof that she was vulnerable to financial abuse. When she couldn't remember if she'd taken her pills, I thought, *Aha! This proves it. She can't live alone.* In my attempt to ensure her safety, I'd been fixating solely on her weaknesses, exactly the wrong approach.

As I dug my feet into the sand, I had to face the fact that my behavior wasn't new. Ever since I'd been a teenager, I'd been creating a vendetta against her. Oh, I had my reasons. Mom's inability to recognize me as a separate person, her unexamined need for control, and her explosive emotions made loving her a challenge. My tallies justified to me that she was unworthy of my love. The list of her crimes kept growing, and I never forgot them. Her courage and generosity rarely made the list, and if I bothered to include them, it was in pencil, so they could be easily erased. Bright, marquee lights highlighted her deficits—little ones, like always hanging up on me; medium-sized ones, like attacking me for being a lesbian before settling down and accepting it; and the biggest one of all—denying her father's abuse.

From the moment Mom put her self-protection first, the neurons in the part of my brain that alerts to danger kept shouting, *She might betray you again.* And so, I demonized her, hardening her transgressions in stone. I cast her in the role of antagonist in order to survive.

But at what price?

AFTER MOM'S DEATH

MOTHER IN LETTERS

Since her death, I've pored over the fat files of letters between me and my mother multiple times. At times, it feels as if the revelations in our correspondence change everything, especially when the written word contradicts or sheds new light on my recollections. But as revealing and evocative as our letters are, they tell only part of the story—the part that *happened in letters*.

I'm reminded of a woman I interviewed for *The Courage to Heal*. Cynthia's relationship with her mother was volatile. Each time they saw each other in person, the visit disintegrated into accusations and misery. Afterward, Cynthia berated herself, *What's wrong with me? Why can't I work it out with my mother?* She'd limp home, devastated, but as soon as she regained her equilibrium, she and her mother would begin corresponding again. The letters felt good, and Cynthia would think, *I must be exaggerating. I probably just didn't try hard enough. I should go see her again*.

The next visit would start with a honeymoon period, but Cynthia's interactions with her mother inevitably turned ugly, and she doubted herself all over again. This pattern repeated for years. Finally, Cynthia stopped tormenting herself by accepting the reality of her situation: "We cannot be in the same room, but at least I have a mother in letters."

That's how it was with Mom and me. Correspondence provided a safe distance that made it possible for us to interact. Letters could be composed, rewritten, edited, nuanced to express exactly what we wanted to say. Letters enabled us to conceal things. In person, there were no such filters, no escape from the painful immediacy of our emotional limitations. Triggers were everywhere. The worst parts of us were activated during our visits; in letters, our best selves shone through. In letters, we were brave, articulate, and loving. Our relationship worked there, but it was an idealized and mediated relationship, one we couldn't replicate in person.

CHAPTER 39

PINK SLIP

958 Days

Mom spat out the words. "He's just a young whippersnapper. A kid, a punk. Why should I listen to him? Who the hell does he think he is?"

After firing a long line of doctors for transgressions that included talking too softly, wearing skirts she deemed too tight or too short, and hiring rude receptionists who demanded her birth date the moment she walked in the door, Mom had settled on Dr. Reed, her fourth general practitioner in two years.

Each time she fired another doctor, I had to find a replacement. When I finally wangled an appointment, we walked in as strangers. Temme Davis was just another old lady who was never getting better. There was no relationship—just records on a screen.

For the past few months, Dr. Reed had been her golden boy.

In December 2011, we arranged to meet at his office. Mom showed up later than usual—five minutes early rather than her usual fifteen. Her shirt was stained. Her jacket looked slept in. This wasn't the first time I'd seen her in dirty clothes, though most days, she still looked perfectly put together: a striking multicolored jacket, the right scarf, perfect shoes, and matching pocketbook, her hair carefully coiffed.

Her vanity was legendary; now it was slipping. It was hard watching her transform before my eyes.

Dr. Reed addressed Mom directly, his tone grave. "Temme, your neurologist told you last summer that you shouldn't drive and asked you to come in for a follow-up. You didn't."

What? I'd been trying to get Mom's doctors to stop her from driving for years, but no one had been willing to intervene. At the one appointment I'd missed, her neurologist told her not to drive? Of course Mom hadn't told me. *Damn it.* Now Dr. Reed was saving me from the one task I'd dreaded most.

"Temme, if you don't tell me right now that you're going to stop driving, I'm going to call the DMV and make a report."

Why hadn't I thought of that?

Mom's face collapsed, and her foot trembled. When Dr. Reed stepped outside for a moment, she spat out the words. "That young fuck! How dare he tell me to give up my keys."

I loved her fiery spirit, but I was definitely rooting for Dr. Reed. As gently as I could, I said, "Mom, a couple of years ago, you had a hit-and-run."

She stared at me in defiance. "I did not!" Of course she didn't remember, but even if she had, she would have denied it.

"Have you noticed that Lizzy hasn't been in your car? Karyn and I decided it wasn't safe for her to ride with you."

She blazed back. "You two are always exaggerating. I just drive a little slower, that's all."

"Actually, Lizzy's scared to be in the car with you."

Mom's eyes filled with tears. I reached for her hand, but she yanked it away—exactly what I didn't want.

When he returned, Dr. Reed rolled his stool right up to Mom. "Temme, you're going to have to give your daughter your keys."

She squared her shoulders and glared at him. "I'm not going to do that! So, put me in jail."

"No one's talking about putting you in jail. But you have to stop driving."

Mom sagged. I pulled my chair closer and placed my hand on the small of her back. Waves of heat wafted off her, but she didn't shrug me away.

She pleaded with Dr. Reed. "Please don't call the DMV. I regulate my driving. I don't drive at night or on the freeway. I only go to the grocery store."

A flush rose in Dr. Reed's face, and for a split second, he turned away.

Mom saw her opening and took it. "Can't you wait until the next time I see the neurologist?"

Dr. Reed sighed. "All right, Temme. If you agree not to drive, I'll hold off on contacting the DMV until your next neurology appointment."

Shit. No way.

Mom straightened up with a victorious smile on her lips. *Unbelievable.*

Dr. Reed leaned forward; his voice regaining its strength. "And, Temme, when you see her, I'm going to ask her to evaluate whether it's safe for you to live independently. It's not a question of if; it's a question of when."

Mom's eyes froze like a cornered animal. "I'll tell you one thing. I'm not going into that place." She gestured with her arm, covered with black and purple Coumadin bruises. "That place between the hospital and the graveyard."

"Dominican Oaks?" I asked. One of the best assisted-living facilities in town.

"Yes, that place. I went there for a play-reading group, and it was so depressing." Mom's voice broke as she fought to maintain control. "You walk in, and there's a whole row of wheelchairs. And at five o'clock, there's a lineup of zombies in the dining hall, staring off into space, waiting for someone to feed them. I'm not going to live in a place like that."

I took Mom's hand. It was trembling uncontrollably.

"So, what are you going to do, Temme?" Dr. Reed had recovered; now he was holding firm.

"I'll have someone come live with me."

Bingo.

—∞—

Once the awful appointment was over, Mom and I walked across the street to Safeway so she could buy a small bag of groceries. When she wasn't looking, I slipped a bar of her favorite chocolate into the cart. At the checkout line, she turned to me, lips quivering. "This is as bad as the day your father walked out on me."

Oh, Mom. And there I'd been, cheering for Dr. Reed during one of the worst moments of my mother's life.

I hadn't been there for her when Dad left us, but I wasn't fourteen anymore. I put my arms around her, right there at the check stand. Not Good Daughter—me. I held her like I'd held my children when they woke from a nightmare, feeling scared and alone.

Customers averted their eyes and walked around us. When Mom finally straightened up, she placed her food on the conveyor belt and paid for her little bag of groceries. She grinned when she saw the chocolate. I carried her groceries out into the warm afternoon.

Mom's mood had lightened, and so had mine. As we headed back to the parking lot, I remembered her promise to Dr. Reed. I asked as gently as I could, "So, should I start looking for someone to come live with you?"

Mom's smile vanished. "Why would you want to do that?"

"Because you just told Dr. Reed you would."

"I said no such thing! I am perfectly capable of living alone."

I stared at her in the middle of the parking lot. I should have known it was only a temporary surrender. Now she was Miss Independence again.

I wanted to get away from her. And from the look on her face, she felt the same. We reached into our purses simultaneously, fishing for our keys. When we pulled them out, we looked at each other and started laughing. "Mom, you just promised not to drive."

She gave me the same pleading expression she'd used on Dr. Reed. "It's only half a mile."

What kind of bizarre movie was I in?

The afternoon was warm, the sky clear, and there wasn't much traffic. She only had to make three turns and she'd be home. I was already late picking up Lizzy. I opened her car door and set her groceries on the seat. "Okay, Mom, but this is the last time."

That night, I Googled "Department of Motor Vehicles." Two clicks later, I was staring at the form, Request for Driver Reexamination. I filled it out, explaining why I didn't think it was safe for her to drive. "She should be tested," I added in the notes section, "but don't tell her I said so. It would destroy our relationship if she knew I turned her in."

The Department of Motor Vehicles sent Mom a formal letter, saying she had to take a road test if she wanted to continue driving. Thankfully, it didn't say, *Your daughter, Laura Davis, says you're a menace on the road.* I pretended to be surprised and listened as Mom railed against this latest outrage. She told everyone she was going to sue the DMV, but she lost the form and missed the deadline for turning in the paperwork.

She never drove again.

CHAPTER 40

CONSPIRACY

894 Days

Two months later, Paul offered to fly out for a family session with an elder care attorney, who skillfully guided us through the process of signing a durable power of attorney, the final document we needed to manage Mom's finances and health care for the rest of her life.

His last night in town, I wanted to thank Paul for initiating the trip. "Want to spend some special time together?"

After Karyn and Lizzy went to bed, I built a fire in our woodstove. Paul and I sat on opposite ends of the couch, feet tucked under the same cozy blanket. It had been a long time since Paul and I had really talked about our lives. As the fire crackled, he told me about the woman he was dating and the latest on my niece, Sonya. I dug deeper than the headlines as I described my life with Karyn and the kids. I caught him up on Bryan's life. Talked about my challenges growing my business, and Paul gave me some promotional ideas. Like me, he was a creative entrepreneur, and he had a good head for business. By the time we exhausted that topic, it was almost midnight, but I wasn't ready for the good feelings to end. I put another log on the fire. Paul pulled out his guitar and played some old rock and roll. I joined in on the choruses, relaxing in a way I rarely did around my brother. Why didn't we do this more often?

After a haunting rendition of "House of the Rising Sun," Paul put away his guitar and sat next to me, closer than before. He looked at me with more intensity than I was comfortable with and said, "Laura, there's something I've been wanting to talk to you about. I've been studying a lot about our banking system, and since you're my sister, I really want to help you protect your assets. I've been learning some shocking things about the Federal Reserve. There's this video I want to show you . . ."

That great, relaxed feeling started to fade.

Paul reached for his laptop and navigated to a video on YouTube: *Conspiracy: The Secret History. Masters of the Universe: The Secret Birth of the Federal Reserve.* "This is really important, Laura. If you continue keeping your money in banks, you'll lose everything."

I felt myself go flat, like air hissing out of a tire.

Paul turned on the documentary. One minute into the opening credits, I knew it definitely wasn't for me. I checked the time stamp: forty-five minutes. I looked at my brother's earnest face and tried to think of a polite way to excuse myself. I hated to disappoint him, but five minutes later, I pushed Stop. "I'm sorry, Paul. I don't want to watch this."

"Don't you care about the security of your family? This could . . ."

"You're so gullible, Paul. You believe everything anyone tells you. That 9/11 was perpetrated by our government; Guru Maharaj Ji is Lord of the Universe; and spirit guides tell you how to live your life. This is just one more conspiracy theory." That hurt look I knew so well spread across Paul's face. The gulf between us gaped again.

"Laura, these are proven facts."

"Well, they're not facts I'm interested in."

"You don't have to be so closed, Laura."

"And you don't have to be so weird." I regretted it as soon as I said it.

Paul stared at me with hurt eyes. "Do you really think so?"

Oh no. I did not want to get mired in a heart-to-heart with my brother. It was like walking into a honeycomb, all those sticky surfaces. "Look, I'm sorry. I should never have said that." I gave him a hug. "It's late. You're catching a flight tomorrow. We got a lot done for Mom, and tonight was great. You've been terrific. Let's focus on that."

The next morning, as a peace offering, I cooked kale and eggs for Paul, his favorite breakfast. He thanked me, and things felt good until I mentioned my plan to take our new power of attorney to Mom's bank. When I said the word "bank," that hurt look rekindled in his eyes. As I stood up to clear the table, a voice inside me whispered, *Why can't you be nicer to your brother?*

Paul's eyes lingered on mine. Then he left to gather his things.

CHAPTER 41

FIONA

866 Days

Mom's neurologist passed the buck on telling her she shouldn't live alone. I was furious. In desperation, I hired a geriatric social worker to do an in-home evaluation. After their meeting, Mom grudgingly acknowledged she needed help because she could no longer drive.

When the first caregiver arrived, Mom spent the whole morning holed up in her bedroom, TV blasting, refusing to speak. "I hate her. I can't have her in my house."

"Give her a chance. She just started. You'll warm up to her."

"I'll never warm up to her. She's a sourpuss. I hate her."

So, I called the agency and requested someone else. Two days later, Mom rejected her, too. "I hate the new girl. She talks down to me like I'm an imbecile."

"Mom, she's not a girl. She's a full-grown woman, and you're not giving her a chance!"

"It's never going to work. I don't want her in my house."

Mom seemed to tolerate the third caregiver. I thought she was great: communicative, experienced, compassionate, even with a curmudgeon like Mom. But just as I was starting to relax, Mom's distress boiled over. "She just sits around watching me."

I called the agency and asked for Number Four. We were getting a reputation.

I made an appointment with Dale Thielges, head of the local Alzheimer's Association. She suggested I try finding Mom a roommate—someone who could drive her around, dispense her pills, and do simple household tasks in exchange for rent. She gave me a referral that led to Fiona, a woman my age who was down on her luck.

When I told Mom, she balked. "I don't need a goddamn roommate."

"It will be like having your own private chauffeur. Fiona will take you anywhere you want to go." That's what I said to my mother. But I had a different agenda: someone—*besides me*—to make sure she took her pills properly. Someone—*besides me*—to be there if she fell. To make sure the house didn't catch on fire. Someone who could be my eyes and ears, so I could be with my family, run my business, and live my life.

But Mom wasn't cooperating with my plan. "I don't want her living here."

"Look, it's either one of the three you've rejected, or it's Fiona."

"Just wait till you're my age. Lizzy's going to do this to you someday."

I pulled out the big guns. "You want to stay here, don't you?"

She glared at me. "All right, I'll try it."

Two days later, Fiona moved in with a single suitcase, a cardboard box, a litter box, and her beloved cat. She drove Mom where she wanted to go, shopped for groceries, gave Mom her pills day and night. She reported to me every other day.

Before Fiona, Mom had lived alone for more than forty years, doing things her way. Now, a stranger was living in her mobile home, leaving lint in the dryer, cooking on her stove, and talking to her cat as if she were a baby. The fact that Mom hated Fiona was no surprise. She treated her like a servant and discussed her in the third person, as if she weren't there. "I'm better off than she is. I don't want to be her damn social worker." Mom burned at the injustice of having an intruder in her house. "The damn cat is always running across the dining room table. And the litter box—ugh! It stinks up the whole house. That woman and her cat have got to go."

I repeated my mantra, "Mom, you said you'd try it," and repeatedly apologized to Fiona for my mother's rude behavior. Mom was desperate to remain in her home, so we all settled into an uneasy truce. The first week stretched into the second, and the second week stretched into the third. For now, Fiona was the best stopgap we had.

CHAPTER 42

GENETICS

845 Days

A few weeks later, I invited Mom over for dinner, promising to pick her up and drive her home at the end of the night. We talked politics over a make-your-own-taco dinner with Lizzy's famous guacamole. After we ate, we called Eli in Boston so he could say hello to his grandmother. Karyn did the dishes, and Lizzy excused herself to do homework in the next room. Mom and I remained at the kitchen table, discussing education.

"Genetics prove it," she said. "Some people are just smarter than other people."

My spine stiffened. "What are you talking about?"

"Just what I said. Some groups are smarter than others."

"Mom, you can't say that."

"Of course I can. It's true. They've proven it. I should know. I worked as a school social worker my whole career. I saw those families. I worked with those kids. Those *schwartzes,* they just aren't as smart."

I cringed and stared at the eighty-four-year-old woman in front of me. My mother had worked in an all-Black school district for years.

She'd been a hardworking member of the child study team. Advocating for kids. Advocating for families. This was her conclusion?

"They've done studies of Nobel Prize winners, and a very large percentage of them are Jewish."

"God, Mom." Who was this woman? "Some people have more opportunities. Some people have had to deal with racism their whole lives. Those kids were born into poverty."

"So what? Your grandparents grew up in a *shtetl*. Jews have had to deal with anti-Semitism for thousands of years. We're just smarter, that's all. Look how many Jews are at the top of their professions: doctors, bankers, scientists. They're all Jews."

I watched Karyn at the sink, her back rigid and unmoving. Karyn wasn't Jewish. Her stiff back spoke volumes.

"I can't believe what you're saying." I strode over to the thin red pocket door between the kitchen and the dining room and slammed it shut in one sweeping motion. I didn't want Lizzy hearing her grandmother claim she was genetically superior. "Mom, this isn't like you . . ."

"I know, but as I get older, these things become clearer to me. It's obvious Jews are smarter. That's why we're so into education. Look at your kids. Eli's at MIT. Lizzy's at the top of her class . . ."

"Being Jewish has nothing to do with it."

"There's evidence, Laurie. They've scanned people's brains. Jews' brains are larger."

I looked at Karyn, her stiff back framed by the kitchen sink. Her mother-in-law, the one she showered with generous kindness, had just proclaimed that she was inferior. I stood up, grabbed Mom's turquoise cotton jacket, the boxy one with embroidery on the yoke, and thrust it at her. "Get your purse. I'm taking you home."

"You don't have to get so huffy. I'm just telling the truth."

"That's not the truth, Mom, and I'm not going to let you talk like that in our house."

I drove her home in silence, seething and confused. Dementia had erased the politically correct censors on what Mom was willing to say. Did that mean my liberal Jewish mother had always felt this way?

When I pulled up at her unit, neither of us made a move to get out of the car. Mom sat wedged against the passenger door, her chin trembling.

"Mom . . ."

"You didn't have to do that to me." She lashed out, a darting snake.

My body was still red-hot with anger, but I was not going to react. This was about me setting a boundary. *My* family. *My* spouse. *My* home.

"Actually, Mom, I did need to do that. I didn't want your granddaughter hearing you say that. I'm sorry, but I get to decide."

"You're making a mountain out of a molehill." Mom spoke like a petulant child.

"Mom, Karyn's not Jewish. How do you think she felt?"

Her chin trembled again. "I didn't think of that."

"I know you didn't. I'm not going to argue with you about it, but it's not okay for you to say things like that in my house."

Regret filled the air between us. "I can see that now. I wasn't thinking about Karyn." Yeah, and all the other non-Jews in the world. But I wasn't going there. I had to hold steady. Protect my family *and* maintain my relationship with Mom.

A wave of doubt broke over her face. "Are you still going to invite me over?"

"Of course we will." I spoke to her the way I'd speak to a fearful child. "Let me walk you to the door. It's been a long night."

On our way up the stairs, she gripped my arm and leaned heavily against me. She struggled up each step. At the top, she fumbled with the key. When she finally unlocked the door, she turned to face me, uncertainty marring the softening skin of her face.

CHAPTER 43

CAMPUS QUEEN

836 Days

Ever since Mom's arrival, I'd been scoping out all the assisted-living places in town. I knew Fiona was only a temporary solution. Sooner or later, I was going to have to move Mom out of the little home she loved. It looked like the best choice was Sunshine Villa. It was conveniently located near Lizzy's school and pretty much every other place I went, so it would be easy for me to drop in to see Mom in the middle of my busy days. More important, as her mind deteriorated, they'd still have a place for her; there was a memory care unit downstairs.

Sunshine Villa was a state-of-the-art facility: beautiful, immaculate, with impressive gardens and elegant furnishings. Everyone, from the janitors and cooks to the nurses, was trained to help people with memory loss feel relaxed, oriented, and empowered. The whole environment was designed to minimize the kind of stress Mom was experiencing every single day.

But I knew she wasn't ready. People at Sunshine Villa looked old, and Mom hated to be around people who looked old. My mother looked ten years younger than her age, thanks to a combination of natural vitality, good genes, beautiful skin, and the face-lift she'd gotten in

Mexico—her solution to the trauma of turning fifty. I knew she'd take one look at the residents of Sunshine Villa and want to bolt, but she agreed to visit anyway.

Walking into Sunshine Villa with its wide hallways, floral carpets, elegant furniture, and crystal chandeliers was like entering a grand hotel. But we were immediately confronted by a dozen people sitting near the front door, staring placidly into space. Tuesday was doctor day at Sunshine Villa. If you made an appointment with a doctor on a Tuesday, the Sunshine Villa bus would take you there. These folks were waiting for that bus.

One look at those old people and I knew Mom wanted to flee. I did, too. As much as I worried about her living in her little mobile home, I looked around and thought, *Not here, not yet.*

But we went on the tour and met with Maureen, Sunshine Villa's face to the world. Maureen was lovely, with light blue eyes and well-scrubbed good looks. She talked slowly and calmly and put Mom at ease. She assured us that 25 percent of the residents were completely independent and went out during the day. That's why we weren't seeing them.

By then, we'd heard enough. We'd dipped our toes into the water.

On our way to the car, Mom grabbed my arm and whispered, "I could be Campus Queen of this place." I looked at her, waiting for the laugh track, but she was perfectly serious.

—∾—

Sixty-five years earlier, the reigning Miss America, Bess Myerson, had crowned my mother Campus Queen at City College of New York. Now Mom wanted to reclaim her former glory. She'd started life as a poor girl with immigrant parents, graduated from high school at fifteen, then fought with her father to accept the free education available at City College. When she was nineteen, her good looks won that crown. Winning the contest led to a photo shoot and a part as the ingénue in her first play, the first of many in a fifty-year theatrical career.

As a little girl, I'd loved poring over the photo album of my mother's special day, filled with glossy pictures of her with the other competitors: Mom in the swimsuit competition, Mom in a smart tailored suit, Mom looking back over her shoulder at the camera, Mom wearing a fancy dress and a string of pearls, Mom beaming, wearing her sparkly crown.

My mother's beauty was larger than life. I never tired of watching her "put on her face" before she went out. She'd spread on a thin coating of Noxzema, then foundation, brush on light blue eyeshadow, paint on eyeliner, dab her finger in a pot of rouge. "Always smile and stroke upward onto your cheeks."

I loved the gold wand she pushed into the mascara case, her mouth in a soundless O as her lashes magically lengthened.

Carefully rolling nylons up curved calves, she fastened the tops into garters dangling from her Playtex Living Girdle. My question was always the same. "Ew! How can you wear a girdle?"

"You'll understand when you grow up." She gave me a knowing smile. "Women suffer for beauty."

Now at eighty-four, unable to remember what had been said a moment earlier, my mother wanted to be Campus Queen again. I could see why. Sunshine Villa was not a place she wanted to go, but the possibility haunted her future. Living with me wasn't an option. Our house was small, but that wasn't the issue; extended families often live together in much smaller spaces than ours. The truth was that after a lifetime of scrimping and saving, Mom could afford a place like Sunshine Villa. And with our history, neither of us could imagine living in close proximity. Mom pushed every button I had. She'd *made* most of those buttons. Wake up to her each morning? Help her dress? Wipe soup from her chin? I could no more imagine that kind of closeness with my mother than I could picture living on the moon.

But her time at De Anza was running out. We just happened to be at war about the timing. I worried every day that she lived there, imagining catastrophe; she wanted to stay as long as possible. If moving to a place like Sunshine Villa was in her future, why not be Campus Queen?

—∿∿—

West Cliff Drive is a narrow street, flanked by a curved pedestrian path that snakes above the Pacific, the go-to place for rollerbladers, bicyclists, hikers, and anyone who wants to watch the sunset. It stretches between the Santa Cruz Beach Boardwalk and Natural Bridges State Park, right below the mobile home park that Mom called home. After helping her into the car, I tossed the glossy Sunshine Villa brochure into the back seat and suggested we stop at West Cliff before I took her home. "Mom, let's go for a little walk and sit on a bench." Since Karyn had pointed out my fixation on Mom's failings, I'd been trying to spend more easy, enjoyable time with her. I'd cleared my schedule to make this happen. Mom loved the ocean and happily agreed.

We had walked only a little way before she tired. We sat on a bench, staring out at the surfers and the deep blue Pacific. It was windy, and she was underdressed. I had the impulse to put my arm around her but hesitated to touch her, as I always did. A voice inside me said, *You want to be a good daughter? Put your arm around your mother.* I scooted next to her and pulled her close. She stopped shivering and settled into my warmth.

For the next hour, as the sun set and streaks of color filled the sky, my mother was thoughtful and calm. No panic. No anger. No confusion. The fickleness of her memory drove me crazy.

"Laurie, I don't want to stay alive and be a burden on you. I don't want to drain my money and the government's money just to stay alive a couple more years. Write this down."

"You've already signed papers that say the same thing. We've made your funeral arrangements. I know what you want."

"I want to be sure."

"I did this with Dad. I stopped them from reviving him when he had a do-not-resuscitate order. I can do what needs to be done."

Mom leaned her head on my shoulder as the last glow of sunset kissed the horizon. Three surfers wiped out in a row. One caught a perfect wave and rode it all the way to shore. I squeezed Mom's hand. She squeezed mine back. "I don't want to commit suicide, Laurie, but I want to quit while I'm ahead."

I hoped, for her sake, that she would get her wish. I tightened my arm around her shoulders. Warmth emanated from the place our bodies touched.

CHAPTER 44

TESTS

833 Days

I remember the day Mom got her diagnosis. And I'm not sure now whether it was a good idea. I pushed for it. I wanted to be part of the Early-Stage Memory Loss Support Group at the Santa Cruz Alzheimer's Association, a weekly group where those with memory loss meet with a facilitator in one room while their caregivers meet in another. I hoped the group would help Mom, but really, I was the one desperate for help. In order to join the group, Mom needed an official diagnosis. So, I called the Stanford Alzheimer's Center and made an appointment to get her tested.

Now, I just had to get her to agree.

I exerted pressure every way I could. It was one of my worst talents. I pulled out my inner steamroller whenever there was something I really wanted: getting Mom to say yes to the reconciliation book, forcing Paul to show up, getting my way with Karyn and the kids. I wasn't proud of it, but it had its uses, and I needed it now. I called Mom's doctor, her sister Ruth, and Paul, and asked them to join me in a full-court press, telling Mom that testing was essential. Mom didn't want to go, but we talked her into it. Let's get real—*I* talked her into it. I made it sound like there was no other option.

But I see now that there was. I could have left her in peace. Did I really need to rub her face in what was so painfully apparent to the rest of us? Mom couldn't remember what she'd said five minutes earlier. Thirty seconds earlier. She was angry and frustrated and lashing out. She had all the signs. Why did I feel the need to prove it? Because I wanted to go to a support group? Yes, that was part of it. But there was a lot more to it; I just couldn't admit it at the time.

So, I went ahead; I orchestrated her acquiescence. Mom needed me and wanted to please me, but I think the real reason she agreed to go was that she was sure the tests would show nothing. Her memory was just fine. So, maybe a few synapses weren't firing. It was just normal aging, nothing more. Mom was certain she was about to be vindicated and that I was wrong.

On April 12, 2012, I drove Mom to Stanford in the pouring rain. They led her away, and I waited for hours. When she finally emerged, she looked diminished. Shrunken. Exhausted. She drooped. Then she put on her game face and said, "I might have missed one or two things, Laurie, but I did pretty good on those tests." Her breezy confidence made me wince.

By the time I got her home, she was spent. She went directly to her bedroom and closed the door. Soon, her TV was blaring through the walls.

This was the opportunity Fiona and I had been waiting for. Every two weeks, the two of us refilled Mom's weekly pill vials and created a new master list of medications that reflected the latest changes, complete with sample pills taped on. Fiona and I hunched over the table, twenty pill and vitamin bottles spread out before us. As a dozen baby aspirins tumbled into my hand, we could hear Mom calling her sister Ruth in Florida. The walls were so thin, it was as if the conversation were being broadcast: "That woman, Fiona, she and her damn cat, I want them out of here. I'm perfectly capable of taking care of myself."

As rain poured down the gutters, Mom shouted into the phone. "Yes, I'm going to tell her. I'm going to tell her right now."

She burst into the room. "What are you two doing? I need to know what you're doing. They're my pills."

"Well, pull up a chair." I was too busy snapping the top on the Coumadin bottle to look up. "You can watch."

Agitation wafted off her tightly coiled body as she paced behind us. "I don't want to just watch." Heat seared through her clipped words. "I need to be able to do it."

You want to do it? We could barely do it. The five-milligram prednisone pills looked identical to the one-milligram prednisone pills. There were two sizes of Coumadin, which was also called warfarin. The exact same medication, dispensed from different pharmacies, came in different shapes and colors. Three of Mom's vitamins looked identical. Some pills had to be taken in the morning; some in the evening; some twice a day. You needed a PhD to fill her pillboxes.

"Mom, this is something we have to do for you." Then considering how much she distrusted Fiona, I added, "That *I* have to do for you. We can't afford to make a mistake with your pills."

Mom's face flushed. "I'm not incompetent." As the rain intensified outside, she slammed her hand down on the counter with a smack. "You're treating me like an invalid."

I flashed back to an odd fact from eighth-grade English class. "Invalid" was a homonym. If you were an invalid, you were invalid. And here I was brushing my mother away as if she were a two-year-old, insisting that she be the one to crack the eggs. I pressed down the lid of her pillbox, the one with "A.M." Magic-Markered across the front. It was bulging and could barely close. Finally, I got it to shut with a satisfying snap. "There are a lot of things you can still do for yourself, Mom, but this isn't one of them."

She glared at me. I could almost see steam rising off her rigid body. "What if I stop taking my pills?"

"You could. But if you stop taking your pills, you might have a stroke." I paused, wondering about the best way to approach this eighty-four-year-old child in front of me. "You're the one who said you wanted to keep taking your pills."

"I do want to." She stamped her foot, just like her grandson Eli, King of Tantrums, used to do. "But I have to be in charge. They're my pills!" We faced off across her kitchen aisle, battle lines drawn. Fiona backed into the living room, trying to be invisible.

"Mom, I'm not changing my mind."

She wheeled on Fiona. "I don't want to have to fight in front of a stranger!" Fiona got the message and went outside to stand in the rain. There was nowhere else for her to go.

Mom's hands were shaking. I tried not to stare at the purple Coumadin bruises up and down her arms. She shouted, "Anyone can make a mistake."

"One mistake could cost you your life. And there have been lots of mistakes."

"I don't remember that."

"I know. That's the problem." I hated talking to her like this. I might as well have been yelling, *You are a senile old woman, too stubborn to admit it, and you are ruining my life.* I didn't want to talk down to her like that. Though maybe part of me did. Was this fight really about her safety? Or did I just want to win?

Mom rose on shaky legs, her aura extending way beyond her four feet, eleven and a half. "I can do it myself!"

I remembered Eli at two, the way he'd get on his tiptoes and scream, rage radiating all the way out to his fingers. But my mother wasn't a two-year-old. She was the woman who'd pulled me into the world, dressed me in onesies, sewn me gingham dresses. And now, I was batting her down like an unruly child.

Outside, rain pounded the cheap striped awnings. Fiona stood pressed under the meager shelter as a neighbor drove by. Mom shouted, "Maybe it would be better if I was dead! I'm eighty-four years old. What am I supposed to do? Live forever? I'd rather die than lose everything. Keeping my autonomy is much more important than death!"

I stared at her, shocked and secretly delighted. She'd nailed it, but I couldn't give her the satisfaction of having the last word. "I'm leaving!"

I slammed the door on my way out. But because she lived in a mobile home, with thin, cheap doors, it wasn't a satisfying slam. I felt like a child myself.

I drove across town to my evening class, where a dozen students were waiting for me to inspire them. When I was halfway there, my phone rang; I put Mom on speaker. "I'm sorry, Laurie. Sometimes I can be such a bitch. I'm just so frustrated, but you shouldn't be my target. You spent all day with me; you're trying to take care of me. I couldn't have a better daughter. I know that, but I just hate what's happening to me. I shouldn't take it out on you."

"I love you, too, Mom. I should have been more patient. I'm sorry." As the wipers caught across the windshield, my throat tightened. I was not being the caregiver I wanted to be. All those years of careful reconciliation had worked when we could control set and setting, when it was possible for us to retreat into our separate corners to regroup and lick our wounds. But we were living in a new world now, and the old rules were obsolete. The hard-earned peace I'd been so proud of was feeling fragile, and I could feel myself fraying. I wasn't sure how much longer the seams could hold.

CHAPTER 45

FAMILY CONFERENCE

832 Days

The next morning, I called my brother. I did not want to make this call.

"Hey, Paul, I took Mom in for her tests at Stanford yesterday."

"How did it go?"

"Exhausting for both of us, especially Mom. Then we had a big fight."

"You're doing a great job, Laura."

"I appreciate that. It's not easy teaching, running a business, taking care of kids, and managing Mom." I paused. I had to get the whine out of my voice. My tone had to be just right—matter-of-fact. "So, Paul, we're going back to Stanford in three weeks, on May third, for a family conference to get Mom's results. I need you to come. I looked online. Southwest is having a big sale . . ."

"I'd love to, but this is a really busy time for me. I have two seminars coming up, and I've put down a deposit for Master Sha's Intensive Karma Cleanse workshop that week. Can't you go?"

"Of course I'm going. I need you to be there, too."

"I'll be happy to call and talk to the doctor."

"Paul, this requires more than a phone call. It's her Alzheimer's results."

"I've already bought a ticket to see her in August."

"That's four months away."

"I was just there last month."

"Yeah, and I'm here every day."

"Look, if I could come, I definitely would, but . . ."

"Remember the night we talked about Mom moving out here? You promised you'd show up whenever I needed you. Paul, I need you."

"I'd love to, but . . ."

"This is no ordinary appointment. This is going to be one of the worst days of Mom's life. She's going to need both of us to support her. She needs you there. In person." I paused, then went for the coup de grâce. "They don't call it a family conference for nothing."

There was a long silence on the other end of the phone.

"I'll call Southwest tonight and email you my itinerary."

CHAPTER 46

SAFE SPACE

828 Days

Because I'd taken her to get tested, Mom and I were welcomed into the Early-Stage Memory Loss Support Group the following week. When I told Mom where we were going, she balked. "I'm not like those people." But when I explained that I needed to go, that it would help me take better care of her, she acquiesced.

We arrived at the Alzheimer's Association with five minutes to spare. Soon, ten of us gathered around a large table. The two facilitators took turns introducing the group, speaking slowly and calmly. They used simple, concrete language, yet it never felt like they were talking down to anyone.

The whole room felt serene: no sense of hurry, nowhere to go, nothing to accomplish. They were modeling exactly what I'd been reading about in the Alzheimer's caregiver books stacked on my bedside table. I soaked up their words like a thirsty sponge.

After brief introductions, the caregivers moved into the adjacent room with one facilitator. The people with memory loss stayed with the second one. We followed the same predictable pattern at every meeting. Everyone in my group was struggling with similar concerns, and the hour and a half went quickly. Several group members suggested I make an appointment with the Caregiver Resource Center downtown—and I did.

I loved my new support group, and, luckily, when I met Mom at the exit door, she was smiling. She liked the people and felt she belonged. Thank God. I lived for that group. It saved my life every Tuesday.

CHAPTER 47

WEST CLIFF

821 Days

Mom was eighty-four years old when she went back into therapy for the last time. She'd been seeing a counselor, on and off, for as long as I could remember. Now at the end of her life, she was back in therapy again. The losses were piling up too fast for her to process. She needed to vent about the person she depended on who was taking over her life: me. But mostly, she went to therapy because she was lonely, no longer capable of making a friend. She needed a compassionate ear and was willing to pay for it, even though she couldn't remember anything said in those sessions. And of course, her therapist couldn't tell me.

His name was Shaw Coleman. Or was it Coleman Shaw? Neither of us could ever remember, and when our memories failed simultaneously, it was always good for a laugh.

One day, Mom asked Coleman to mediate for us. She wanted to get rid of Fiona, and I was the obstacle standing in her way. I couldn't leave Mom unsupervised, but she hated Fiona and wasn't ready to "move in with the zombies." I had to find an alternative. I knew that negotiating with Mom, with dementia, was bound to fail, but I reluctantly agreed. Maybe there'd be a miracle.

That afternoon, Mom rose out of her mental fog and rocked the mediation. She was articulate and charming. No one would have guessed there was anything wrong with her brain. Coleman took notes, and in fifteen minutes, we negotiated an agreement:

April 24, 2012
Temme and Laura agree:

- *Someone will come each morning to assist Temme with medication management, possibly her neighbor, Jane.*
- *Laura and Temme will hire a caregiver they both agree on, to come three times a week, for three hours each time, to assist with driving and errands.*
- *Laura will give Fiona thirty days' notice to move out.*

I knew our written agreement wasn't ideal. I was giving up a lot, but Mom had finally agreed—in writing—to have help. That was a huge step.

"Mom, thanks for being so cooperative."

She teared up. "Oh, darling, I knew I could count on you." And just like that, we were golden. As Mom struggled out to the car, I carried our newly forged agreement in my hand. Maybe God was giving me a gift.

Five minutes later, as we drove to pick up Lizzy, I broached the subject. I kept my voice light. "So . . . let's talk about how to find someone to help with your pills."

"I don't need help with my pills." *Oh no you don't. Not again.*

"You just agreed!" I held my voice steady, like a metal ice cube tray headed for the freezer.

Mom glared back. "I said no such thing."

I slammed on the brakes at the next traffic light, reached into the back, and threw the evidence onto her lap. "Read it!"

She glanced at the piece of paper. The ink had barely dried. "You just made that up."

"I did not. Your therapist just wrote it down for us."

"Well, that's not what I meant."

I felt flammable. Pricks of energy raced over my skin. Was this her dementia or just the same gaslighting mother I'd always had? The one who'd forced me to perform, then insisted it was my idea. I'd spent my life listening to her say "I never said that" and "You don't feel that way." Making me feel like the crazy one. *Not this time.*

I jammed the car against the curb in front of Lizzy's school, where she'd soon emerge from tenth grade. Gossiping teenagers surrounded the car, their laughter ricocheting off the hard glass windshield. I spoke through pursed lips. "We just made this agreement. Let's read it together."

"Oh, yeah, yeah," Mom said, suddenly remembering. "I'll call my neighbor, Jane, tomorrow. Maybe she knows someone who can drive me."

I yanked the emergency brake upward like an accusation. "You need more than just a driver!"

Lizzy bounded down the steps with her skinny jeans and curvy hips. She threw her heavy canvas book bag in the back and gracefully slid in. A dad I didn't know stood on the steps. He came over and peered into the car. "How sweet! Three generations!"

Mom put on her beauty queen face, beamed him a megawatt smile. "Well, hello there! We're here picking up my granddaughter. She's such a smart girl—at the top of her class. And who's your child?"

Really, Mom? Now you're going to flirt? Now you're going to brag? The man smiled. Obviously, he was clueless; he couldn't feel the venom wafting through the car.

I slammed my foot on the gas and peeled away. The dojo where Lizzy taught martial arts was just a few blocks away. I glanced at her in the rearview mirror and consciously released my grip on the steering wheel. For ten minutes, I could play Good Mom. Dealing with my mother would have to wait.

I gave my daughter a big smile. "How was your day, sweetie?"

"Fine."

I wasn't the only one on good behavior. With Lizzy in the car, Crazy Woman in Denial was replaced by Benevolent Grandma. "So, darling, tell me, what are you doing this summer?"

Mom had been asking Lizzy the same question for months, several times each visit. Lizzy patiently answered every time, speaking slowly and clearly, rather than mumbling the way she did when she addressed me. "I'm going to study French and international relations in France this summer. Thank you, Grandma. I wouldn't be going without your help." Mom radiated pride and glowed with satisfaction. I had to hand it to her. She was generous and cared about education. When I was young, she'd offered to take me to Israel, and I'd spurned her offer. She'd scrimped to save for my college education, and I'd spat on her opportunities.

Lizzy reached across the seat and squeezed her grandma's shoulders. She did it easily, effortlessly. I wished I could touch my mother like that.

Mom beamed all the way to the dojo. When Lizzy hopped out, I checked the clock. I still had to take Mom home, redo her pills, fire Fiona, then drive back across town in rush hour. My class started in two hours. I wrenched the car around. I'd wasted my afternoon at that appointment when I damn well knew better. *Dinner? Forget it. I'm not living in the sandwich generation. I'm living in a fucking vise.*

But Mom was happy. Ten minutes with Lizzy had made her day. "That Lizzy. She's really something. Eli, too. You and Karyn did such a good job with those kids. Who says lesbians shouldn't have children?"

Despite myself, I had to laugh. "Thanks, but a lot of it was just dumb luck."

Both of us enjoyed the momentary truce Lizzy's presence had created.

—∾—

The shortest way to Mom's house was also the prettiest. Five minutes after we dropped Lizzy off, I turned right onto West Cliff Drive. It was a sunny spring afternoon. I slowed the car to a crawl and rolled down my window. I needed this: The Pacific on my left. Surfers dotting the rising and falling waves. The clackety-clack of skateboard wheels. The bark of sea lions. Laughter on the wind. West Cliff was the picture of the health and beauty that is Santa Cruz, but all I could think was *How can I keep her safe now?*

In the Alzheimer's group, we'd learned that people with dementia need clear, limited choices, like the ones Karyn and I used to give the kids when they were small: "Eli, would you like to put away the blue blocks or the red blocks?" I decided to give it a shot. "Mom, I really appreciate you inviting me to see your therapist. It's so great that we have an agreement. Now we just have to find someone to help you a few mornings a week. We could go back with an agency, or I could follow up on referrals from the support group. An agency costs more, but if you don't like the person, they'll send someone else. Which do you want?"

"Oh, I'll just call Jane when I need a ride. You can set up my pills like always, and I'll be fine."

I slammed my hand against the steering wheel. "You won't be fine! I just wasted two hours going to that therapy session—that you asked me to go to—and you agreed to have help!"

"I never agreed to that."

"Yes, you did!" I wanted to smack her.

"No, I didn't!"

My voice grew, filling the car and broadcasting our fight. "You need help, Mom! You don't remember anything, so how can you possibly remember whether or not you've taken your pills? You can't even remember an agreement you made five minutes ago! If you don't agree to get help, I'm not firing Fiona."

The sound of congas rose up from the beach. "I'm perfectly capable of living alone!"

"You are not! You know what one of the symptoms of Alzheimer's is? You insist there's nothing wrong with you! There is something wrong with you! Your brain is broken, and you're not safe. It's my job to take care of you, and you won't let me! You have to do what I say!"

"You're not the boss of me!"

Oh yes I am. "I hate this. I hate taking care of you!"

"And I hate that you keep treating me like I'm losing it!"

"Well, you are losing it!" My voice echoed through the car. I could feel my eyes bulging. "I don't want to do this anymore! I'm sorry I invited you here."

"And I'm sorry I came."

I ran a stop sign. A bald guy on a ten-speed banged on the side of my car and yelled, "Fucking maniac!" I ignored him. I slammed on the brakes, right in the middle of West Cliff Drive, so I could hate Mom with my full attention.

"I don't want to be your daughter anymore. I want my life back!" I yelled as cars honked behind me, a cacophony of horns, but I didn't hear them. All I could hear was the inferno blazing in my head.

A vein next to Mom's right eye pulsed. "At least you have a life."

"I hate my life!"

"Well, I hate my life, too!"

I stared at her. My vision narrowed. A sledgehammer pounded in my ears. I couldn't stop shaking. I screamed with a voice that had never come out of me before. "I wish you'd have a stroke and be done with it!"

My words reverberated through the car and out onto the street. Mom flinched, and her head jerked back. Her chin trembled. A scared child crawled out from the depths and peeked at me through ancient eyes. Then Mom turned away, wrenching her body as far from me as she could get, as far as the tightly buckled seat belt would allow. She reached for the door handle with a shaky hand, but it was childproofed. I'd locked her in.

Suddenly, I could hear again—the bicycles, waves smacking the seawall, the bellowing chorus of horns behind me, blaring their reprimand.

It was ten minutes to Mom's place. Ten minutes on one of the prettiest roads in the world. But I saw nothing. I was aware of one thing and one thing only—the hell that was my life. I drove in silence as Mom cowered beside me. Voices echoed in my head: *Bad daughter, selfish daughter.* But I didn't listen. Those voices were wrong. This was all her fault. She'd moved out here and ruined everything. She was crazy. She was manipulative. She made me say those things. *Fuck you, Mom. Fuck you!* I drove in a trance, my body trembling.

When I finally reached her unit, I braked hard. "So, you want me to fire Fiona? Okay, I'll fire her. Then I'm going to do your pills, and then I'm leaving. And I plan to stay away for a long time!" I yanked out the keys. "Go ahead—live alone! It's your life!"

And it's going to be your death.

I slammed the car door, leaving her behind. Bolted up the steps. Thrust open the door. Strode into Fiona's bedroom. "We need to go for a walk." Fiona's face darkened. She took one look at me and knew. She was about to lose her home.

By the time we headed out, Mom was in her bedroom, railing to her sister Ruth on the phone.

—∞—

As Fiona and I walked to the lagoon, I tried to focus on the clear blue sky, the warmth of sun on my skin, the smooth glide of the swan Mom loved. I pressed my feet into the earth with every step, reaching for the molten center of the earth, until finally, my breath slowed. My chest filled with regret. What had I done?

Fiona and I chose a small bench overlooking the water. For better or worse, I was giving Mom what she wanted. "I'm sorry, Fiona, but this is not working."

"I know." Being fired was not a surprise.

"I'm giving you thirty days' notice." What I was going to do next, I had no idea, but there had to be something better than this.

Fiona looked out at the swan. It had a reputation for biting people—its days were numbered, too. We both knew Fiona had nowhere to go. Now, we both had to start over.

Mom was still holed up in her bedroom when we returned. The theme music for *Jeopardy!* boomed through the door. Good. She was busy.

Fiona and I moved fast, methodically plunking pills into Mom's caddies while I redid the master list. As I was taping on the final pill, Mom burst through the door, stormed over, and grabbed the list. "I need that!" I yanked the paper back, and my careful work was ripped in two.

Mom gestured at Fiona dismissively. "What if she drops dead? How am I going to get my pills then?"

"Fiona will be here all month, Mom." I held the torn paper out of reach, smoothed the damaged halves, zigzagged a piece of tape across the ragged tear. "I just gave her notice, but she needs time to find a new place to live."

"I want her out of here right now!"

"She has thirty days. That's just how it is."

Mom's cheeks flushed with fire. She wheeled on me. "You're really pissing me off! I want you out of here!"

I glared back at her. "I want to get out of here, too!" I slapped the medication list high inside a cupboard. I was nine inches taller than Mom and used it to my advantage. "I have to go to work."

Mom gripped the edge of the kitchen counter, knuckles white, her whole body about to ignite. Spiky energy radiated all around her. Everything about her said to me, *Go on; get out.*

With pleasure. I grabbed my purse and pivoted toward freedom. In four long strides, I was at her front door. I reached the knob and hesitated for a second, but momentum carried me forward. Rage propelled me. Regret did not stop me. I turned the knob. I did not look back. I couldn't bear to see her enraged and ragged face. Maybe I'd have an accident on the way to class and never have to deal with any of this again. I wrenched open the cheap, hollow door and fled.

By the time I got home from teaching, Karyn was already asleep, so I sat down next to Lizzy, who was watching *Dr. Who* and doing homework. She paused her show.

"I really blew it with Grandma today. I yelled at her like I've never yelled at anyone before. It was really bad." That's as much of a confession as I was willing to make. Lizzy was only fifteen, and I was ashamed to let her see the ugliest part of me.

"You need to apologize."

"I don't want to." Apologies were always hard for me. And apologizing to Mom was the toughest of all.

"She can't help it. It's the disease."

"I know, but sometimes it's just so hard." I looked at Lizzy, so young, so full of promise. "Well, you've certainly been provided with a great gene pool. Heart disease, diabetes, cancer, and now Alzheimer's disease."

"Yeah, thanks. But I'm not worried. By the time I'm old, they'll have cured all these things."

If *only.* I turned to my daughter and took her warm, slim hand in mine. "Lizzy, when I get old, if I live that long, I hope I never give you such a hard time. If I ever start resisting your efforts to help me, remind me what happened with Grandma."

"I will Mom, but . . ." And here, Lizzy paused for effect. "You won't remember."

We both cracked up.

—~—

That night I couldn't sleep. The wind was rising from the south, bringing the bark of sea lions from the harbor and the yipping of coyotes from the nearby woods. But these wild sounds, deep in my suburban neighborhood, did not provide their usual pleasure. The rhythmic whoosh of my CPAP machine ricocheted in my head, amplifying my jagged breath. I ripped off the mask, slid out of bed, and drew a bath. Green Epsom salts. The hottest water I could stand.

I slid into the steaming water, stretched my legs onto the smooth white porcelain. Cranked the window open. Cool night air blew against my face, a welcome counterpoint to the searing heat. An alto chime sang in the ornamental cherry tree, but its mellow tone failed to soothe me. I had to face the truth. I was an awful person and a terrible daughter. I had betrayed my mother completely. Our grand reconciliation had all been a sham, and this proved it.

I wanted Mom to have help, so she could stay in the little home she loved, doing the things she loved for as long as possible. I wanted to take care of her, in theory anyway, but I wasn't actually sure I'd ever be able to do more than just go through the motions. Could I ever be wholehearted, or was I destined to remain an ambivalent caregiver?

This tragedy was heading only in one direction. And I wasn't sure I could survive until the end. I'd made Mom a promise, and I wanted to find a way to keep it, but I desperately needed to know: How much longer was this going to take? When would it be over?

—~—

The next morning, just as I was about to call Mom to apologize, I found a chipper message from her on my voice mail: "Good morning, Laurie. I want to apologize for yesterday. I don't know what's happening to me. I'm going nutso. You absolutely don't deserve any negativity from me. You have been fabulous, and I'm not sure what's going on for me to react like this. Totally uncalled for. You don't deserve that. Okay, bye!"

My God. She didn't remember what I'd said. She and I were the only witnesses to my crime, and she didn't remember a word of it. Because I was her lifeline and she needed me, she had blamed herself. I'd gotten away with it. And I could get away with it again. I could say and do anything. I could vent my rage, exact my revenge, and no one would ever know. I had all the power now. And all the glory. "You're such a good daughter." I heard that every day. "You take such good care of your mother. I wish I had a daughter like you."

I had never understood elder abuse before, but now I understood it perfectly. I had the freedom. I had the license. I had the opportunity, and somewhere buried inside me, I still had the motive. The woman who'd screamed at my mother had been waiting a lifetime to come out. For fifty-six years, Mom had told me I was a liar, that it hadn't happened, that I was wrong. For years, this crazy streak of hers had been kept under wraps, but dementia had exposed the bare wires. I was being triggered in a way I hadn't been in decades. All the rage I'd ever felt as her daughter for gaslighting me was right there, blistering my tongue. And I'd let it out. Me. I'd done that. But there was more. The worst part was that it felt good. Screaming at Mom was primal. It felt good to lose control. I'd been so controlled all my life. Finally, I had let the raging demon out. But I couldn't let it happen again. She was defenseless. I had to be her mother now.

AFTER MOM'S DEATH

THERAPY SESSION

Tucked in our correspondence, I discovered a single page of notes I'd written after the therapy session Mom and I had during the worst period of our estrangement. At the time, she was fifty-seven and still living in New Jersey. I'd just turned twenty-nine and was living in San Francisco. It had been a year since I'd remembered the incest, and Ellen Bass and I were hard at work on *The Courage to Heal.* My whole life was dominated by incest, and there was a huge gaping hole where family used to be. I still secretly hoped that Mom would take me in her arms and say, *Oh, honey, I'm sorry I didn't protect you.* I knew that would never happen, but part of me was still holding out for a miracle. Mom was praying for a miracle, too, hoping I'd recant. That, too, would never happen. I'd crossed a line and was never going back. The two of us were at a standstill. An impasse. At war. And during this terrible time, my mother agreed to fly to California for a session with me and my therapist. To open that session, I read out loud a letter I had composed—a fantasy version of the letter I wished Mom had written to me. I wept as I read her these coveted words:

Dearest Laurie,

I'm sorry you are in so much pain. It has been very difficult for me to believe you because I didn't want to face that my father could have hurt you that way. Frankly, denial has been the easiest way for me to deal with the unpleasant things in life. But now that I see how deeply this has affected you, I must step past my own denial and support you. I believe what you have told me. What my father did was an atrocity. No wonder it has so deeply affected you. Sometimes it must seem like it would have been better to have never remembered at all, but now at least you can put to rest some of the deep questions you've had about your life.

I am so sorry it happened. Sorry I didn't see it, didn't stop it, sorry you are living with it still. My biggest regret is that I didn't protect you, but you have to remember, such things were not even thought of back then.

Unfortunately, nothing can be done about that now. Yet here we are in the present, two adult women. As your mother, I want to give you whatever love and nurturing I can to help you get through this thing. I'm not saying this to rush you. I know it will take time for you to heal. You've lived with this secret festering inside you for more than twenty years. That's got to have taken its toll. I want you to know that you have my full support for as long as it takes us to lick this thing. He's not going to win. You're not going to let him, and neither am I.

Laurie, I think you're incredibly brave to do this work. I am proud of you. I only hope I can face my own life with as much grit and determination. It is only with this kind of truth that we can forge the kind of healthy mother-daughter relationship that we have both always wanted. I truly believe this healing can bring us together.

All my love,
Mom

When I finished reading the letter that I wished she'd written to me, I looked up. Mom sat gripping her pocketbook. After a long silence, she spoke. "It's like the Laurie I love so much and want to comfort is sitting right there. And there's this other horrible monster next to her, making these accusations about my father."

When she said that, something tore inside me—the last shred of hope that she'd take my side. I pressed my legs against the nubby cushion, willing myself to stay present. I glanced over at my therapist, sitting in the armchair between us. I felt her silent encouragement: *Say what you need to say, Laura. This is what we've been preparing for.*

"They're just one person. It's a package deal. It's taken me a year to accept and love that 'monster,' and I can't afford to split her off from me anymore, not even for you."

Mom sat alone, looking so much smaller and less threatening than the mother in my head. She dug in her pocketbook for a tissue, snapped the gold clasp shut. Then she repeated the litany I'd heard so many times before: How every choice I'd ever made was to spite her. How I was making up the incest for revenge. How she was the real victim.

Each word felt like a blow, only this time, I had a witness. I wasn't crazy. My mother wasn't the innocent, wronged mother she made herself out to be.

I became myself in spite of her, not to spite her.

That therapy session made things clear, and I guess that was the point. For me to give up hope. To let the impasse stand. To stop waiting for my mother to magically turn into someone she couldn't be.

Until now, that's all I remembered from that session: her denial.

Mom flew home, heartbroken. I went home, brokenhearted. The next time I saw my therapist, she said, "Your mother is the most narcissistic person I've ever met." Maybe she shouldn't have said that, but she was sick of me always questioning myself, tying myself in knots to stay connected to a mother who could never really see me.

For years, I waved my therapist's assessment around like a flag. I loved having that word to describe my mother: "narcissistic." But then she and I reconciled, and I forgave her, and she forgave me. Who cared about labels?

But now there was an open box in my lap. And in my hands, a single sheet of paper. Notes I'd taken immediately after that session. Written in ink, in my own hand.

I didn't remember anything I had written on that page. It was as if I were reading it for the first time.

My mother told me about the time her sister Ruth had played her tapes of their father's ninetieth birthday party. Mom said, "When Ruth played me those tapes, I started to cry, and I didn't know why. Could it be that we were all celebrating him, but it was all wrong?"

I didn't remember that.

Mom said that her therapist had explained to her that women often remember abuse many years after it happens, and that I might have, too. Mom said, "As my therapist pointed out to me, 'Why would Laurie go through all of that just to spite you?'" Then Mom added, "I realized you wouldn't."

I didn't remember that.

The final note on the page was a direct quote from my mother: "I had a flash of my father telling us stories Saturday morning. He wore pajamas with a hole at the crotch. I remember thinking how ugly his penis looked. It must have been erect or I wouldn't have thought it was so ugly."

Under that quote, I'd jotted down my reply: "Mom, that's when he abused me. That's how it started—when he told me stories."

I didn't remember that either. I didn't remember any of it.

All I remembered about that session was my mother's hard, cold, steel wall: her refusal, her denial. That once again, she chose her dead father over her living daughter. That was all I was able to recognize at the time; it's how I've held that session in my mind for all these years.

But I forgot Mom's courage. Even when she was up against something she absolutely couldn't bear to face, she tried. Thirty years later, holding this brittle sheet of paper in my hands, I can see that she tried to look into the past. She asked herself the question "What if Laurie is telling the truth?" She dug down as far as she could bear to go, until she couldn't bear to go any farther, and she did it because she loved me. Because she didn't want to lose me. She didn't want to lose her horrible, lying, traitorous daughter. And so, she wrestled with it. She peered into the vast untenable darkness. She looked into those flames.

My mother must have been in hell. I can see that now. I can also see that she tried. She didn't cut me off. She didn't sit *shiva* and proclaim me dead. She flew across the country to face pain and misery. I can see how much she loved me.

PART IV

"Some people say the longest path we will ever walk is from our head to our heart."

—Pancho Ramos Stierle

CHAPTER 48

VALIDATION

820 Days

The day after I screamed at Mom in the car, I emailed her final doctor and left a message, asking him to call me back. I wanted to confess and needed his support. I scrapped my plan to spend the day writing my newsletter and disappeared downtown instead. Went to an early matinee at the Nickelodeon. Bought myself a steaming soy chai and a chocolate truffle at Chocolate. Stopped at Sockshop Santa Cruz to try on a new pair of hiking sandals for my upcoming writers' trip to Bali. I did not return Mom's call.

I was buying toothpaste when her doctor called me back. I told him what had happened. We discussed simplifying Mom's medications and adding an antidepressant. Everyone else in the Early-Stage group was on one, and he thought it might stabilize her moods. Then he added, "I hate to say this, but as she gets worse, things are going to get easier for you."

An hour later, I arrived for my intake at the Caregiver Resource Center, the agency I'd learned about in the support group. They administered a test, called the Burden Scale, to rate my stress as a caregiver. I was handed five laminated cards, each with a different phrase written in bold dark letters: **Never, Rarely, Sometimes, Quite Frequently, Nearly Always.** I was told to hold up the card that best represented my answer. The test went like this:

Do you feel that because of the time you spend with your relative that you don't have enough time for yourself?
NEARLY ALWAYS.

Do you feel stressed between caring for your relative and trying to meet other work and family responsibilities?
NEARLY ALWAYS.

Do you feel strained when you are around your relative?
QUITE FREQUENTLY.

Do you feel angry when you are around the care receiver?
QUITE FREQUENTLY.

Do you feel you have lost control of your life?
NEARLY ALWAYS.

Do you feel you should be doing more for your relative?
NEARLY ALWAYS.

There were many more questions on the test. A score of sixteen to eighteen was considered a serious level of stress. I scored a thirty-nine.

Driving home, I left a message for a therapist the intake worker had recommended. Clearly, the support group I was attending, the reading I was doing, the walks I was taking, the good food I was eating, and the friends I was talking to were not enough. I needed help separating my old relationship with my mother from what was happening now.

CHAPTER 49
RESULTS

812 Days

Three weeks after I took Mom to get tested, it was time to return for the results. On our way to Stanford, we picked Paul up at the airport, and the three of us went out to lunch. I asked Mom, "Are you as incredibly happy as I would be to be with both my kids together?"

"Yes, I love being with the two of you." She beamed, and we shared a knowing smile, not as mother and daughter, not as frustrated caregiver and recalcitrant patient, but as two mothers who never saw enough of their kids.

When the bill came, Mom pulled out her credit card with trembling hands. I watched her hesitate over the tip. The bill totaled thirty-six dollars; she added thirty dollars for the tip. I glanced at Paul, then smiled at Mom. "Here, let me." Quickly crossing out what she'd written, I wrote in "$7.00" instead.

Paul helped her into her coat. "Ready?"

Mom nodded. "You'll see. The tests will show nothing. It's just normal aging—nothing more."

As we slid into the car, Paul squeezed my hand. "I'm glad I'm here. Thanks for encouraging me to come."

—~—

Forty minutes later, the three of us sat across from Helen Davies, the psychologist who gave people their test results. I wondered how she did it, every single day.

Paul flanked Mom on one side; I flanked her on the other. My palms were clammy. Paul and I traded glances over Mom's head.

Her scores were tallied on a spreadsheet, each representing a different area of brain function. Some of the lines—a lot of them—scraped the bottom of the chart.

Paul and I leaned closer, energetically bookending Mom. She stared straight ahead, gripping the handle of her patent leather pocketbook.

We knew what was coming, and she didn't.

Helen carefully went over each devastating result, looking Mom in the eye. "Our diagnosis for you, Temme, is dementia. There are several possible reasons: Alzheimer's disease. Medication reactions. There have also been some cerebrovascular incidents." Her fainting spells.

Fear and confusion clouded Mom's features. I wondered if I should take her hand.

I glanced at Paul. He held my eyes in his clear, steady gaze. I couldn't do this without him.

Helen closed the folder and waited for the news to sink in.

Mom finally had an official diagnosis. Dr. Asshole had been right. Her deficits weren't caused just by normal aging, and the authorities at Stanford Alzheimer's Center had just given it a name. Dementia was the booby prize Mom had received for her longevity.

Having a diagnosis would make it easier to get her services. For us to chart a course for the rest of her life.

Mom's blank, empty face told me that she was receiving news she didn't expect or know how to process. Like a lost child searching for an anchor, she turned toward me, her eyes filled with so much need and bewilderment, I had to look away.

Helen kept her gaze fixed on Mom alone. "Dementia is a loss of cognition and memory. Things can stay stable for a while, but for your safety and to stay independent, you'll need help to keep functioning."

Hallelujah.

Helen paused. "Temme, do you have any questions?"

Mom's voice shook. "You know I'm eighty-four years old. I want to quit while I'm ahead."

My God, she's talking suicide.

Helen's tone remained steady, matter-of-fact. "Have you thought about doing that?"

"No," Mom said. "But you know what I think. 'Ignorance is bliss.' There's an expression in Yiddish, *Mach zuch nischt visindick.* It means 'Pretend you don't know.'" Mom's chin trembled as she grasped for something to hold on to. "I'm sorry I came here. I have a label now. I wish I didn't know."

I could barely breathe. The devastation on Mom's face was *my* fault. I was the one who'd steamrolled her here, who needed her to get a diagnosis. I'd gotten what I wanted, but as I looked at Mom slumped beside me, defeat and shock framing her face, I did not feel like a winner.

I reached out and took her hand.

—∞—

By dinnertime, Mom had forgotten all about our trip to Stanford. She forgot she had dementia. But I'd never forget what had happened in that room. I had to face the truth. My reasons for bringing Mom to Stanford weren't just about joining a support group or accessing services. I'd brought her there for far more complex reasons. For decades, I had wanted—no, *needed*—someone to tell me that I was right and that she was wrong. That my perceptions were real. That I wasn't crazy. Now, I'd gotten my proof, in the form of the most crushing news Mom had ever received. That was my validation. My big win.

She might forget what I had done, but I wouldn't.

—∞—

After Mom got her diagnosis, Paul stayed a few more days. Money was one thing he could handle long distance, and he was determined to organize Mom's bills so he could manage her finances from Phoenix. While I taught an all-day workshop, he sorted her chaotic paperwork.

That night, the two of us cooked a simple dinner while Mom napped. As I seasoned the chicken and slid it into the oven, Paul stir-fried the chard. “Her desk was a huge mess, but I’ve taken care of everything. I left her one credit card, one checkbook, and closed out everything else. All her financial, tax, and business documents will come to me now. One fewer thing on your plate, little sister.”

“Thanks, Paul. I really appreciate it.”

Over dinner, Mom began questioning whether firing Fiona had been a good idea. “I’m feeling more vulnerable now. Maybe I should have her stay.”

I tried not to pounce on her statement with too much enthusiasm. Fiona’s departure was a week away, and I didn’t know what I was going to do when she left. Mom wasn’t ready for Sunshine Villa, and I dreaded facing a revolving door of caregivers. My whole life was about to be swallowed up by Mom’s chaos. Now I might be getting a reprieve from Mom herself; I knew Fiona wanted to stay.

I shot Paul a glance: *Let’s not blow this.*

We spent the next hour discussing the pros and cons. Together, we decided that Fiona was still our best option. For once, I didn’t feel like I was railroading my mother.

That night, his last in town, Paul pulled out his guitar and serenaded us with old Beatles songs, played a few of his originals, then took requests. Mom and I sat on the couch, clapping and singing along. Then we all cozied up to watch *The Day After Tomorrow.* Paul and I loved disaster movies, especially apocalyptic ones where a raging firestorm or meteor wipes out entire populations. Mom preferred period films, foreign movies, and British high drama. Disaster wasn’t her thing, but she loved sitting sandwiched between her two children, both of us holding her hands.

CHAPTER 50

AIRPORT

811 Days

The next morning on our hour-long drive to the airport, I flipped on NPR. Paul reached over and lowered the volume. "Let's talk, Laura. We haven't really connected this whole time."

I cranked it back up. "We've been together for the last four days. I've barely seen my family."

Paul switched the radio off with a decisive click. "But we haven't really talked."

Oh God. Can't we just drive to the airport?

I passed several cars and slid back into the slow lane. "Sure, Paul. What do you want to talk about?"

"Our lives. I feel like I don't know you anymore."

"My life is an open book. I take care of Mom. I have a family. Two kids. A stepson. I run a business. I'm squeezed every single day. What more do you want?"

"I know what you *do*. But how are things for you on a soul level?"

"Paul, my soul is just *fine*."

My rebuff stopped him, but only for a moment. "You're my only sister, and I feel like you're not interested in my life."

I ignored the longing in his voice. “Look, Paul. We don’t see eye to eye on a lot of things. But I really appreciate everything you’re doing for Mom. You’ve been great.”

“That’s just it. All you care about is my function. You never really ask about my life.”

I sped up into the passing lane. “I ask about your life.”

“Hardly. And it’s all superficial. You don’t really want to know me.”

I swerved to avoid a slow truck. Paul was right. It had been that way for decades, ever since I told him about the incest. Paul’s response had been “It must have happened because of something terrible you did in a past life.”

I hadn’t confided in him since.

“Laura, you’re my only sibling. We incarnated into the same family for a reason.”

Yeah, maybe so we could both take care of Mom? I checked the clock on the dashboard. Ten more minutes to the airport. I stepped on the gas.

But my brother wasn’t done. He spoke honestly, telling me his truth, with that earnest voice of his. “You’re the one person in the world who knows me the best. That I trust the most. And it feels like you don’t care about me.”

As I sped up the highway, the weight of obligation thickened the air between us. More obligation was the last thing I needed. *Why did Paul have to be so needy? Why did I have to be so cold?* I cracked open the window and checked my rearview mirror. “Of course I care about you, Paul. You’re my brother. We’re in this together, right?”

When I pulled up at the airport, disappointment bathed my brother’s face. I hopped right out and grabbed his suitcase; it was only then that he opened his door. As I handed over his bag, I gave him a quick squeeze, and he held on too long. When he finally released me, I dove back into the car. From the safety of the driver’s seat, I called through the window. “Hey, Paul. Thanks for everything. So glad you could come.”

My mother wasn’t the only person I hadn’t yet learned to love.

—∾—

Fiona agreed to stay on—though we all acknowledged it was temporary—and Mom began appreciating her help. Mom returned to Sunshine Villa for a candlelight dinner where they seated her with some of the more with-it residents. If things deteriorated fast and Mom needed more help than Fiona could provide, Sunshine Villa was the place I was counting on. Best of all, Mom's new antidepressants kicked in. She was more grounded, less anxious, no longer teary and accusatory. I could actually start to relax around her. It was amazing what one little pill could do.

But it was more than that. Because I was changing, too. Karyn's words had taken root. When I was with my mother, I consciously worked to focus on the good things, and it was far easier than I expected. I was surprised how pleasurable it was to create a positive list: Laughter over a card game. The softness of her hand in mine as we watched *Jeopardy!*. Her loyalty to Karyn and our children—how she never failed to ask about their lives. I sought these things out as assiduously as I'd once sought out her flaws. I celebrated her humor. Her fortitude. Her courage in facing a horrible disease. As I hunted for things I could respect and admire, *I* felt so much better. Karyn had been right.

In the days that followed, I breathed easier. The air felt lighter. Water tasted better. I started really seeing Karyn and Lizzy again. I called Eli to chat about his semester. We invited Bryan's family over for a barbecue. I'd spent two months in crisis mode. Now I could relax and let things unfold. Whether this respite lasted a week or a month, six months or a year, was completely unknowable, but I could finally see my mother as someone to enjoy, rather than as an intractable problem to be managed.

AFTER MOM'S DEATH

PARADIGM SHIFT

Thirteen months after Mom died, I dropped Lizzy off at the airport to fly back to Boston for her sophomore year of college. At the terminal, she gave me a warm, melt-into-your-body hug. She whispered in my ear, "Great visit. I love you, Mom." I knew she meant it.

We did have a great visit. Six weeks having our baby back under our roof again. Six weeks of fires in the backyard, chats around the kitchen table, elaborate barbecues with roast peaches, Padrón peppers, salmon and figs. Six weeks of sexy bras on the drying rack. Six weeks of time together and apart. Six weeks of dishes left in the sink. Six weeks breathing the same air.

We loved having our youngest at home.

The amazing thing was, I wasn't devastated after I dropped her off. I wasn't even sad. I felt happy. That's when I realized I'd made the shift—grown accustomed to Lizzy being gone. A year earlier, when we'd dropped her off for freshman year, our goodbyes had been wrenching. But this time, I felt fulfilled by our visit, grateful for my own rich life to return to. After twenty-five years raising children, I was experiencing the giddy freedom of not having kids at home.

It occurred to me for the first time that this might be how Mom felt when she dropped me off at the airport. After our good visits and our difficult visits, she went back to her own life. She had a life that had nothing to do with my being her daughter. She was a social worker, an actress, a bridge player, a crossword-puzzle solver, a world traveler, a storyteller, a movie hound, a student, a poetry lover, a sister, an aunt, a daughter, a volunteer, a poll worker, and a friend. She had a life that did not include me. There was more to my mother than I would ever know.

I'd known this in theory, of course, but I never really knew it in my bones. Not until I dropped Lizzy off with excitement rather than dread. That's when I finally understood. Mom was just like me. Liberated when we left her. Free to re-create a new Temme Davis, to forge life on her own terms. I can't believe I'm saying this for the first time now, but my mother wasn't just a foil for me; she was *real*.

CHAPTER 51

THE MOVE

571 Days

The day Mom left De Anza Mobile Home Park for the last time, she stepped out onto the cement steps that descended to her driveway. In one hand, she carried her black pocketbook, the sides caving in like the mouth of a toothless old woman. Mom's pocketbook held her blue handicapped parking placard, old red wallet, Medicare card, a credit card, and a bit of cash. A few wadded-up tissues. A pair of scratched reading glasses with a bent frame. That was all. In her other hand, she gripped her multicolored cane, the one she was more likely to wave around than lean on. She wore brown stretch pants, sensible brown flats, and a white jacket, a color she never would have worn in New Jersey after Labor Day.

I was a few steps behind her when she fell. If she hadn't caught herself, her body would have slammed down the steps. I couldn't have gotten there in time.

It was December 30, 2012, and that moment confirmed what I already knew. Even with help, Mom couldn't live here anymore. I knew it; Paul knew it; and Fiona knew it—I'd given her notice again; she was looking for a new job and a place to live.

Together, we maneuvered Mom into giving up her final home.

We employed "fiblets," the strategy recommended by the Alzheimer's Association for dealing with people with dementia. As Dale Thielges, program director of our local chapter, explained, "Just think how much more stressful it would be for Temme if you told her she'd never see her home again. It's better this way."

Paul and I told Mom that the move would be on a trial basis. "Just for a month. If you don't like it, you don't have to stay." But the term "month" meant nothing to Mom. It might as well have been forever.

I hired a mother-daughter team whose specialty was moving seniors. They measured her new apartment—the width of the walls, the height of the ceilings, the size of the bedroom, closets, medicine cabinet, shoe rack, and living room. I enlisted Mom's best friend to get her out of her house for an afternoon, and in her absence, I went through every room with the moving team, telling them exactly what to take and what to leave behind.

Every time I moved her, the rooms got smaller.

—ꝏ—

The night before the move, I had Mom sleep at our house. Karyn showed her the garden's latest blooms. Mom and Lizzy discussed *Romeo and Juliet.* Eli called from Boston, excited about the origami conference he was going to attend, and Temme got to say hello to her grandson. Mom and I played a few hands of 500 rummy until she started to yawn. Karyn made her up a bed in the living room.

I built a fire in the woodstove and played Paul's latest guided meditation CD; his voice lulled Mom to sleep every night. Pretty soon, her snores filled the house. But in the middle of the night, she woke in a panic, unable to find the bathroom. She'd been to our house hundreds of times but had no idea where she was. Thank God she recognized Lizzy, who woke up and led her to the bathroom. When I finally got Mom calmed down, I knew we were making the right choice.

The next morning, as we ate breakfast, the moving team brought Mom's things over to her new apartment: a beautiful suite with two rooms, high ceilings, and windows with soft white curtains that let in the afternoon sun. Their job was to re-create her environment as closely as possible, to place her couch and chair in the same configuration, her masks in the same sequence, to mount the artwork I'd chosen, and set up her bed with the same white comforter and striped throw pillows. They set the *New York Times* crossword puzzle and her favorite pen on the coffee table. Set up her desk, her computer, her answering machine. Connected her to the internet. Made sure her phone would ring. Hung her clothes in the closet and lined up her shoes.

I wanted to do this right. I'd special-ordered a book online, *How to Move Your Parent with Alzheimer's Disease.* Late at night, in the days leading up to the move, I had dog-eared its pages, highlighter in hand.

When we got the all-clear, Karyn, Lizzy, and I drove Mom to Sunshine Villa. As we slowly padded across the floral carpets, Karyn and I flanked Mom while Lizzy flitted up and down the hall, chatting up her grandma. "Wow, check out this activity room! Look, they have concerts. Movies every night. Grandma, you're going to love it."

I entered Mom's new room first. The living room wall was the same salmon color she'd loved at De Anza. Her couch was there. Her masks. Her crossword puzzle. Her computer. Her answering machine. The striped pillows. The fluffy white comforter. Her Mexican table lamps framed her headboard. Our moving team had done a fantastic job.

It was all familiar, but it wasn't the same.

Mom stepped in behind me. She took it all in: the high ceilings, the light streaming through the windows, all of her things. Then she smiled. Oh my God, she smiled! The apartment was smaller, but it was beautiful. Peaceful. Calm. She liked it. This was going to work out.

Her eyes swept over everything again. Then her face crumpled in confusion. Her lips trembled. "This isn't my home." She looked around again and stamped her foot. "This is not my home!" I led her to the couch and sat down beside her. I took her hand. "Mom, you have to give it time. This is just the first day."

"I want to go home. Take me back to my real home!"

The years slipped away, and I was right back with Bubby in the nursing home. *I had a home. I could cook. I could sew.* But I stepped over my regrets, and survival kicked in. "But, Mom, you said you'd try it for a month."

Karyn squatted down and stroked Mom's other hand. "Temme, it's going to take a little while."

Mom sank deeper into the couch, looking dazed. The three of us—daughter, daughter-in-law, and granddaughter—spoke in optimistic tones, reassuring her that it would all work out. Lizzy promised to visit often. Karyn was encouraging and sweet. I highlighted a list of benefits. But underneath my bravado, I was sick with dread. We stayed till dinnertime, when they led Mom to a table with assigned tablemates for the first time. I plastered a fake smile on my face for Mom's sake but cried all the way home.

—∾—

Each day, Mom begged to go home. Did I have room in my heart to hear her side? I did not. "You said you'd try it for a month." That was my mantra. I wanted her complaints to go away.

But on the fifth day, there was something different about her face. A softness I didn't recognize. She patted the couch. When I sank down beside her, she spoke in a clear, cogent voice. "I've decided I'm in the perfect place. I like the color of my wall. I love the people at my table. You set up my masks perfectly, and my cards are right within reach. I love this place."

I breathed a little deeper. Maybe this was going to work out.

"My memory so far is not a health hazard."

I smiled. I had no reason to comment on her memory anymore.

"I got over my snotty attitude that I'm better than everyone else. I can see that I belong. I like it here."

Thank God. Sunshine Villa was going to be the oasis I'd hoped for. For me and for her. My timing had been spot-on. It had just taken her a little while to adjust.

"Laurie, I hope you have an old age just like mine."

What would she come up with next?

—∾—

That night, for the first time in months, I enjoyed a peaceful dinner with my family. Lizzy settled down to read; Karyn practiced headstand variations in the living room; and I started working on a new story. I was halfway through the first paragraph when a three-tone ring announced Mom's call.

"Laurie, tonight, after dinner, they showed *Leave It to Beaver*, and the place was packed. No one else could fit in there. *Leave It to Beaver*?"

"So . . ."

"So, I'm more intelligent than the people here." Her voice rose in outrage. "You have to get me out of this place—tomorrow."

"Mom, it's not that you're more intelligent. I'm sure there are a lot of smart people there. Can we just say you're more cultured?"

She thought it over for a moment. "Yeah. I'm more cultured. I'm from New York. Thanks, darling."

Then she hung up on me. Click.

Crisis averted.

—∞—

There was a staff member at Sunshine Villa whose job was to orient new residents. She brought Mom to meet the bridge players, but Mom couldn't remember which tricks had been taken, so those "old biddies" didn't want to play with her. She introduced Mom to a Jewish woman who'd been a social worker in New York, just like Mom, but that woman showed no interest in being her friend. Mom couldn't remember what had just been said, so she couldn't engage in conversation. How could she possibly make a new friend?

Mom complained constantly. The people at her table were boring. The activities were stupid. The only things she didn't complain about were the food, the nightly movies, and the scoop of ice cream they served with every meal.

As her grievances escalated, my concentration fell apart. I snapped at one of my students, and my apology wasn't very good either. Thick bags bloomed under my eyes. I cursed Paul for living in Phoenix.

Each day, I visited Mom like a dutiful daughter. And each day, she asked, "Laurie, when can I go home?" Guilt and frustration snaked through my bowels. There was no way to do this right.

CHAPTER 52

MAGNET

550 Days

Mom's unhappiness wasn't the worst of it. It was how quickly she declined.

It's not that I hadn't been warned. In *How to Move Your Parent with Alzheimer's Disease*, the authors laid it out plainly: each move would reduce a person's functioning. But I had no idea Mom's decline would be so swift and relentless. After she moved to Sunshine Villa, she never sent or received an email, never played online bridge again. Her computer sat, lonely and forlorn, on her tidy, unused desk, but she wouldn't let me take it away. Mom, the queen of plans, never again consulted a calendar. Within a week, she was using adult diapers. The week after that, the staff asked me to buy a walker, and pretty soon, she was shuffling down the hall, her room key dangling from a curly turquoise band around her wrist. But worst of all, the fight went out of her. My fiery mother was replaced by a passive woman who acquiesced to everything. Seemingly overnight, she became unrecognizable. Aides dressed her, bathed her, made her up in the morning. She took her meds without complaint. Each night, they queued up one of Paul's CDs, so Mom could fall asleep to the reassuring sound of his voice.

That big dopey smile that I grew to love and hate appeared on her face. "Laurie," she crooned each time I walked through the door, "you're the best daughter in the whole world."

But who was I daughter to? A mother I didn't recognize.

As if drawn by an invisible magnet, I visited every day. Fifteen minutes here. Half an hour there. Down the wide flowered hallways to room 103. How could I forget that number? I'd written it in Sharpie on the labels of all her clothes.

Mom's doctor told me to get her up and moving. So, each time I came by, I urged her to go for a walk. On good days, she said yes.

As we made our way down the hall, I shortened my stride, moving so slowly, it felt like walking meditation. Mom teetered nearby, a sweet, empty expression on her face. We passed the music room and the binder where residents signed up for outings: the monthly movies, the scenic drives, trips to the drugstore to stock up on Depends.

The first time I saw the Sunshine Villa bus, a year earlier, I'd looked at the huge letters on both sides, shouting out for all to see—Sunshine Villa Assisted Living and Memory Care—and thought, *My mother wouldn't be caught dead on a bus like that.* I thought the same when I visited on Saint Patrick's Day and the halls were full of cardboard leprechauns. For the entire month of December, canned Christmas carols rang out from speakers everywhere. That would be hell on earth for my proud Jewish mother, to live in such a *goyisha* place. It was like a preschool holiday curriculum on steroids. Why did they think that's what old people wanted?

But now, just ten months after my first visit, Mom was being helped into the van with the letters screaming "Memory Care" on the side, enjoying scenic drives to nowhere.

And I was visiting every day—because somehow at fifty-six for me and eighty-five for her, a new umbilical cord tethered us. How could it be, that despite my spouse and children, my mother had once again become the most important person in my life? She was the one I woke up thinking about, the one I fretted over as I fell asleep, the one I had to see, to check in on.

498 DAYS

Late one afternoon, I stopped by to see Mom. By the time we got back from our walk around the building, she was wheezing, exhausted by my "healthy" outing. When we reached her door, she pulled the blue stretchy cord from her wrist. Shaking, she held the key up to the lock the wrong way, three times. Everything in me wanted to pull out my key—the one that lived in the detritus at the bottom of my purse—but this was one thing she could still do for herself.

"Got it!" she exclaimed, a proud grin on her face.

Mom set her cane by the door and fell heavily onto the couch. When she landed, her body was at a slant, and I had to straighten her. I reached for the deck of cards that always sat on her coffee table, and dealt out our first hand of 500 rummy.

Playing cards with Mom was my own mini mental-status exam. She still knew what a meld was, but the whole concept of holding her cards so that I couldn't see them—she'd lost that entirely. Her melds sprawled over the couch cushions like leaves in a storm, but the three, four, and five of hearts were still in the right order.

I'd stopped keeping score long ago.

After a few hands, I reached into my bag and pulled out the pumpkin foot cream I'd bought at Trader Joe's. "Mom, can I rub your feet?"

"Oh, I'd love that!"

I pulled her right foot into my lap. The cream was thick, viscous, and white. I spread some on her instep, worked it around the top and sides. Mom purred with pleasure. I loved the fragile weight of her foot in my hands.

Light and warmth streamed through the tall bay windows. There was something I needed to ask her, and she seemed clear enough for me to ask it now. Having dementia was like tuning in and out of a radio station with poor reception. That day the signal was clear. I might not get another chance. I spread cream around her ankle and took a deep breath. "Mom, I'm thinking of writing another book about us. A memoir. About our relationship."

I nestled her foot, the one with red nail polish and a crusty toe. She looked up and smiled, that sweet, empty dementia smile. "Our relationship. It's perfect."

I stroked her foot gently, careful not to irritate the thin, tender skin. "It hasn't always been."

"No, it hasn't."

I moved on to the other foot, spreading cool cream on her instep. "But it's good now."

"Yes, it's good now. I couldn't ask for a better daughter."

But she hadn't really answered my question, so I asked again. "So, the book . . . about us. What do you think?"

She beamed at me. "Go ahead and tell our story, darling. It has a happy ending."

As I massaged the callus on her heel, I took in her smiling, open face. Could it really be that simple? For Mom, it all boiled down to a happy ending.

I smeared a gob of cream between her toes. She giggled. I smiled back. "Mom, do you ever think about Vicki anymore?"

Her answer was immediate. "Darling, I never stopped thinking about her."

Warmth spread through me. Mom still understood. She was the only one who ever would. As I caressed her foot, I whispered, "Sometimes I feel like she's still hanging around."

Curiosity filled my mother's eyes. "You were identical. I've always wondered what it would have been like if she had lived."

"My whole life would have been different."

She nodded. "That's true, darling. Both of our lives."

When Mom said that, my hands stilled. I stepped into that secret place where I fantasized how life might have been if Vicki had lived. If I'd fallen asleep to her heartbeat every night and awakened to it every morning. If she'd been with me in that back bedroom with Poppa. If we'd faced the glare of Mom's high-beam expectations together. If I'd been born with a built-in best friend rather than a heart torn asunder.

I'd carried that grief and wondering my whole life, but I had always framed it as *my* loss. But now I realized it was Mom's loss, too. She had lost a daughter.

I squeezed her feet and held them in my hands. When I spoke, my voice was husky. "Thank you, Mom, for giving her a name."

She nodded. Then a shadow crossed her face. "Laurie, my time's running out. I can die at Sunshine Villa, can't I?"

I put the lid on the jar and left it out for next time. "I hope so."

CHAPTER 53

CURTAIN CALL

455 Days

A month and a half later, as I walked into her room, Mom exclaimed, "They had a fashion show here today. I'm upset they didn't ask me to be in it. They had some very unattractive people in it. Do you think it's because of my walker?"

"I don't think so. Almost everyone here has a walker."

"Well, there is something else I've been wanting to talk to you about."

I patted her hand. "Tell me."

Concentration and frustration bloomed and then vanished from her face. "I'm just feeling down. I'm not accomplishing anything."

"What do you want to accomplish?"

"I don't know. I guess I'm feeling ennui."

Ennui? Did she just say "ennui"? A word I never use for fear of pronouncing it wrong?

Mom traced the embroidered pattern on her pillow. "I need a new direction. Things are okay here, and I like my room, but I need to do something different. I just don't know what it is." I stayed silent, but it was a new silence. Not the angry silence of withdrawal, but a spacious, open silence.

I stroked her hand. "Mom, maybe it's best to just accept things as they are."

"I don't know, darling. Maybe I should start a theater group."

I smiled. Mom couldn't remember what she'd said a minute ago. How could she start a theater group? Yet her spirit was still alive. Mom, the doer, once again making plans.

I suddenly remembered a message the activity director had left on my voice mail. "Mom, Rachel called to tell me that you're going to be in a play tomorrow. She asked me to come."

"Who's Rachel?" Mom said, her face blank. "I don't know anything about a play."

I let the matter drop but called Rachel on my way home. "Are you sure my mother's in a play?"

"We've started a theater group, and your mom is in it. They don't have to remember lines or anything."

"But Mom didn't seem to know anything about it."

"Yes, well, some of our ladies do tend to forget." She paused. "Can you come?"

"I'll be there."

—∞—

A table with a red-and-white-checkered tablecloth and four chairs had been set up at the front of the activity room. Three "Wanted Dead or Alive" posters were taped to the wall. This was the stage. One actress was already sitting in place, wearing a white sequined shirt and a red sweater vest, two strands of Mardi Gras beads around her neck. An empty Jack Daniel's bottle and a shot glass in front of her. She held a script in her hand.

Three rows of chairs were filling with white-haired residents, most arriving with walkers or in wheelchairs. I was the only visitor and the only person under seventy. Mom was nowhere to be seen. Her aide went to fetch her.

Moments later, Mom's distinctive voice rang out from the hallway. She proclaimed, "Oh my God, I'm in it?" Her voice broadcast throughout the room. "What's the play?"

Her aide responded, "It's the Western."

Mom didn't hesitate for a minute. "Well, where do I sit?"

She sat at the table as the other actresses took their seats. Rachel helped Mom into her costume: a long-sleeved black-and-white flannel shirt with a red cotton bandana around her neck.

Mom looked down at her script and immediately started reading out in a strong voice, "Howdy, ma'am."

Rachel hurried up to Mom and said, "Temme, not yet."

Mom replied, "Aren't we starting?"

"Our audience is still arriving."

Mom looked out and noticed me. "Well, look who's here! I can't believe this," she said as the stage lights lit up inside her. "A whole audience."

Finally, Rachel gave Mom the signal; she had the opening lines. "Howdy, ma'am! What's a fella gotta do to get a drink in these parts? It gets mighty dry out here on the trail." Mom read her lines with perfect diction, a hearty swagger in her voice. She followed the script flawlessly, never needing prompting like her fellow actors did.

As the audience applauded, Mom looked at me, smiled broadly, and winked. When we got back to her room, she said, "I'm a ham. I love performing, even if it's a dumb play." As she headed to lunch, she added in a loud stage whisper, "But I should have had the leading part."

At that moment, I loved Sunshine Villa.

CHAPTER 54

CANDLE

420 Days

A month after Mom's play, Paul flew out to help me with a task I'd been dreading—clearing out Mom's mobile home. The keys had to be returned by 5:00 p.m. the next day.

Paul tackled the financial papers he hadn't gotten to the last time. I worked on the file cabinets crammed with Mom's personal effects. I designated one carton for things I wanted to keep, another for those I'd go through later. I was determined to get rid of the rest.

I sorted as fast as I could, but sometimes, I just had to stop. Like when I found my parents' wedding album. Or the old shoebox filled with years of correspondence between me and Mom.

For the next several hours, Paul and I sorted, packed, and passed each other on our way to the dumpster. As Paul carried out his tenth load, he said, "I thought you'd want to hold on to more things. I knew I'd be ruthless."

I sealed another giant garbage bag and headed out the door to the rapidly filling dumpster. "Ruthless is my middle name."

As the winter sun crossed the sky, Paul and I crisscrossed each other in the emptying rooms, repeatedly whacking our heads on the cheap chandelier that hung above Mom's former dining table. Fourteen hours after we began, the truck driver Paul hired took two loads to Goodwill and one to the dump. Everything else, we crammed in my car.

At the airport the next morning, I thanked Paul for coming. Then I hesitated. I'd been practicing apologies at home, but they still didn't come easily. But I owed my brother one. For the past year, Mom's doctor and I had been gradually weaning her off almost all her medications. "Paul, you were right about all the meds she was on. She's doing much better without them."

"I appreciate your saying that, Laura."

"You know, we make a good team."

When we reached the terminal, our hug lasted longer than usual, and I had no urge to pull away.

—ᴧᴧ—

Back at De Anza, I had just enough time to do one more sweep before returning the keys to the manager. As I stepped inside, mildew assailed me. The stains on the carpet were visible now that the furniture was gone. Without Mom's beautiful things, it was just a shabby mobile home.

I scooped the last remaining items into a carton: a plastic honey bear, a tired pack of matches, a yardstick. The dented lid of a pan. A clock radio. As I tossed in a half-empty box of *Shabbos* candles, I remembered the ritual Karyn and I had created with the kids the last time we moved: walking through our emptied house with a candle, reminiscing about the life lived in every room.

I pulled a *Shabbos* candle out of the box, lit it, and carried it into the living room. "Mom, I remember all of us watching TV here together: the Oscars, election returns, the Olympics—all the special occasions that made us wish we had cable. But we came here instead."

In the kitchen: "All those meals you cooked for us—chicken marsala, sweet-and-sour meatballs. You always urged us to eat more." I glanced at the lime-green island. "We had one of our worst fights here—the day I screamed at you and fired Fiona. I'm sorry I said those terrible things. I'm glad we're better now."

The bedroom mirror reflected the flame. "You blasted your TV in this room, and I did everything I could to help Fiona sleep. The day I asked you to try wireless headphones, you said, 'Fuck Fiona. She has it so good living here.' God, Mom, you could be such a bitch."

The candle flickered as I entered Fiona's room. "You hated her living here, but she was good for you. Because of her, you got to stay longer."

Hot wax cooled on my fist as I walked into Mom's bathroom. "Paul installed these handrails. When he came, he always worked hard for you."

Circling back to the living room, I licked my thumb and forefinger and pinched the wick. A plume of smoke swirled up toward the ceiling. "You were happy here. I'm sorry I had to make you leave."

I slid down the wall onto the stained carpet, pulled out my phone, and called Mom. My feelings were complex, but I did my best to dumb them down. "Your house is empty. I just took the last things out."

She thanked me. "Laurie, what would I do without you?"

"I feel kind of sad. It's the end of . . ."

I could hear her aide calling her. "Temme, it's time to go to dinner."

The line went dead. I stared at the phone.

"Bye."

Click.

—∾—

On my way home, I stopped on West Cliff to catch the sunset. An orange slash blanketed the sky. Surfers were catching their last waves, and the smell of weed was in the air. I walked down to the bench I'd shared with Mom. Watching the sun descend, I couldn't shake the feeling of emptiness. The drab emptiness of her bare apartment. The hollow emptiness of her voice on the phone. That familiar emptiness in my chest.

A family played on the beach below me. A mother. A father. A little blond-haired girl. She danced with the freedom of an innocent child. Watching her, I started to cry and couldn't stop. That's when I understood. Mom had crossed a line. She was never going to look me in the eye and acknowledge the truth about her father. We would never have that heartfelt moment when she finally said it outright: *Laurie, I believe you.* Or *It happened to me, too.* Such a conversation was beyond her ability now; perhaps it always had been.

I thought I was past this kind of longing, but I must have been holding on to one last shred of hope. Maybe Mom would find the courage. Maybe Mom would do the work. Maybe the truth would rise up inside her like it had for me, and she'd have no choice but to face it. Maybe she would love me enough to admit it. Maybe she would feel loved enough. There had always been that tiny secret flame of possibility.

But not anymore. It wasn't about courage anymore. It wasn't about love or healing or commitment or surrender. It was about brain cells. Simple capacity. That truth-telling reconciliation session that I hadn't dared to hope for was simply out of reach. Mom had come close—in that therapy session and on that road trip in the pouring rain—but she had never been able to go all the way and say it out loud, *I believe you. I know what you're saying is true.*

And now it was too late.

For nearly thirty years, my mother and I had agreed to disagree, and that bargain had taken us far. The adult me was fine with the way things were. Incest hadn't been in the forefront of my consciousness for decades. Yes, it was still a thread in the tapestry of my life. It had shaped me, forging strengths and vulnerabilities that I would carry forever. I accepted that. It was a fact of my life but no longer a trauma. So, I didn't think it mattered if Mom believed me. I'd convinced myself I didn't need that from her anymore. Until it was out of reach. Until that tiny flame was snuffed out. That's when I realized that I had never stopped hoping. And now—the love that we'd patched together and practiced, the love with a hole in the middle of it, was going to have to do.

What we had wasn't perfect. But it was enough.

The last surfers were out of the water now, and the little dancing girl was gone. The temperature had dropped as it always did when the sun went down, but I didn't feel cold. In fact, I felt warm, like a fire had been kindled inside me. I thought about Mom, half a mile down the road, and I extended that globe of warmth to her. I imagined her laughing in the movie room, eating ice cream, a key dangling from the turquoise cord on her wrist.

CHAPTER 55

OASIS

197 Days

In the months after her play, Mom continued her precipitous decline. I often found her sitting upright, asleep, mouth open, teeth on the table in front of her, $6,000 hearing aids buried in the couch cushions or gathering dust at her feet.

This is how she'll look when she's dead.

Each time I saw her with that death mask on her face, I resisted the urge to flee. I pushed past my aversion and gently shook her. "Mom. It's Laura." She startled awake with a blank stare, panic in her eyes: *Where am I? Who am I?* She stared at me without recognition until the neurons connected in her brain. I watched myself take shape before her eyes. Her lips widened into a smile; her eyes caught flame; and she beamed her life force, every bit she had left, into my eyes. The fact that I'd walked through her door made her whole day worthwhile. And all I could think was *How soon can I get out of here?* Shame swept up my throat.

I did the Buddhist thing, reciting in my head, *Old age looks like this.* I breathed out pity and revulsion and breathed in compassion. And I stayed. I put my body next to her body and looked into her slack face and smiling, toothless mouth. Finally, I could relax around her because she was my oasis, and I loved her. I had always loved her, but now I didn't have to hold her at bay. Now, all she beamed toward me was love. The kind of unconditional love a mother ought to always have for her daughter. I was fifty-seven years old, and, finally, I was able to let in her love, now that she was no longer the mother that I had feared and rejected, fought, blamed, and pushed away. Now that she was no longer herself, she was mine. Finally, it was safe to love her.

CHAPTER 56

EMPTY NEST

165 Days

As Mom gradually disappeared, Lizzy was disappearing, too. It was the second semester of her senior year. She was waiting to hear from colleges, and senioritis had set in. Lizzy was working three part-time jobs: scooping ice cream, teaching martial arts, waitressing at a pizza joint. When she wasn't working, she wanted to be with her friends. She had inherited Temme's car, and now that she had wheels and her own gas money, she'd gone from *asking* whether she could go out to *telling* us she was going out. I attempted Lizzy sightings late at night, lying on the couch with a book, doing my best to look interruptible, hoping she'd come in and choose to chat, rather than heading straight to her room to stream *Buffy the Vampire Slayer.*

You'd better get used to it, I told myself. *Six months from now, she's going to be gone. Really gone.* When Lizzy left for college, Karyn and I would become empty nesters.

But not completely. There was a new baby in our family. Bryan and his wife, Brinn, had welcomed baby Ellie the previous summer. That offered some serious consolation. Bryan and Brinn lived only an eight-minute walk away, so Karyn and I got to breathe the scent of our new granddaughter's head on a regular basis—welcoming one child while letting go of another.

CHAPTER 57

SISTERS

153 Days

If it hadn't been for Karyn, Mom would never have seen her sister Ruth again. The baby of the family, Ruth was Mom's last surviving sibling. She lived in Florida with my uncle Howard, her husband of sixty-one years. Throughout my mother's decline, Ruth was a loving mainstay, calling Mom several times a day. The two of them shared a unique history, and the far past—the era they shared—was the one place Mom's memories were still intact.

Ruth and Howard were two family members I'd lost when I published *The Courage to Heal*, but over the years, from afar, we'd worked our way back into each other's lives. We never directly addressed our divergent perspectives on my grandfather. Like all the relatives on my mother's side of the family, they believed my accusations to be false. But at fifty-seven, with three decades of healing under my belt, I no longer needed their acknowledgment, and I can only assume they no longer needed me to recant. Our desire to be on Temme's team superseded all of that. I felt nothing but affection for my elderly aunt.

I was grateful for Ruth's devoted presence. She didn't mind having the same conversation with Mom repeatedly. Funny and warm, she was a solid pillar Temme could rely on, until Mom could no longer dial or answer the phone.

Geography being what it is, my mother lost contact with her sole surviving sibling.

Soon I was the one talking to Ruth every day, giving her updates, leaning on her strength. I knew how much Ruth and Mom loved each other and was sad they were going to die without ever seeing each other again. It had been seven years since their last visit. Ruth had advanced diabetes and was going blind, and Howard was on dialysis. The two of them weren't able to travel anywhere—definitely not all the way to California.

I couldn't imagine taking Mom across the country. She was frail and disoriented in unfamiliar situations. Her life ran smoothly because of predictable routines. I found it hard to take her to the movies, out to lunch, to Lizzy's dance recitals. Even bringing her to our house for dinner had become an ordeal. How could I possibly take her across the country? And then there was the issue of my having to be her caregiver. At Sunshine Villa, someone else cleaned her and pulled up her Depends. I had learned to hold her hand, but I couldn't imagine taking on that kind of physical intimacy with my mother. Besides, I was already away a lot, traveling for work. Did I really want to add another trip? But in the middle of the night, when I couldn't sleep, that little voice kept telling me, *You should do it, Laura. You really should.*

—~—

In February 2014, Karyn got a call from one of her sisters. Their oldest sibling, Charlene, was dying of cancer in Florida. Two of her sisters were flying to Sarasota to spend the weekend with Charlene, and they invited Karyn to join them.

In bed that night, Karyn and I discussed her relationship with Charlene and how important it was for her to see her sister one last time. As Karyn settled into her decision, she raised the idea of our traveling to Florida together. "I'd really like Temme and Ruth to see each other. If we all travel together, the two of us could manage your mom on the plane."

I smiled at her across the pillow. "It would be amazing for them to see each other again."

The next morning, I called Ruth to run the idea by her. She was thrilled. So, I drove over to Sunshine Villa to ask Mom. "Would you like to see your sister Ruth?"

Her face lit up like she'd just won the lottery.

—~—

A week before our departure, I sat down with Rosa Fernandez, Mom's caregiver at Sunshine Villa. I was going to be doing her job and wanted to know what was required. Rosa described Mom's morning routine: how she helped her get out of bed, gave her a shower, dried her body, washed Mom's private parts, put on her Depends, chose her clothes, and helped her dress. Then she put on Mom's makeup and did her hair. "Don't worry," Rosa assured me. "Your mom is very easy."

As she insisted how "easy" it would be, little hairs stood up all over my body. I wasn't sure I was ready for this, but I also sensed it was an opportunity. I wanted to seize that opportunity.

—~—

The afternoon before our departure, I went to pick up Mom's meds and her suitcase. As we went over the contents, she asked, "What about makeup?"

I'd been hoping to slide by on makeup. I hadn't worn any in more than thirty years, and I really didn't know how to put it on. If I tried to make Mom up, she'd look like a clown. "Do you really need it?"

"Of course," she replied indignantly. I walked into her bathroom and found a cracked, dusty, half-full compact of blush and a tawdry tube of lipstick. She happily tucked them in her pocketbook. Now she was ready.

—~—

Lizzy offered to drive us to the airport at 6:30 a.m. I knew it would be impossible to pick Mom up that early, so I had her sleep at our house.

I put her to bed in her clothes, just like we did with Eli and Lizzy when they were toddlers, back in the days it was hard to get them out the door for preschool. That way, I could wake Mom up, and all she'd have to do was rehook her bra, slip on her shoes, and pop in her teeth. We'd have breakfast at the airport.

That night, while I was making up her bed, Mom looked at me with the vulnerability of a child. Fear passed over her usually placid face. She asked, "What's going to happen to me once I get to Florida?"

I turned to face her. "Karyn and I will take you to Ruth's house."

A look of shock crossed her face. "You're coming with me?"

"Yes, Mom." I stroked her blue-veined wrists. "I'll be with you the whole time. I'm staying with Ruth, too."

"Where are we going after we go to Florida?"

"We're not going anywhere. We're just going to Florida and back."

"And why are we going to Florida?"

I smiled and squeezed her hands. "We're going to see your sister Ruth. And her husband, Howard."

"Wow, I guess I'm a little nutsy. Is there anything else I need to know?"

"Well, their son Michael died."

Shock waves rippled Mom's soft cheeks. "Michael's dead?" Michael had died several years earlier, but for Mom, he had just died all over again.

"I'm so sorry to have to tell you. He was still a young man."

"Well, darling, I'm so glad you told me. I wouldn't have wanted to make a big boo-boo saying the wrong thing."

The next morning, Mom was disoriented. She'd pulled off her clothes in the night, but I dressed her easily and helped her in the bathroom. When it came time to slip on her Depends and lift her off the toilet, I felt nothing but tenderness. I was no longer an angry teenager or an estranged, distant adult.

CHAPTER 58

THE VISIT

130 Days

Traveling with Mom was exhausting. Every five minutes she wanted to go to the bathroom—seat belts and regulations be damned. It definitely took two of us to manage her incessant, loud demands. As we followed her wheelchair off the plane, I turned to Karyn and said, "I'm giving her Ativan on the way home." *Why hadn't I thought of that before?*

Eleven hours after leaving Santa Cruz, we arrived at Ruth and Howard's condo, part of a huge development dedicated to senior living. Ruth was waiting outside with her walker, wearing a brown stretchy pantsuit with a leopard-print shirt poking out around the collar. Howard, at least fifty pounds thinner than the last time I'd seen him, stood stooped in the doorway. I pulled Mom's red walker out of the trunk and set it on the sidewalk. Mom's eyes locked on Ruth, and Ruth's eyes, magnified by thick glasses, stared back. Mom grabbed the grips of the walker and took off with an urgency I hadn't seen in months, shoving the small, stiff gray wheels over cracks in the pavement. A whimper escaped her lips. "I can't believe it. Ruth, it's really you."

"I can't believe it either. My big sister. You're really here." Ruth's familiar New York accent mingled with the sticky air, enveloping me completely. I fell into the cadence of her words, a lost childhood melody. She strained over her walker, eyes riveted on Mom's face. "You look so good, Temme. You're still the pretty one."

Mom propelled herself faster, panting, erasing the distance between them. "No, you are. You're so beautiful to me." At two feet away, she let go of the handle grips and surged toward her sister.

Ruth's voice rose in alarm. "Temme, don't! You'll knock us both over."

"My baby sister." Mom teetered on unsteady feet.

I ran over, guided her back to her walker, and the five of us slowly made our way into the living room. When the two sisters finally settled on the couch, they couldn't stop hugging, staring at each other, and hugging again.

"I can't believe you're really here," Ruth said. "I never thought I'd see you again."

"Ruth, *mein schvester*," Mom said back. My sister.

I gave Karyn a long look, the kind parents share when their kids do something wonderful—pleasure, pride, and joy, all rolled into one. Karyn had been right about this trip. I mouthed the words, "Thank you."

—∾—

The next morning, Mom woke up disoriented, certain that we'd dropped in and were imposing. She wanted to go home to Santa Cruz and asked me to pack her things. But by the time Karyn drove off to meet her sisters, Mom had settled down. Pretty soon, the three octogenarians and I were eating a huge spread of bagels, lox, and cream cheese—retro foods not usually in my diet.

Mom slept most of the day and perked up over dinner. I couldn't believe how much she slept. Ruth and Howard brought in a big tray of cold cuts—turkey, pastrami, corned beef, chopped liver, rye bread, potato salad, coleslaw, and a vat of half-sour pickles. Mom and I scarfed down the chopped liver. I hadn't eaten any in ten years, but it was a sacrament to the gods of my childhood. I made myself a fat pastrami and mustard sandwich on rye, and it tasted great—soul food from a different era.

Over dinner, Mom and Ruth discussed their brother and sister who had passed on. Then they moved on to their mother. Mom asked Ruth, "I dream about Bubby sometimes. Do you?" Still in the grip of memory, she went on. "I remember visiting Bubby in the nursing home. She was so sad and begged me to take her home."

I remembered that visit, too.

Ruth recalled her own last days with Bubby. "People asked me, 'Why do you bring your daughter? She's a little girl. It's so painful.' And I'd say, 'This is what life is. This is her grandmother.'"

Remembering their mother's suffering, Mom said, "I hope I die quickly. I want to quit while I'm ahead."

Howard responded in his low, deep voice. "You have no choice about that unless you take your own life. I've been on dialysis for seven and a half years, and most people don't last that long. But I'm still here. As a friend said to me, 'At least at this point, we don't have to worry about dying young.'" Then he looked at his wife of sixty-one years, his childhood sweetheart. "I'm only here because of her."

When it was time for bed, I helped Mom out of her clothes. I cleaned her teeth and pulled up her Depends. She lay on the couch in the room next door to the little alcove where I was sleeping. When I tucked her in, she looked at me with her teeth out, her mouth caved in. I wanted to turn away from her sagging hollow cheeks, her empty mouth, and slurred speech, but I didn't. I knew Mom wouldn't trust anyone else to see her like this. I stayed where I was. I smiled down at her.

"I love you, Laurie. Thank you for bringing me to Florida."

—~—

The next three days were golden. I took Mom to the Morikami Japanese Gardens, borrowed a wheelchair, and pushed her around its mile of accessible paths. It was a perfect day with a slight breeze, and Mom was certain she'd been there before. "Weren't we here yesterday?" she asked repeatedly. A strange synapse was firing in her brain. There was no point in arguing. She was a regular.

Back at Ruth's, Mom and I napped on separate couches. I woke after an hour; she slept for three. Ruth and Howard and I sat in the den and talked. "I'm really glad I came," I said. "If I hadn't brought Mom to see you, I'd never have seen you two again."

I was speaking the truth, and we all knew it. Howard, usually a man of few words, said, "It's good you came. I have two siblings I'll never see again."

I felt such love for these two tough survivors. They'd been raised poor on the Lower East Side and had been through hard times—but always together. They'd known each other for sixty-seven years; they'd become sweethearts when Ruth was only fourteen.

We woke Mom for dinner. As she polished off the chopped liver, she launched into a familiar litany. "I like where I live. I can't drive anymore, but they take care of everything. The only thing is I don't have any intimate friends."

Howard interrupted. "At this stage of life, Temme, we don't make friends. We lose friends."

Mom said, "Getting old sucks."

Howard replied, "Yes, but consider the alternative. Getting old is no tragedy. I've had two cancer surgeries. I could be dead right now." Howard paused. "We buried a son. It's life." He reached for another pickle. "You know what real tragedy is? My grandmother had thirteen children, and only my father and one of my uncles got out of Poland. All the rest were exterminated. Now that's a real tragedy."

I quietly pulled out my iPhone and shot a video of the three of them. The conversation moved on to my grandfather's butcher shop. Howard recalled how Poppa always left twenty dollars in the till at night so if he got robbed, the robbers would come away with something and not find it necessary to trash the place.

Mom drifted in and out of the conversation, occasionally chiming in. I just listened. At one point, Mom turned to me and asked, "Did you ever meet my father?"

Ruth and Howard turned to me, waiting to see what I would say. I could have answered a million different ways. Thirty years earlier, I would have felt compelled to talk about what he did to me when he tucked me in. How he inspected the girls' breasts when they hit puberty. But I had no need to do that anymore. I had my memories, and they had theirs. "Yes," I finally said. "Of course I knew him. I remember him making schnapps. He made his own sauerkraut and his own whiskey."

I got up to wash the dishes as Howard, in his black sweatpants and signature yellow cardigan, struggled to rise from his chair. "We'll wax more nostalgias tomorrow." Then he headed off to bed.

—∞—

It was our last full day in Florida. By the time Mom got up, ate, and finished her two morning naps, it was 1:00 p.m., and I really needed an outing. Mom and Ruth and I headed to one of the many swimming pools gracing their complex.

I put on my bathing suit and pulled Mom's old suit from the bottom of her suitcase. I wasn't sure I could manage getting her in the water, but I wanted to try. Mom had loved the beach at Coney Island as a girl and raised me at the Jersey shore. I could still see her wearing a wide-brimmed hat, sitting in front of a cabana, playing bridge. Whenever she got too hot, she jumped in the pool and swam with her head out of the water so she wouldn't mess up her hair. For more than eight decades, Mom had always loved the water.

At Ruth's condo complex, the pool was full of senior citizens, covered in deep wrinkles and dark, even tans. There were lots of men with silver hair, white hair, or no hair, most with moderate to huge bellies. Women stood in clusters with full makeup and bright lipstick, perfectly coiffed hair, lacquered fingernails and sunglasses, ropes of gold jewelry adorning their necks, ankles, and wrists.

"Let's get in the pool." I had Mom maneuver her walker as close to the stairs as possible. There were five wide steps going down into the shallow end. Sturdy railings with blue grips led all the way into the pool. I stood in front of her, ready to catch her if she stumbled. She held on to the railings, and I called out, "There's another step." Each step was a major accomplishment, but soon, she was standing on the floor of the pool. I took her by the hand and led her to the side where she could hold on.

"This is the perfect temperature!" Then she kissed me on the cheek, a huge smile on her face. "I just felt like doing that. We're in Florida!"

At that moment, I felt as buoyant as the water around us.

Slowly, I walked backward, leading Mom around the pool, just like I'd led Eli and Lizzy when they were small. We talked about some of the troubles happening in our family. She volunteered, "I've never had any troubles in my life."

I looked at her in disbelief and started to laugh. "Yes, Mom, you have. When I came out to you as a lesbian, you were very troubled by that. The first thing you said to me was 'You've confirmed my worst fear about you.'"

Mom bobbed in the water. "Well, I don't feel that way now. I love Karyn. She's like a daughter to me. If you ran around with a lot of women, I probably wouldn't like it, but Karyn's my daughter-in-law, and she's very good to me."

"Do you want to try floating, Mom?"

Like a trusting child, she lay back in the water, and I pulled her forward, her body bobbing like a cork, light and unencumbered. I supported the back of her head and neck and pulled her gently, steadily backward around the pool. I walked faster, swishing her body from side to side. Eli and Lizzy used to love it when I did this for them, and I'd loved it when Dad did it for me.

When I set her back on her feet, she tried to dive in and swim, but she just lay there, flopped down on her stomach. I lifted her up, and she tried again. "I can't swim anymore." It was true; she had forgotten how.

"Are you ready to get out, Mom?"

"No, just a little longer. This is perfect."

"Are you happy?"

"I'm happy with you," she said, beaming at me. "I couldn't be happier."

I knew just how she felt.

—∾—

That afternoon, Karyn returned from visiting her sisters in Sarasota, and we went for a long walk. As soon as we were alone, I asked, "So, how did it go with Charlene?"

"We talked at a level we'd never talked before. She opened up about some painful times in our childhood that I hadn't known about. I just sat on her couch and listened. It was the most real conversation we've ever had."

"I'm glad. It's been great here, too. And it never would have happened without you."

Our last morning in Florida, I woke early to the sound of Mom's voice down the hall. "Laurie, Laurie, I need to go to the bathroom."

The sky was dark. Karyn snored gently beside me. I reached for my phone. 3:00 a.m. *Shit.*

Mom's voice rose. "Laurie, can you help me?" A stab of annoyance pierced my concern. Ruth and Howard were asleep in the next room, and Mom was going to wake them. We had a huge travel day before us.

A moment later, Mom called out again, her voice frantic. "I need help!"

I tiptoed over to the couch where she was sleeping. *Oh no.* She was sprawled diagonally across the cushions, legs dangling off the side. She had tried to get up. Now she lay tangled in the covers, nightgown twisted around her thighs. She was panting from her failed exertion. The sharp points of her dental implants pierced the gaping cavity of her mouth. *My God, Mom.* I looked away, but her eyes sought mine, searching for a place to land. I forced myself to meet her gaze.

"I really need to go to the bathroom. Help me, Laurie."

Adrenaline slapped me into high gear. I reached under Mom's back. Lifted her. She was heavy. Dead weight. "Can you stand?"

"Yes." She pushed off against the bed with her hands. Rocked her body to establish momentum. Swung her feet around to meet the floor. She pushed, and I pulled, until finally, she stood wavering in the darkness.

"Let me lean on you." She slumped against me, her weight substantial. I urged us toward the bathroom. "No," she cried out. "Don't rush me! I can't make it that far!" Panic edged her voice.

I pushed her down the hall, wrestled her through the doorway, aiming for the toilet. Both of us breathless. "Mom, can you pull down your pants?" "Pants" was a euphemism. She was wearing giant diapers that sagged below her waist.

"I can't!" Her voice burst into flames, that quick rush to anger I'd known all my life. From zero to one hundred in a second. It still shocked me every time. She spat, "I can't pull down my pants. If I could do it myself, you think I'd have asked for help?"

I felt slapped. My body sagged beneath her weight. I struggled to keep my voice steady and reassuring, but it was a command. "Hold on to the sink."

Immediately, she was compliant again. She grabbed the porcelain, fingers straining with effort. I reached for the top of her diapers with both hands. "Hurry up, Laurie. Pull them down. I have to go right now! I can't wait any longer."

Oh my God, I can't do this. But I have to. I wrestled the poofy diaper down around her knees. My voice a tight wire. "Sit. The toilet's right behind you."

"I can't!"

"All you have to do is sit!"

"I can't."

"Just sit down."

"I can't! My knees don't work." She wavered. I gripped harder. Her voice rose. "I can't hold it. I've got to go."

And she did. She went everywhere. Diarrhea poured out of her. It poured down her beautiful, still lovely legs. Onto the remains of her Sunshine Villa pedicure and her crusty toe, the one with the fungal infection that never went away. It sprayed the sink and puddled on the floor. The front of my pajamas, wet and brown. The back of her nightgown, a brown lake. Shit speckled the walls. Like all the walls in this condo, they were white.

Oh my God, Mom. I gagged and looked away.

"Ah . . . that feels better."

Vomit rose into my throat, and I swallowed hard. Mom's shit did not smell like the sweet poop of my new baby granddaughter. I breathed through my mouth. It had all come down to this. The two of us standing in this bathroom. I looked at Mom's face. So soft, so familiar. The face I'd known and run from all my life. The beauty queen. The actress. My mother. Her cheeks smooth, without the age spots that mottled her arms. Even with her teeth out, she still looked beautiful.

An embarrassed, elderly child looked back at me. "I'm sorry I made such a mess, Laurie, but I just couldn't wait any longer."

Oh, Mom. This is the child who lives inside of you. Inside all of us.

I wanted to comfort her, but my mind skittered into the future. Twelve hours from now, we'd be on a plane heading back to California. The flight out had been a nightmare. I was going to dose her with Ativan, but how was I going to deal with this?

"Hold on to the sink." It was a command, but I tried not to sound curt. "Stand still."

Mom bellowed back. "What do you think I'm trying to do? But my legs won't stop shaking." There it was again. Humiliation turning into rage turning back into humiliation. Was this where the monster came from?

"Lift up your arms." Mom's hands reached up in surrender as I lifted the nightgown over her head. Threw it in the corner. Knelt down on the floor in front of her. I knew what I was kneeling in. Ripped off her Depends. Tossed the shit-stained diaper.

This can't happen on the plane. What the hell am I going to do?

Mom stood naked before me, teetering, goose bumps on her skin. Her belly still round, her legs narrow, shapely sticks, her breasts soft half-moons sagging on her chest. I spooled toilet paper off the roll into my hand, dampened it, and wiped her down. There were flecks of brown everywhere. I made sure the water was warm.

"Wipe me again. I think you missed a spot."

Rage spiked through my chest and passed as quickly as a heartbeat. That's when I remembered the Imodium stashed in my CPAP bag for travel. *Bingo.*

I helped her onto the toilet seat and wiped between her toes.

Finally, she was clean. The walls and floor would have to wait.

As I swung open the door to take her back to bed, Karyn stood in the hallway, waiting, a clean nightgown in one hand, a bucket of soapy water in the other. A yellow sponge floated on top. Karyn was never one to shirk the dirty jobs.

Our eyes caught. *Bless you,* my eyes said, finally filling. *I'm here for you,* her eyes said back. *I'm here for both of you.* I reached for the nightgown, and our fingers brushed under the worn cotton. Karyn carried the bucket into the bathroom as I pulled the clean nightgown over

Mom's head, feeding her arms into the holes, as I'd done for my granddaughter the week before. I led Mom back to her room, helped her into a new pair of Depends, and tucked her in. As I pulled the covers up to her chin, I stroked her hollow cheek. Her skin as soft as baby Ellie's.

"Oh, Laurie, thank you. I never wanted you to have to do this for me." Her dry lips quivered. "What would I ever do without you?"

"I love you, Mom." I kissed her goodnight, prayed she'd go back to sleep.

A minute later, I came back with two white tablets and a glass of water. The Imodium would keep her plugged up for at least twenty-four hours. She took the pills without question. Two minutes later, she was snoring.

—✿—

Mom slept the entire morning. Karyn and I finished cleaning the bathroom, tried and failed to go back to sleep. Howard had dialysis and had to leave early, so he wouldn't be there to see us off. We shared an awkward, gentle hug—I didn't want to knock him over—and I thanked him for his hospitality. As he made his way slowly to the car with his lopsided gait, his cane tap-tapped down the long walkway. He carried a worn insulated lunch bag, the same bag he carried three times a week to every dialysis appointment: a turkey sandwich, a bottle of iced tea, ten grapes, and two graham crackers. The same lunch for seven and a half years, made by his wife, handed to him as he stepped out the door. I watched from the doorway as he plopped heavily onto the driver's seat. I knew I'd never see him again.

Karyn, Ruth, and I spent our last morning at the kitchen table. I floated on the tangy edge of Ruth's New York accent. I could listen to her stories all day.

I woke Mom at noon so there would be enough time to feed her and get her ready. She had no memory of what had happened the night before, and I prayed that the Imodium would hold. Karyn cooked her a soft-boiled egg and a piece of buttered toast. I made her a cup of peppermint tea. Mom and Ruth started talking, and I turned on my recorder. Mom said, "Ruth, *mein shvester*, I'm never going to see you again."

Ten minutes later, the two of them were singing Yiddish songs from their early childhood. For the first time since I was a little girl, I didn't hide my tears from my mother.

I wanted to linger, but our bags were packed. Mom was dressed, and I'd done the dishes. Karyn zipped up the suitcases. I had the two sisters sit for some final pictures. Then Mom and Ruth, the last of their generation, embraced for what I knew would be the last time.

Ruth walked us out to the car. I buckled Mom into her seat and closed the door. She looked out the tinted window, her face like that of a lost little girl. As I gave my aunt a hug, Ruth looked me in the eye. "If Temme dies before me, I won't be able to go to her funeral, and if I die, she won't be able to come to mine. This is it. The final chapter. I'll never see her again, but then, I never thought I'd see her now, so thank you."

When we dropped off the rental car, I pulled Mom's red walker out of the trunk. Karyn stacked our suitcases on the curb, then reached back in and pulled a grocery bag out of the trunk. The bag was fat and unmarked, with the top rolled down, one fold, two folds, three. Karyn looked at me, a quizzical expression on her face.

"Never saw it before."

As she helped Mom out of the car, Karyn handed me the bag. When I opened it, the smell of turkey rose up to greet me: three sandwiches, a bag of grapes, graham crackers, and tea.

CHAPTER 59

FRACTURE

101 Days

Three weeks after we returned from Florida, I flew east again, this time with Lizzy, so she could visit the colleges that had accepted her: two in Washington, DC, and two in Boston. She was hoping to fall in love with one of them.

To celebrate our first night in the nation's capital, we chose an outdoor Greek restaurant. It was a humid night. Half a dozen young men performed flamboyant skateboard tricks nearby. Twenty minutes into our meal, Lizzy went to the restroom, and I checked my phone. Alerts blazed across the screen: two texts and three voice mails from Karyn. Three messages from Sunshine Villa. Panic pulsed through me. *No. No! Please God, no.*

Mom had fallen. She was in pain, and an ambulance had taken her to the emergency room. By the time I listened to the final message, the X-rays had come back. Mom's hip was broken. I imagined her writhing in pain as Lizzy—beautiful, vibrant, young—bounded back from the restroom. Her hair flowed softly over her shoulders. She looked radiant.

Lizzy slipped into her chair, took her first bite of scallops. "Yum. These are amazing! Have you tried them?"

I said nothing. My whole body was buzzing on high alert. I had to call Karyn. But I couldn't. Not yet. But I had to.

Lizzy took one look at me, and her face filled with concern. "Mom, what's wrong?"

"Grandma fell and broke her hip. They've rushed her to the hospital."

A shadow crossed Lizzy's face. Her narrow shoulders slumped.

In that split second, I thought about all the years I'd been caring for Mom. About Karyn's loyalty to her mother-in-law—I knew she'd step in. I thought of Paul. He'd have to come. I was with my daughter now. This was our time.

"I'm not going anywhere, Lizzy."

Her face remained grave. "You can if you need to."

"Then how would you get around?"

"But Grandma . . ."

"I'm not going anywhere."

It wasn't until I said it the second time that Lizzy's shoulders relaxed. I smiled at her, picked up my fork, and stabbed a scallop. The seasoning was perfect. "Yum," I said.

"Yum," she said back.

Paul flew in, and he and Karyn managed the crisis. I talked to one or both of them every day, quick phone calls and late-night texts, but all the decisions were in their hands.

Lizzy and I drove to Boston, saw Eli as much as possible. I tried to stay upbeat, but I wasn't fooling anyone. The kids bore the brunt of my worry and distraction. A week later, we flew home, mission accomplished; Lizzy loved Tufts.

Mom's surgery had been successful. She was recuperating at Kindred Rehabilitation Center, ten minutes from our house. Paul had scored her a bed with a sliding glass door to a courtyard—a real coup on his part. He and Karyn had done a first-class job.

Lizzy and I drove straight to Kindred from the airport. We crowded into Mom's side of the room. "Grandma," Lizzy announced, "I'm going to Tufts!"

Mom beamed at her. "That's wonderful, darling. I'm so proud of you!"

"You're going to get to come to my high school graduation, Grandma."

"I wouldn't miss it for the world!"

93 DAYS

The next morning, I met with Mom's care team at Kindred. They made it clear she wasn't making adequate progress. When someone has a hip replacement, there are three things they are not allowed to do: bend from the waist at more than a ninety-degree angle, pigeon-toe their feet, and cross their legs. The staff at Kindred went over these restrictions with Mom multiple times a day. The physical therapy team reinforced them, and Paul pasted them in huge letters on her wall. But Mom could never remember more than one rule at a time, if she remembered any at all. Usually, she forgot she'd broken her hip, and when we reminded her, she insisted it wasn't true. She was impatient and wouldn't wait for someone to take her to the bathroom, so she tried to get out of bed on her own. Breaking her other hip was only a matter of time.

81 DAYS

Two weeks later, she refused to get up at all.

"Mom, you have to!"

"I'm too tired, Laurie."

"You've got to try."

"Maybe tomorrow."

I knew that staying in bed was the worst thing Mom could do. My friend, an occupational therapist, had told me, "Once they get stuck in bed, it's all downhill, and it goes downhill quickly."

"Mom, don't you want to go to Lizzy's graduation? You can't go if you stay in bed."

"I don't know, dear. I'm just feeling lazy."

Three ascending notes rang out on my phone, announcing a text from Lizzy. "OMG Mom!!!! I was just at the all-school meeting, and they announced I'm the saludictorian!!!"

I laughed out loud and texted back. "You mean salutatorian?"

"Yeah, whatever."

"Congratulations! Can I tell your grandma?"

"Sure."

I squeezed Mom's gnarled hand. "Now you've got to get out of bed. Lizzy's giving a speech at graduation."

CHAPTER 60

SUPPORT GROUP

75 Days

That weekend, Lizzy and I shopped for her graduation dress. She chose a white one with tiny flowers. It had a lot more cleavage than I liked, but I smiled, said nothing, and whipped out my credit card. When we got home, she modeled the dress for Karyn. I could tell she wanted to pin the bodice closed, but she, too, merely smiled.

That afternoon, I got a call from the facilitator of the Early-Stage Memory Loss Support Group. The last time Mom and I attended the group had been before our trip to Florida.

"Laura, I just wanted to check in with how you're doing, touch base about your mom and how she's using the group. We're not sure the group serves her anymore. It is an 'early stage' group. Some of the people are still driving. They're dealing with their diagnosis."

Please don't take this away from me.

I tried to keep it light. "Are you kidding? Temme still thinks she's better than everyone else."

"Well, maybe I need to talk to her." If she did, Mom would tell her the truth—that she only came to the group because I cajoled her every week. *I* was the one who needed the support.

"Whenever anyone goes through a major change, we reevaluate their appropriateness for the group. Even if she doesn't come back, you can still come to one last session."

I considered the others in the group; they were declining, too. Why were we being singled out? But then I recalled Mom's refusal to get off her bedpan. Her wheelchair and her empty smile. My voice was thick when I finally replied. "I'll come alone on Tuesday to say goodbye."

That afternoon, I drove over to see Mom. When I walked through her door, a voice in my head whispered, *Look at her. See who she is today.* So, I looked. I really looked. And this was what I saw: A gown stained with mashed potatoes. Bluntly cut white hair flying around her face. No makeup. No jewelry. A woman who'd gone from watching the sunset at Mount Fuji to happily staying in bed. Satisfied with the view out her window—the way the waning light filtered through the sliding glass doors at dusk. Content to sleep and read the paper all day. Did she still read, or was she just turning the pages out of habit? There was no way for me to know.

I was determined to keep making good choices on her behalf, but Mom was winding down. Her palms were open. Each moment held the simple pleasure of light and color, shadow and warmth, nourishment and rest. She wanted nothing, and when before in her eighty-six years had she wanted nothing? Temme Davis had swum through life, a hungry shark, devouring experiences, always wanting more. There was a reason she had needed three calendars. But not any longer.

For the first time in her life, my mother wanted nothing more than what she had—she was a woman without ambition. She was content to spend the rest of her life in a wheelchair, the very thing that had terrified her the most when we visited Bubby in the nursing home. Mom was tranquil in her decline. She was shrunken and serene. Content with who she was and where she was. She didn't need a support group. She didn't need anything but us close by.

CHAPTER 61

THE DECIDER

68 Days

A week later, I was in Mom's rehab room at Kindred, searching for her Pocket Talker, the miracle device that had enabled her to hear again. No matter how many times I explained to the staff what it was for and how to use it, I had to search for it every day—and usually discovered it on the floor or in pieces.

My request that they get Mom out of bed had been ignored. Her dentures hadn't been cleaned, and she was wearing yesterday's clothes.

I drove over to Sunshine Villa to pick up some of her things. The moment I walked into her room, the grief that I'd been holding gave way. Her wall was still painted the salmon color she loved. Light slanted through the windows, casting a soft glow. Mom's familiar art covered the walls. I scanned the room: the Dell computer she no longer used, the La-Z-Boy she never sat in, the desk she hadn't touched since the day we moved her in.

I'd always made fun of Sunshine Villa for its 4:30 p.m. dinners and tacky holiday decorations, but Mom had been happy there. Sunshine Villa had been her home. I missed the way the aides dressed her in pretty clothes and made her up each day. They had preserved her dignity while attending to her needs. I considered moving her back, but her needs had changed. None of the expensive bells and whistles mattered anymore. Mom would never act again. She'd never take another scenic bus trip to nowhere.

There was also the question of money. At Sunshine Villa, every new bit of care was itemized on the monthly bill: ka-ching, ka-ching, ka-ching. What would it cost for Mom to stay in her sunny private room now? If I moved her back, would she outlast her funds? She'd told me dozens of times that she didn't want the money she'd saved, scrimping for decades, to go into the pockets of one of the fastest-growing wealth sectors in America.

I asked the social worker at Kindred for advice. "If she were my mother," she replied, "I'd move her into a smaller, more homey setting."

So, List Laura did the research.

55 DAYS

I knew Mom was living at Kindred on borrowed time. Medicare would pay for ten hours of therapy a week as long as the patient made progress—but if Mom refused physical therapy and couldn't follow basic commands, she couldn't stay.

I didn't know if any of the places I'd researched would take her. Mom was a fall risk, and her dementia was getting worse. I didn't want to put her in a nursing home and couldn't imagine bringing her home to live with us.

The last time I'd moved her, Mom's decline had been swift and precipitous. What would happen this time?

I was the decider. The one who'd be called upon to enforce the papers Mom had signed years before, the ones that said no to extraordinary measures, that insisted, "Do not sustain my life when I no longer have a life." I'd been with her when her doctor went through her options and made sure she understood them. But the mother I had now wasn't the mother who'd signed those papers. That mother would have been horrified to use a bedpan, but the mother I had now wasn't horrified in the least. Her mantra was no longer "Just take me out back and shoot me." It was "I hope you have an old age just like mine."

So, I grappled with the essential question, What makes a meaningful life?

I'd soon be attending a care conference with the staff at Kindred to discuss my mother's case. They were going to ask me what I wanted for her. Did I want them to try to make her walk again, so she could return to her shiny red walker? She'd fallen six times in the past year. If she stood, she was certain to fall again. I didn't want her to break another hip, to be rushed to the hospital, bewildered and in pain.

Twenty years ago, a broken hip meant death, but no more. Mom was happy now, but if I aggressively treated her, would I be consigning her to round after round of hospital admissions, each with diminishing returns? Maybe it was time to arrange for palliative care rather than pushing for recovery. For years, Mom had told me, "I've passed the acceptable age for death. No one would call my death a tragedy. I want to quit while I'm ahead."

And so, I wrestled with the question, *How do I honor her wishes now?*

CHAPTER 62

GRADUATION

41 Days

The day before Lizzy's graduation, I drove to Sunshine Villa. I'd hired Diana, Mom's favorite caregiver, to transport her to and from the ceremony and to tend to her personal needs. Now all I had to do was choose Mom's clothes.

As I flipped through her closet, I ignored the fancy outfits—too tight, too restrictive. I chose a simple pair of light cream pants, baggy but tailored, a blue shell and matching jacket made of a soft fabric that wouldn't chafe her tender skin. I ran my fingers through her shimmery scarf collection and chose a multicolored silk that glittered when it caught the light. A pair of simple flats. They were scuffed, and the back heels were worn down, but they were comfortable, one of the few pairs that still fit her swollen feet. With a little polish, they'd look just fine.

I rooted around the bathroom until I found an ancient compact with rouge on one side and a mirror on the other, an old tube of lipstick in Mom's favorite shade—still creamy enough for one more application.

40 DAYS

On the afternoon of June 14, 2014, Karyn, Paul, and I filed into the lobby of the Sanctuary of Peace United Church, Diana and Mom beside us. Mom looked beautiful. Her Pocket Talker rested in her lap. I prayed she wouldn't disrupt the ceremony.

Lizzy rushed up in her cap and gown to greet us, saving her biggest hug for Mom. "Grandma, I love what you're wearing! I'm so glad you're here."

"Darling, I wouldn't miss it for the world."

Lizzy ran off to line up with her friends. I rolled Mom's wheelchair to our reserved seats. As the first strains of "Pomp and Circumstance" rang out, I reached for Karyn's hand.

Slowly, the teachers of Georgiana Bruce Kirby School filed down the center aisle to their assigned seats. Rustling filled the room as everyone turned their heads, craning their necks to see their special student. The graduating class of 2014 promenaded to their seats in time to the music, thirty-eight robed young people ready to take on the world.

The head of school greeted the students and welcomed the crowd. "We're going to start with the first of our speakers. I'd like to introduce the salutatorian of the class of 2014."

Lizzy's classmates cheered as she made her way to the podium, a chrysanthemum lei around her neck. She took in the crowd: four hundred seats, all full. She set her notes on the lectern and spoke in a strong, clear voice.

I squeezed Karyn's hand. She squeezed mine back. I looked at Mom. She was fully engrossed in her granddaughter, her eyes gleaming. I stroked her arm.

"When I told my parents that I was going to be salutatorian, they congratulated me. When I told my martial arts instructor, he responded, 'What is that?'"

The audience laughed. A huge smile erupted on Lizzy's face. I watched the realization take shape in her eyes—this wasn't a one-way street; it was a conversation. She paused, feeling the audience, enjoying the audience, letting them fill her sails. "Next year, there will be many firsts to enjoy: Setting up your own dentist appointment. Doing the laundry and accidentally dyeing all your whites pink. There will be late nights frantically writing term papers, frat parties, hookups, and falling in love. You'll make friends. You'll lose friends. But what do I really know about life after high school? All of my expectations about college come from HBO."

The whole room roared with that one. As she waited for the laughter to subside, she looked at us, the joy of performance transforming her face. "Every person in this class has something they're passionate about. Whether we want to design the next generation of self-driving cars, start a goat farm, or practice law, medicine, journalism—or another profession that has no jobs—we're prepared. We know how to work hard, solve problems, form community, and to laugh."

She closed with a line from Dr. Seuss. She smiled, gathered her papers, and the audience erupted in applause.

After the recessional, we chose a spot to take pictures. Lizzy alone. Lizzy with her moms. Uncle Paul and Lizzy. Lizzy next to her grandmother. Paul said, "I want one with my sister," and the two of us slid into a cozy pose. Just as we were about to disperse, Karyn said, "One more. Three generations." Lizzy squatted on one side of Mom's chair; I squatted on the other. Lizzy gave Grandma a hug, and so did I.

Mom turned to me, eyes shining. "Laurie, I'll never forget this moment."

It would be Mom's last public outing.

CHAPTER 63

NAME GAME

38 Days

Two days later, I was lying on Mom's bed, chatting with her through her Pocket Talker, filling her in on Lizzy's graduation party. I liked lying on her hospital bed, pushing buttons on the remote to make the bed go up and down. Mom was sitting beside me in her wheelchair, eating Salisbury steak, overcooked green beans, mushy white rice, and gummy peach cobbler, each in a separate segment of the molded plastic tray. Foods I would never eat, not in a million years. I hope to God that institutional food improves before I end up in one of those places. In the assisted living of my dreams, they teach mindfulness meditation, offer hash brownies for anxiety, serve tofu and garlic kale for lunch. Yoga in the morning. Meditation in the afternoon. Cat Stevens, Aretha Franklin, and the Beatles piped in. Wi-Fi in every room. But Mom was eating with gusto. The social worker told me she was the only person in the history of the place who had ever complimented the food.

Each time Mom brought a bite to her lips, I gritted my teeth, watching the slow, uncertain trajectory of her arm. As green beans and rice tumbled down her shirt, I wanted to grab the spoon, but I gave her the dignity of feeding herself.

Mom looked up from a bite of green beans, a quizzical look on her face. She seemed to be trying hard to figure something out. "Who are my children?"

My breath caught, but I gave her my full attention, kept my voice light. "Who do you think they are?" I was truly curious. Exploring the vagaries of Mom's memory had become a fascinating spectator sport for me.

She thought for a while. "Sonya?"

"No. Sonya is your granddaughter." I reached for the remote and raised the head of the bed, bringing my face closer to Mom's.

She thought a while longer. "Eli?"

"Nope. He's your grandson."

Mom stopped eating and fully focused on the problem before her. "Is it Paul?"

"Yes, Paul is your son."

She looked right at me, a puzzled expression on her face. "And who's my other child?"

I said it simply, with a light touch. "You're looking right at her."

Mom's whole body sagged in relief. She laughed, rejoicing in recognition: "Oh, now I remember! You're my only daughter." She beamed me one of her megawatt smiles. "And you're the most important person in my life."

I responded with a flat voice. "Yes, Mom, I know."

"Where would I be without you? You take such good care of me. And you and Karyn have done such a great job with those kids. They've never given you a moment's trouble. Who says lesbians shouldn't have children?"

Mom was right back in one of her favorite conversational loops, but I couldn't share her joy at rediscovering me. She'd looked right at me and drawn a blank. The one bullet I had always hoped to dodge. Everything in my body was vibrating, and my skin felt too tight.

I stared out at the garden. The glass door was smudged with dirty fingerprints, and a fat fly was trapped inside the glass. Who was I if Mom didn't know me? From the moment she'd stood outside my Isolette and pulled me into the world, Mom had always been at the center. At the center of my love. At the center of my hate. At the center of my feigned indifference. I had never stopped revolving around her.

I had never escaped her gravitational pull. Now suddenly, I had been released from orbit and was hurtling through space alone. Nothing tethered me to the earth anymore.

CHAPTER 64

REDWOOD GARDENS

31 Days

The decision about Mom's future was taken out of my hands. She'd reached the dreaded plateau, "failure to progress." She'd be discharged from Kindred in a wheelchair. No one expected her to ever walk again.

I had to find her a new place to live, and quickly.

I found her a room at Redwood Gardens, a twenty-bed assisted-living home a block and a half from our house. Where she lived was up to me, and I chose proximity. When I told her that we were going to be neighbors, she clapped her hands like a child. "It will be like living with you, but you'll still have your privacy."

I prayed that this new placement would work.

Mom's new room had just enough space for a hospital bed, a dresser, a chair, and a small television. A sliding glass door looked out onto a courtyard.

Karyn and I went over to set up her things. We placed a few of her masks on the wall, squeezed in one of her Mexican table lamps, and set out pictures of her three grandchildren. We made the bed with her familiar white fluffy comforter and placed one of her orange-and-turquoise striped throw pillows at the top of her bed.

Everything else had to go.

When we showed Mom her new room, she immediately asked, "Where's my bookcase?" I winced. Bookcase? I'd not only gotten rid of her bookcases; I'd gotten rid of all her books. Thank God I'd kept a few play collections for sentimental value. I could bring them over as window dressing, so she could see that her world was in order.

But she wasn't done complaining. "How come I don't have a couch?"

"There's no room for one, Temme," Karyn said, stating the obvious.

"This room is so tiny. It feels like a cell." She was right. With three of us in the room, it felt crowded. "What if I have guests? Where will they sit?" It never ceased to amaze me how Mom's social impulses remained when so much else had been lost.

"There are a couple of chairs in here," I said. "If you have a crowd over, you can use the patio."

"How many chairs are out there?" Mom wasn't letting this go. I was shocked. She'd been so happy and carefree at Kindred that I had assumed this move would be easy. I thought she'd crossed a line where environment no longer mattered. Apparently, I was wrong.

I peered out the sliding glass doors and counted. "At least half a dozen."

"Are there tables?"

"Yes, Temme," Karyn chimed in, determined to cinch the sale. "Two tables." Mom finally seemed satisfied.

When it was time for her first lunch, Ian, the manager, came in to escort her. He said it would be better if we waited in her room. Karyn and I sat on the stiff hospital bed. Comfort was out of the question. I sighed. "I have a bad feeling about this."

"She'll be fine. She just needs time."

Twenty minutes later, Ian wheeled Mom back. As soon as he left, she said in a loud stage whisper, "I don't like this place. Nobody talked to me at lunch. I think it's because I'm Jewish. I want to know what my other options are."

Other options? I knew what her other options were. There weren't many, and they were a lot worse than this place. The walls of her tiny room were closing in on all of us.

Anxiety lapped at the edge of Mom's voice. "I'm going to call my friend Gail. Maybe I can live where she is. That place in Scotts Valley . . ."

"Oak Tree Villa? Mom, you can't live there. They won't take you."

"Why not?"

"You have a dementia diagnosis."

"I don't have dementia. There's nothing wrong with my memory."

Here she was, thinking she was too good for this place; I was praying she'd be good enough.

Ian returned and gave us the "It's time you two leave and let us deal with Temme" look. My growing dread was not assuaged by the "Let's hope for the best" expression in Karyn's eyes.

We said our goodbyes and walked out into a sunny summer day.

—∾—

That afternoon, I wandered down the brick path that meanders alongside our yard. The sun was warm, edging toward hot, coupled with a light breeze. Karyn's dahlia garden was in full bloom. The Meyer lemon tree was weighed down with unpicked fruit. I sat on the granite bench by the firepit. Despite the heat of the day, the coolness of the stone seeped through my jeans. We'd had so many celebrations in this yard. Mom had been here for many of them. Now she was living a five-minute walk away, and I didn't know whether she'd ever see our house again.

My fantasy about Mom being happy at Redwood Gardens was just that—a fantasy. Her future was spiraling in only one direction. There was nothing I could do to stop her decline or ease her suffering. I couldn't control it. Lord knows, I had tried.

In her book *Final Journeys*, hospice nurse Maggie Callanan says that as people approach the end of life, they and their family members become more of who they already are. For me, that meant being an information gatherer, a networker, a worrier, and a doer. List Laura had done it all, and for five and a half years, Mom had benefited from my connecting, resource gathering, and advocacy, but it was time for List Laura to retire, for me to give up my caregiving crusade. The time I had left with Mom was short. The losses were snowballing downhill, gaining momentum. She would not be getting better. What Mom needed from me now was for me to simply be her daughter. To love her and to bear witness. The time for doing had come to an end.

An hour later, the phone rang: Ian from Redwood Gardens. Mom had forgotten she wasn't supposed to get up by herself. Her caregiver had walked out for a minute, and when she came back, Mom was lying facedown on the floor. They hadn't called the ambulance because nothing new was broken—for now.

CHAPTER 65

THE SCREAM

23 Days

It was at Redwood Gardens that Mom started screaming. I began getting insistent, angry calls from the owner, Jackie. Whenever Mom was left alone, she yelled for help. Shouting day and night, she scared the other residents; she was their worst nightmare, the specter of who they might become. On my way to teach or to pick up toilet paper, my cell would ring, Redwood Gardens flashing on the screen.

The moment I picked up, Jackie demanded, "You have to do something about your mother! I can't have her screaming like this. You have to make her stop."

Each time she called, I went over, but Mom never yelled while I was with her. But as soon as I left, Jackie would call to tell me that Mom had started screaming again. I wondered if she was exaggerating. We were paying her a lot of money. Why couldn't she handle the situation? This was her business. How bad could it be?

The real truth was I wanted the problem to go away. I'd finally let go of managing Mom and trying to control her. I wanted to enjoy her for the time she had left. To just be her daughter. And now this. I dreaded every phone call.

Jackie's tone grew more urgent. "If you don't do something, I'm kicking her out."

I contacted every resource I could think of. Dale Thielges suggested I get a DVD of *Jeopardy!* and play it in a continuous loop. Karyn thought Mom's masks might be frightening her, so we took them down. Paul overnighted a new guided visualization he made to calm her. I called in the palliative care team. They tried various drug cocktails. But Mom just kept screaming.

CHAPTER 66

LULLABY

9 Days

The night before my annual writing retreat at Commonweal in Bolinas, I was shopping for Lizzy at Trader Joe's when a call from Redwood Gardens flashed across my phone. It was 7:45 p.m.

Shit. I can't do this. They know I'm leaving town. I have to get ready. The checkout lines are short. Just give me five more minutes.

I shoved the unanswered phone in my pocket. Grabbed three boxes of Lizzy's frozen mac and cheese. Raced to the cashier. Grabbed my groceries and ran to the car.

Sliding into the front seat, I hit Play. Ian's voice filled the car. "I'm afraid I have bad news. Your mom's okay, but she forgot she wasn't supposed to get up and fell on her face. She's cut up pretty bad. The EMTs are on their way. You need to get here as soon as possible."

Shit. Shit. Shit. Fuck. Not tonight.

I called Karyn. She was closer; she could get there sooner. Then I raced home. Tossed the frozen mac and cheese to Lizzy: "Grandma fell. Gotta go."

"How is she? Is she going to be okay?"

"I don't know. I'll text you."

I grabbed the big purple binder with Mom's Medicare information, medication list, medical power of attorney, and the bright pink Physician Orders for Life-Sustaining Treatment or POLST, the one document that matters in California if you want to refuse treatment. If you want the right to die.

It was a two-minute drive to Redwood Gardens. Mom was sitting in her blue recliner, holding an ice pack to her cut and bloody face. Karyn knelt below her, holding her hands and whispering reassurances. Four tall EMTs waited outside her door with a gurney, ready to load her into the ambulance. Elderly residents in pajamas peeked out from their doorways. What was going to happen to the woman who never stopped screaming?

I squeezed into the room and knelt beside her. Smiled up at her, assessing the damage. Mom's eyes were wide open. She didn't smile back. A giant lump was rising on her head. Wasn't that a good thing—that the swelling was going out instead of in?

Everyone was staring at me. Waiting for me, the Decider.

I'd promised Mom that she'd never have to go to the hospital again: no more bright lights, IVs, or needle sticks. The hospital is the worst possible place for a frail old person with dementia. Mom was disoriented and confused enough already.

I looked at Ian. "I don't want her to go."

He handed me his phone; I knew it was bad cop Jackie. "You have no choice. Temme isn't on hospice. She has to go to the hospital. It's a question of liability."

This is how the game is played. An endless cycle of forced admissions to the ER. Frail, demented people tortured by procedures they don't want or understand.

"What if I spend the night in her room?" *But I can't. My retreat starts tomorrow. I have to pack.*

"No. She has to go to the hospital. If she doesn't go, she can't stay at Redwood Gardens."

I looked at the four burly guys, the residents staring up and down the hall, Ian waiting, Mom in the chair, Karyn stroking her hand.

No way could we care for her at our house, and there wasn't another facility in town that would take her like this, screaming day and night. I didn't want her doped to oblivion in a nursing home. I had promised.

Everyone stared at me, waiting. I sought Karyn's eyes. They said *Yes* and *I'm so sorry.* I slumped against the wall. Mom was screwed, and so was I.

"Take her."

—∞—

I followed the ambulance in my car. I imagined Mom strapped in the back—disoriented, confused, with only a stranger for comfort. *This isn't what you wanted. I'm so sorry.*

I jammed in my Bluetooth earpiece. "Call Paul Davis." My brother had moved to Tiburon, just north of the Golden Gate Bridge. He could be here in two hours.

I kept the ambulance in sight. Three rings. Four rings. *If he leaves now, he can be here by 10:00 p.m. I can get home, finish packing, and still take off by nine tomorrow morning.* Five rings. *C'mon, Paul. Pick up the phone.* Six rings. When he finally answered, I was five minutes from the hospital. "Paul, thank God! It's Mom. She fell and really hurt her head."

"Is she okay? What happened?"

"Of course she's not okay! She's in an ambulance right now. We're heading to the ER."

"How badly is she hurt?"

"I don't know! We haven't gotten there yet."

"I'm so sorry to hear that. Look, Sonya's here. Call us as soon as you have news."

"No, you don't get it, Paul. You need to come. You have to drive down here right now! My big retreat starts tomorrow morning."

Across town, my suitcase sat half-packed in the living room. I had to be at Commonweal by noon. I owed the retreat center $20,000. This was my livelihood. Eli's college tuition. Our mortgage. My reputation. My biggest annual event.

"Paul, you need to come now."

"No way can I come to Santa Cruz. I'm teaching my biggest seminar of the year in just over a week."

"Mine starts tomorrow."

"I'm sorry, but Sonya just got here. I just picked her up from the airport. She's only here for a few days. I never see my daughter."

"Bring her with you. I'm sure she'd love to see her grandma. And Temme would love to see her." I clutched the steering wheel to still my shaking hands.

"She hasn't even unpacked. She just walked in."

Blood pounded in my ears. *How dare you not obey my command!* "I've got people flying in from all over the country tomorrow!" Twenty-one students were arriving to study writing with me for a week. I had to be there. I couldn't lay this on Karyn, not again. It wasn't fair. "I will not ask Karyn to do this. She's already done enough. This is your mother, Paul."

"I have a huge list of things to do, too." His voice rose. "My life is important, too."

I slammed on the brakes at the red light by the hospital. "You promised!"

Paul's voice grew hard, his words clipped. "I'll only come if she's dying."

I hung up on him. I couldn't stop shaking.

I drove through the parking lot like a maniac. Full. All full. When I spied the only empty spot, another car was heading for it, but I cut him off and shot into the space. I ignored the blaring horn, avoided looking at the driver. I would have killed for that spot.

Racing to the ER, clutching the purple binder, I tried to shake off my rage. How could Paul do this to me?

I checked every cubicle, searching for Mom. Huge draperies on giant rings swooshed open as I strode into her room. And there she was. So small, with a warmed white blanket tucked under her chin. She stared at the ceiling, eyes wild, screaming, "Help! Help!" The sound shot right through me, rattling my bones.

I took her hand. "It's okay, Mom. I'm here." But I couldn't catch her eye. She was desperately looking for something, her gaze far from this world.

A nurse, all efficiency and routine, came in to start an IV. "No IV," I said. "She doesn't need one. I'm her health-care proxy. She has a DNR and a POLST." The bright pink Physician Orders for Life-Sustaining Treatment was the most important document in Mom's binder. It told emergency health-care workers exactly what Mom wanted them to do if she was incapacitated.

The nurse turned to face me, taking me in for the first time. "Well, we'd like to give her a catheter. We want to test her urine. Is that okay with you?"

"No. My mother fell. She's here to get her brain scanned and to see if she broke something, and that's all I want you to do."

"Can we take her blood pressure?"

I thought for a moment. "Yes, you can do that."

It was sky high, of course, but we weren't going to treat it, so why bother? The nurse looked at me on her way out to her next patient. "I wish more people came into the hospital with an advocate like you."

There are no chairs in the ER; they get in the way. I scooched Mom over and sat on the edge of her bed. She was looking at me, but she wasn't there. One moment she seemed to recognize me. The next, she stared blankly, yelling "Help! Help!" all over again. It was one thing to be told about that scream; it was entirely different to finally hear it. It was bad. It was awful. She sounded like a trapped animal. Like a wounded child. Like someone so forlorn and alone in the world that no one could possibly reach her. A forgotten part of her was finally rising up to have its say. How many decades had the word "Help!" been trapped inside her?

Mom's ragged voice tore through my solar plexus. The raw sound pinned me in place.

Then I got an idea. Pulled out my phone. Recorded a voice memo of her ragged, naked screams. Attached it to a text. Typed in Paul's number. Hit Send.

Ten minutes later, he texted back. "We're coming. We're leaving now."

For the next two hours, it was just me and Mom, and she never stopped screaming. She screamed all the way down to the diagnostic center, where they took pictures of her hip and a CAT scan of her brain. When we finally returned to her cubicle, I climbed onto the bed and looked into her eyes. Terror and fear and *I have no idea where I am* stared back at me. All her defenses had been stripped away. She was completely untethered. I was seeing the deepest, emptiest places inside her. Fear she'd kept at bay for eighty-six years. I was looking into the eyes of a needy, frightened tenement child.

All I could do was listen and hold her hand.

But then I remembered babysitting my granddaughter, how I'd bounced Ellie on the big red yoga ball in our living room, quieting her to sleep. I didn't know if Mom could hear me, but I put my mouth next to the tiny microphone on her Pocket Talker and sang her the lullaby she had always sung to me. "Hush little baby, don't say a word, Mama's gonna buy you a mockingbird. If that mockingbird won't sing, Mama's gonna buy you a diamond ring . . ."

I'd sung it to Ellie the day before. I'd sung it to Lizzy and to Eli when they were small. And now I sang it to Mom, directly into the microphone, so it was all she could hear, my shaking voice drowning out the frantic shouts of nurses and doctors, beeping machines, patients crying out in pain.

When I got to the last line, "And if that horse and cart fall down, you'll still be the prettiest girl in town," one intact memory rose out of the shambles of Mom's brain. She reached through her delirium and panic and croaked out the epilogue, the one she'd sung to me hundreds of times. She delivered it the same way she had always, in a confiding stage whisper. "I really mean it!"

For that single moment, I had her back.

I squeezed her hand and immediately began another lullaby. "I gave my love a cherry that had no stone. I gave my love a chicken that had no bone . . ." But before I could sing the next line, she started screaming "Help!" again. I held her hand. There was nothing else I could do.

Nurses came in and out. I refused the next blood pressure test and the one after that. "She's on comfort care," one nurse whispered to another. We waited for the X-rays. Waited for the okay that Mom could return to Redwood Gardens, where they might kick her out any day.

All of a sudden, Mom called out in a loud, clear voice, "Laura?"

I brought my ear up close beside her. "What, Mom?"

"When is it going to be over?" Her voice raw. It. When is *it* going to be over. The tests? The horrid bright cubicle? The torment in her brain? Or life itself?

"When is it going to be over?" Each word rasped out over rough stone.

"Soon, Mom. I hope it's over soon." I was referring to her life.

That wild, panicked look came back into her eyes. Like someone being tortured, like someone being ripped in two. "I want it to be over now!"

That's when her trauma passed into me, and I felt the hell that she was in, the hell she had sought to avoid.

I wanted to take a pillow and press it over her face. I wanted to press down hard. I wanted to end it for her. And maybe for myself. But I couldn't. Not in the ER and not ever. But I wanted to. More than I'd ever wanted anything, I wanted to end her suffering. I wanted to end my suffering. I wanted to get that scream out of my head and out of my body. I wanted her to be at peace. I wanted to go home and pack. To get the hell out of town. To shut her up. I didn't want to have to bear her suffering anymore.

At midnight, Paul texted me. He and Sonya had just arrived in town and were on their way. When they swished open the curtain of Mom's cubicle, I hugged them, thanked them, and went home to pack. Six hours later, I left for my weeklong retreat, three and a half hours away.

CHAPTER 67

SANCTUARY

8 Days

Mom was only allowed to return to Redwood Gardens on one condition—if hospice came on board. Paul called them, and they sent a nurse to evaluate her. At first, they wouldn't accept her on their caseload. Mom didn't qualify. She was still eating three meals a day. There was too much meat on her bones. Her dementia wasn't advanced enough. She didn't have any other conditions that were actively terminal. She wasn't "actively dying." But, by emphasizing the reality of her situation, Paul convinced them to take her. She was in agony. She'd broken one hip and was in danger of breaking another. She was about to be kicked out of her home. Maybe hospice could lessen her anxiety with the right combination of drugs. Paul, who'd spent years urging me to treat Mom with natural remedies, asked them to alleviate her suffering with morphine. At his urging, they accepted her onto their caseload on a temporary basis.

The first few days of my retreat, I didn't hear much from home. I became engrossed in my students. I thought about Mom constantly but assumed this was just one more in a long line of crises. I told myself it was good I was away. I was giving Paul the opportunity to step up.

So, I taught. I wrote with my students about my night in the ER. I wrote about how it felt being squeezed between a daughter being launched and a mother about to die. I wrote about elder care and our failing health-care system. It felt good to express the strain of the summer. And of course, my students started writing about their aging parents, their parents' deaths, their own aging. The retreat was rolling.

I had no cell signal at Commonweal, so I could only call Karyn from the phone in the kitchen, with zero privacy, struggling to hear over the loud industrial dishwasher. She didn't say much. She told me that Mom was back in her old room at Redwood Gardens and that she'd taken a turn for the worse. But she didn't tell me how bad things were. That she and Paul were sitting at Mom's bedside eighteen hours a day. That Mom was barely conscious. That she'd looked at Paul and Sonya and failed to recognize them. Karyn later explained, "I didn't want to upset you while you were teaching."

5 DAYS

Two days before my retreat was due to end, I went out for a hike on the headlands above the wild Pacific. On the cliffs, perched above the ocean, there's a little meditation shack—a ramshackle wood hut full of rocks and stones and feathers and totems—left lovingly in remembrance of people who have died. Most of the year, Commonweal is a healing center for people with cancer, and this hut is where people come to pray, meditate, and commemorate the death of their loved ones.

It was a cool afternoon, a breeze blowing in from the ocean. I lay down on my back on the bare wooden floor. I began calling out, "Mom . . . Mom . . ." Soon I was sobbing, and I got a clear message that she was dying. I spoke to her in the silence. "It's okay, Mom. You can go." If she was ready, I was ready. "You don't need to hold on anymore."

If I wanted to see her again, I knew I had to leave right away. Back at the main house, I called to tell Karyn I was coming home. "I'm glad," she said. "Seven crows have been perched outside her room all day."

I sat down with David Colin Carr, the friend and colleague I'd run this workshop with for more than a decade. He offered to facilitate the final days. We mapped out the curriculum. David helped me pack and loaded my car. I had a three-and-a-half-hour drive ahead of me and didn't leave Commonweal until midnight. I had to slap my face all the way over Highway 17 in order to stay awake. What had I been thinking? I arrived home at 4:00 a.m. Redwood Gardens was locked up tight.

Back at home, Karyn met me at the front door and brought me up to date: Paul and Sonya had just left. She, to fly home; Paul, to get ready to teach his big seminar. Eli would be arriving in the afternoon, flying in from Boston.

I crashed for a few ragged hours. At 7:00 a.m., I walked down the street to Redwood Gardens and right into Mom's room. The moment I walked in, I felt it—she was dying. The energetic vortex of birth and death was palpable in the room, that vibration of complete focus necessary when we enter or leave this world.

She was in a deep morphine sleep, and the subtle scent of decay wafted off her body. I could smell it on her breath—the odor of organs disintegrating, systems shutting down. Her face still looked the same, but death was there. I could feel it, and I stepped into the zone with her. Everything else fell away.

Mom's room had been transformed into a sanctuary, the staff no longer hovering. She was no longer a crisis to be managed; we had entered sacred time. My mother, tucked deep inside herself, doing the hard work of dying. Me, there for the duration. I pulled up a chair, as close to her as I could get, and took her hand. "Mom, I'm here." I stroked the soft white hair off her forehead. She was still beautiful, her face soft, her cheeks ruddy and full. She didn't look like someone who was dying. But she was leaving us. She was on her way to freedom.

A few hours later, the hospice team came to meet me. The nurse explained what to watch for. "She could die anytime. Or she could last a week or more." Every day, they sent an aide to turn her, to clean her, to check for bedsores.

Mom had stopped eating the day before and now was refusing water. The nurse taught me to dip a little green sponge on the end of a stick into a glass of water and to place it in her mouth. She sucked it like a hungry baby bird. Was she really thirsty, or was it just a reflex?

Late that afternoon, Mom opened her eyes and recognized me. I could see it in her face: her anchor was back. She tried to speak, but all that came out was a low, rumbling groan. What was she trying to tell me? More than anything in the world, I wanted to know.

—∾—

The next four days were holy. We took turns by her bedside as she labored to die. She would slip under the morphine, then awaken and look into my eyes.

Early one morning, as we traded shifts, I hugged Lizzy in the hallway. As I released her, I realized that the woman who birthed me was leaving; the girl I birthed was leaving, too.

That afternoon, Bryan came by with baby Ellie—luscious, vibrant, ten months old. I played with her in the Redwood Gardens living room. She was doing a combat crawl with one leg stuck straight out to the side, and every time I peeked at her from behind the curtains, I was rewarded with a huge belly laugh. Ellie smelled like life, the top of her head still fragrant with a hint of the world she had come from—the world to which Mom was about to go. I remember that afternoon as incredibly sweet. Playing with my granddaughter; my mother dying down the hall.

Would I ever stretch across four generations again?

—∾—

During my mother's final days, I obsessed over the fact that I didn't know how to help her die. As I watched her struggling, panting, and writhing, I remembered all the stories I'd read about people dying, their transit from one realm to the next eased by shamans, psychics, gurus, and healers. I didn't qualify. I had no spiritual powers. I was just her daughter—a middle-aged woman with a shoddy meditation practice.

One afternoon, as Mom slumbered in a morphine sleep, I slipped out to the patio and called my friend Nancy London, a hospice social worker. We'd been texting back and forth for days, a line here, a line there. "How's it going today, Laura?" And I'd tell her. This was the first time we'd connected by phone, and the moment I heard her voice, I started sobbing. "I've never had a mother die before. I know I'm not doing it right. I'm not spiritual enough. I should have meditated more. I should have read *The Tibetan Book of Living and Dying.* I don't know how to help her cross to the other side. I don't know how to help her through the *bardo*," the Tibetan Buddhist term for the state of existence after death and before rebirth.

Nancy laughed, the rich, melodic laugh I knew so well. "Laura, you have nothing to worry about. Your mother wasn't a *bardo* kind of gal. Just love her. That's all you have to do."

I laughed as relief flooded through me. Love her? I could do that. Finally, after all these years, that was something I could do.

1 DAY

On Mom's last morning in this world, Anna, the hospice aide, asked, "Would you like to help me give your mother a bath?" She explained that we would do it right there, with Mom in bed. "She's working hard. She's sweaty. It might make her feel good."

I trusted Anna and hospice, so I said yes.

It was quiet in the room. No machines beeping or monitors humming. Mom's body free of tubes and wires. The way I wanted it to be. The way I'd promised her it would be.

Anna demonstrated what to do with gestures and quiet words. We worked in synch, rolling Mom over to slip a waterproof pad beneath her. Anna showed me how to use plastic squeeze bottles of soap and shampoo that required no rinsing. With expert hands, she removed Mom's sweaty gown. She began at her head; I began at her feet. Anna moved efficiently, silently, her hands a living prayer. I followed her movements, amazed at how hard she scrubbed Mom's body.

I thought about all the times my mother had bathed me when I was small. All the decades I had recoiled from her touch. Now she was naked before me, and I moved my hands across her failing body with the same awe and tenderness I'd felt bathing my infants for the first time. Mom wasn't emaciated like a cancer patient. Her belly, still full and round. I lay my cheek on her soft, yielding center. I grew in there. *You made me. That's where Vicki and I wrapped our arms around each other. Then she left me. She left* us. Now Mom was leaving, too.

"Goodbye, Mom." I added in a whisper, so quiet Anna couldn't hear, "Tell Vicki I miss her."

It was a sacrament. We washed every part of her except the bedsores that had sprouted overnight. When Anna lathered Mom's hair, Mom moaned with pleasure. The last pleasure she would ever feel. Mom loved clean hair, and I combed it out for the very last time.

The bath lasted much longer than I would have expected. When we finally finished, Anna gathered up the used bottles and wet pads. We dressed Mom in a clean gown. She looked happy and beautiful; her face was radiant. "Thank you," I said, hugging Anna.

"My pleasure," she replied.

"Would you come back after she dies so we can do it again?"

"Yes, I will."

CHAPTER 68

JOURNEY

10 hours

That afternoon, my mother took my hands. She was drifting in and out of a morphine haze, her body shaking as it dissolved in front of me. But then she opened her eyes, grabbed my hands, and didn't let go. I held on to her hands, still warm, and we stared into each other's eyes.

People came and went, but I ignored them. My back screamed, hunched in that chair for hours, but I never moved. Mom struggled to speak. She desperately wanted to tell me something, and I desperately wanted to hear it, but all that came out was a low rolling groan. Her language was gone.

She stared at me with the same intensity with which she'd pulled me into this world, and she took me on a journey. Into a tunnel. A place we'd been before. Stretched out on one side were all the places we'd been together, not just as this mother and this daughter, but before. In that tunnel were all the befores: before I was her child, before I was the two-pound, twelve-ounce preemie, before I was her little girl, the sullen teenager, the strident young adult, before I was the mother of her grandchildren, her protector, her caregiver, the one to mother her.

Past lives had always been Paul's thing, but now, as Mom held me on the edge of life, on the portal of her death, she showed me how big we were. *We have been to all these places,* her eyes told me. Then she pointed the other way. *Those are the places we have yet to go.* Her eyes burned the vision into me—the two of us stretching far out into the future. Her eyes said, *You need to understand that we are so much bigger than this small struggle to love that we've been engaged in. We are so much vaster. Our time together on earth, our dance of love and hate, is just a small part of who we are.*

Mom had been shuddering her way toward death all week, her cells dissolving toward their final rest. She hadn't spoken or eaten in days, yet she showed me that our history was so much bigger than the story we had lived, than the stories I had told.

Crouching over her hospital bed, I was certain I was watching her die. Mom was done with life, flaming right by me like a star, working hard at death, letting go of her vast, imperious grip on this world. But she had one last thing to tell me. Transmitting through her eyes the one thing she hadn't been able to give me in life. *It's okay, darling. You can surpass me.* She gave me permission to stand on her shoulders, carrying her blazing, broken heart in my hands.

PART V

"Blessed is the flame that burns in the secret places of the heart."

—Janet Bieber, after "Ashrei Hagafrur," by Hannah Szenes

CHAPTER 69

SNAPSHOT

+1 Day

I have a picture of my mother, dead, on my iPhone, and I don't know what to do with it. I snapped it after her aide arrived with her 2:00 a.m. dose of morphine on July 24, 2014. I was asleep, curled up in the blue recliner at the foot of the bed. Temme's caregiver, Marta, shook my shoulder and whispered, "Laura . . . Laura . . ." I clawed back from sleep to the smell of decay. Marta's voice was warm. "Laura, she's gone."

After all my mother's suffering, all those weeks of screaming, she had died silently in her sleep.

I uncurled my body from the recliner and touched her cooling face. Her mouth was ajar, her skin still soft. Her chest wasn't moving. Or was it? No, it wasn't.

Because she was in hospice, no code blue screamed. They left us alone. Redwood Gardens was quiet, the residents asleep.

I called Karyn and the kids, and Paul, and told them to come. It would take my brother several hours to arrive. My family needed ten minutes to wake up, five to walk over. I'd be alone for the next fifteen minutes.

I wished I knew the *Kaddish*, the Jewish prayer for the dead, but I didn't, so I sang Mom a lullaby instead. Ran my fingers over her belly. Stroked her hair. Her legs still straight and thin. "You got your wish, Mom. It's finally over."

I reached for my bag, grabbed my phone, and took a final headshot. A tiny icon on my camera roll, never downloaded.

When Karyn and the kids arrived, we sang and cried and touched her. Shared stories about her final days. When they left, I texted Anna, the hospice aide, and she came right over. In silence, we washed my mother's corpse. Repeating the motions from the day before, squeezing, scrubbing, patting, and drying. But it was different this time. Mom's body was dead weight—heavy, stiff, hard. Blood had pooled into her back, lividity discoloring it like a bruise. We had to cut her clothes off, but there was no need to be gentle anymore.

"Do you want to dress her?" Anna asked when we were through. "Or do you want to leave her as she is?"

"As she is. How she came into this world."

I sat with her body, wrapped in a sheet, as I waited for Paul to arrive. He slid in quietly just as the promise of sun was lightening the sky. We sat beside her, holding hands, and talked about being her children. The things we loved. The things we hated. Her quirks. Her magnificence. Her powerful essence. How her epic struggle was finally over.

Nobody rushed us. We sat in our bubble as the residents of Redwood Gardens awakened around us. Before her shift ended, Marta gently tapped on the door and brought us oatmeal—two plastic bowls, a thin pat of butter melting on top. We took small gummy bites with thin metal spoons, Mom wrapped in a shroud beside us.

When we said we were ready, an attendant from the mortuary came to take her body. He asked if we wanted to leave the room. "No, we want to stay." We wanted to see everything.

He transferred her to a gurney, covered her in blue velvet, and wheeled her out, not through the front door, but through the sliding glass doors into the courtyard. It was standard operating procedure. Don't traumatize the old people by wheeling a dead body down the hall. As if they didn't know that they'd be next.

CHAPTER 70

FIRE

+3 Days

When it was time for Mom's cremation, Paul and I wanted to watch. I had attended several cremations in Bali: festivities in which the whole community gathers, parading through the streets to the cremation grounds where they celebrate the burning of the dead. The Balinese believe the dead cannot be released for reincarnation until their bodies have been burned, their ashes returned to the sea. Because most Balinese can't afford the high cost of cremation, they bury their loved ones in temporary graves, and later, sometimes years later, dig up the bones and carry them on biers through the streets. Pallbearers twirl them in sweeping circles at every corner so that evil spirits will be too disoriented to follow. Relatives follow behind, dressed in bright colors. At the cremation grounds, flames roar as the Balinese laugh, chat, gossip, and eat. Tourists are welcome; the more people who witness the cremation, the better.

I'd been deeply moved by this ritual, so several years earlier, when I'd finalized Mom's funeral arrangements, I asked the mortician if Paul and I could watch.

"Yes," he said. "It's called a witness cremation."

"Sign us up."

—∾—

The day before her funeral, Paul and I showed up at the crematorium along with the hearse. When we explained why we were there, the man sitting at the desk had no idea what to do with us. He put us at the desk next to his and got right back to his sales calls, as if we weren't there. On the wall behind us, a long horizontal window looked into the back room—the room that held the crematory, the giant roaring furnace where Mom's body would burn.

The attendant wheeled her body into the crematory and drew the curtain, shutting us out. Paul and I exchanged a glance. In a strong yet polite voice, I said to the man at the desk, "We came here to watch."

He looked away, a flush rising in his cheeks. "I . . . I don't know about that. I'll have to call my supervisor."

"Well, call him right now," Paul said. "It's what we signed up for."

I was prepared to say whatever it took. "Tell him it's our religion." I said it in the sincerest voice I could muster. Paul shot me a big smile, and five minutes later, we were in.

The crematory dominated the cramped back room. It squatted there like any other large industrial machine. All we could see was a huge, closed metal door. It wasn't like an oven with a window and a light inside. Apparently, we weren't going to get to "watch" after all. But Mom's body was definitely inside. Definitely burning. We could hear the whoosh of flame.

The attendant handed us two metal folding chairs and told us the cremation would take three to four hours. "I'll come in periodically to stir the bones, but mostly you'll be here alone."

Paul and I squeezed into the only narrow spot available, arranged our chairs facing each other, knees almost touching.

We'd gotten in. Now what? For a while, we just listened to Mom burning. As I gazed at my brother, love welled up inside me. There is nothing more intimate than sitting together in the room where your mother is on fire.

Paul said, "I've got an idea. Since we're going to sit here anyway, how about doing a forgiveness practice?"

I didn't know what that was—probably a ritual he'd picked up at his latest spiritual retreat—but it seemed like a good idea, considering the gravity of the moment.

I said yes.

Paul took my hands, closed his eyes, and started chanting. I wanted to be polite, but his singsong chanting, in the language of his latest spiritual teacher, went on too long. I felt that familiar mixture of discomfort, guilt, and resentment. *C'mon, Paul. Enough already. Open your eyes.*

When he finally did, his deep blue eyes met mine.

Paul apologized for all the ways he'd ever wronged me, a long litany, starting with the time he babysat me and tied the feet of my pajamas to the coffee table. He'd loved tormenting me when we were young. Now he was sorry. Sorry he'd shut me out when he was a teenager. Sorry he hadn't been there when I was a lost young adult. Paul had a long list of things he was sorry for. Some I didn't even remember. He asked if he'd forgotten anything.

"Well . . ." I hesitated. But holding back was not an option in this room. "There is one thing. When I told you about the incest with Poppa, you said it happened because of something terrible I did in a past life. You actually told me I needed it to grow. It started when I was three years old, Paul! I needed it to grow?"

"I'm sorry, Laura. But I still believe we choose our families for a reason."

"Well, your belief hurt me."

Paul glanced away. "I can see that now." When he looked back, he sought my eyes. "I'm really sorry, Laura."

I met his gaze. "Thank you. That means a lot to me."

The crematory roared in the wake of his apology, Mom's skin blistering, her body drying out. Paul kept staring at me. I had that awkward feeling again. What was he waiting for?

Me. He was waiting for me. It was my turn.

I had a lot of regret where my brother was concerned. My words tumbled out like a prayer. "I'm sorry I've judged you. I'm sorry I shunned you when I left the *ashram*, and you didn't. I'm sorry I've rolled my eyes at your spiritual practices. I'm sorry I didn't show up for you after your divorce. I'm sorry I haven't made special time for you at Thanksgiving. I'm sorry I've held you at arm's length. I'm sorry I haven't made our relationship a priority."

It felt good to finally admit the truth. And Paul knew how to listen. Steady. Present. I could tell he liked my apology.

For a few minutes, the only sound was Mom's body burning. Paul spoke into that searing sound—our mother's muscles charring, soft tissue vaporizing. "Laura, do you want to have a relationship with me? Will you really be my sister?"

Did Paul just say what I thought he said? His eyes held steady and were surprisingly free of expectation. I took a breath. I guess this was the conversation we were going to have.

Paul spoke in a steady stream. "Now both our parents are dead. We're the next in line for death, the last members of our family."

He was right. We were the elders now.

"There's nothing holding us together anymore. Mom was the glue. If we're going to stay connected, more than polite talk at family gatherings, we have to be the ones to make it happen. We don't have to take care of Mom anymore . . ."

We? "Jesus, Paul. It wasn't *we*. It was *me*. You dipped in and out, and Mom acted like you were God incarnate every time you dropped in, but Karyn and I were the ones who did the heavy lifting."

Paul didn't hesitate. "You're right, and I'm sorry. There are times I was selfish. I took the jobs I wanted, that were convenient for me. I didn't want to see the stress you were under."

My throat burned. "The last six years have been really hard, Paul. They've been . . ."

We were interrupted by the attendant, returning with a long metal hoe. He'd come in to break up the bones and asked us to step outside. Paul and I looked at each other. "We want to stay," we said in unison. "It's our religion."

The attendant shrugged, then wrenched open the heavy metal door. The blast of heat made us gasp. Mom's bones lay scattered across the floor of the crematory, but her skull glowed red with fire. Lit up till the end. She looked great. She looked . . . beautiful.

The attendant shattered the remaining intact bones but left her skull intact, luminous with flame. When he closed the heavy door, the whoosh of fire, once again, filled the room.

—∞—

Paul looked back at me. "So . . . ?"

I lifted my eyes. The man who looked back at me was a good man, the sincerest person I'd ever met. I tried to feel my heart, to make it larger, to create space for him to come in. I longed to trust him. But it was easier to hold up his mistakes as a shield. I'd kept my brother in the anteroom, just where I'd kept Mom. I hadn't made myself vulnerable to her, and I didn't make myself vulnerable to him.

As Mom's bones shifted in the oven, I felt a nudge from beyond. Mom had told me I could surpass her, and this was my chance.

Looking into my brother's face, I recognized him. I recognized *us.* My eyes in his eyes. My chin in his chin. The pain and love in his eyes, the same as the pain and love in mine. Paul held pieces of my history no one else would ever know. I wanted to know him.

As I met his steady gaze, heat surged up my spine. All the love I'd repressed and pushed away rushed back. My heart connected to his heart, as if it had always belonged there. I released Vicki's spirit and embraced the man in front of me. My voice broke as I gave Paul his answer. "Yes, I will be your sister."

He smiled and squeezed my hands.

The only sound in the room was Mom on fire.

—∞—

For the next hour, as flames took Mom's right kneecap and left kneecap, her tibia and fibula, her eye sockets and jaw, we talked about her. What we remembered, what we'd miss. What we wouldn't miss.

I told him about Vicki—the sister he had never known. Paul knew I'd been a twin, of course, but to him, Vicki was nothing more than a footnote. "Losing Vicki affected my whole life, Paul."

"That's huge. What a loss for you." It felt good to hear him say it. It felt good for him to know. Risking a smile, he said, "Wow. I would have had to deal with two of you."

I laughed and punched my brother's arm. "You wouldn't have stood a chance."

—∞—

Three hours is a long time. We discussed everything: our work, our kids, our plans for the future. The whole time, Mom kept burning. Each time the attendant wrenched the door open, there was less of her. At the end, her skull collapsed into glowing embers; her bones crumbled, heat transforming the indomitable Temme Davis into shards and dust, until just a small pile of ash remained, with a few unremarkable chunks. Our mother was unrecognizable. Her body was no more.

—∞—

By the time Paul and I emerged, the fog had burned off and the sun warmed our skin. It was a bright summer day. I slid into the driver's seat and turned to my brother. "I want to take you somewhere."

Twenty minutes later, I parked on West Cliff Drive. "Let's take a walk."

As we strolled along the snaking path, I slid my arm in his. Teenagers whizzed by on Rollerblades. Women pushed babies in strollers, and friends walked dogs. Old couples sauntered as if they had all the time in the world. I led Paul to a wooden bench on the cliff, facing the ocean. "This was our bench. Where Mom and I came to sit. This is where we talked about the end of her life, how she wanted to . . ."

"Quit while I'm ahead." Paul finished the sentence, and we both laughed.

I plunked down right next to him, despite ample space on either side. I leaned into his shoulder, and he wrapped his arm around me.

The next day would be Mom's funeral. As soon as we drove back to my house, we'd be swept up in a sea of people: Karyn and the kids. Sonya. Bryan and his family. Relatives who'd flown in. Family friends.

But right now, it was just the two of us, sitting together on Mom's bench.

"Paul, I don't know many people who would do what we just did."

"Do you think it's okay that we watched?"

"Well, she always did love an audience." We both laughed again.

Paul and I leaned back on Mom's bench and stared out at the sea. Two surfers rode the smooth curl of a wave all the way back to shore. "But what she'd love even more is the two of us like this."

I reached out and took my brother's hand.

AUTHOR'S NOTE

I have written *The Burning Light of Two Stars* over the past ten years, but the events in this book have lived with me for decades. I've composed multiple versions of many of these stories over the years. Each new rendering has reflected the level of maturity, compassion, and understanding that I had at the time. Each provides a different lens into the past.

My outlook on many of these events has changed dramatically over the past thirty years. As one of my former students, the writer Debra Fruchey, once put it, "Every time I look in the rearview mirror, the past has changed." Even now, six years after my mother's death, my perspective on us and our relationship is still evolving. If I were to write this memoir ten years from now, the story would take new forms, and I would probably come to different conclusions.

A number of my early readers mentioned that my immediate family members (Karyn and our kids) are not fully fleshed out as characters in this book. This was intentional. I assure you that they are fully three-dimensional in real life, but they're private people who have had to regularly come to terms with my choice to be far more public than they prefer to be. They've been incredibly generous in letting me include them in this story to the extent that I have, so I have chosen to respect their privacy and limit my portrayal of their lives.

My brother, Paul, has supported this project from the beginning and read it through many iterations. He asked for changes in the text, and I adapted my portrayal of our relationship accordingly. One thing I'm very happy to report is that our sibling relationship has improved significantly since we completed the ritual described at the end of this book. Paul and I regularly connect and have grown closer. I chalk this up to Paul's persistence, my willingness to listen and change, and the lessons I received from my mother at the end of her life.

—Laura Davis
December 2020

ABOUT THIS BOOK

The Burning Light of Two Stars is a representation of my relationship with my mother as I remember it. As with all stories that rely on memory, I've done my best to portray events and people as honestly and realistically as possible. To bolster my fallible and biased recollections, I relied on notes and stories I wrote over the course of many years, journal entries—mine and hers—and years of correspondence between us, as well as videos and interviews that we recorded together while my mother was still alive. Yet despite my efforts to create a true rendering of these events, there is always more than one truth. Inevitably, others will recall these same events differently, but this is how I remember them, how they live in my heart and in my body.

One of the main challenges in telling an autobiographical story is figuring out what to leave in and what to leave out. I chose scenes and events that served the greater arc of my story—how a mother and daughter can become so estranged and then find their way back to each other. Because my focal point was the mother-daughter relationship, I honed in on that, minimizing the importance of other characters and relationships, leaving out the huge network of loving people that surrounded my mother all her life. The fact that most of her family members and friends do not appear in this book doesn't mean they weren't vitally important to her, only that theirs isn't the story I chose to tell.

As with most memoirs, I have eliminated minor characters, compressed time, estimated dates, and approximated dialogue, though I could often hear my mother's voice in my head as I wrote. To avoid repetition, I created some composite scenes to better convey the impact of key events that occurred repeatedly.

The letters are transcribed from the original correspondence. They have been shortened and, in minor instances, edited for clarity.

The following people are identified by pseudonyms or former names: Anna, Bea, Cynthia, Michael, Dr. Reed, Ruth, Fiona, Gail, Gwen, Ian, Jackie, Jane, Howard, Paul, Coleman Shaw. The name of the last facility where my mother lived and died has also been changed.

IF YOU'RE DEALING WITH A PAINFUL ESTRANGEMENT

For some readers, the theme of estrangement explored in this book is a real and painful reality. Now that you've read *The Burning Light of Two Stars*, you know how complex and challenging, and ultimately rewarding, the reconciliation process was for me and my mother. As she noted in one of our visits at Sunshine Villa, our story had "a happy ending." Not everything was resolved between us, but enough was that we were able to successfully renew our relationship. This required commitment, flexibility, humor, and hard work—over many years—from both of us. Because of what we ultimately achieved, I was able to be my mother's caregiver at the end of her life, a passage I am grateful to have been able to share with her. When my mother died, I felt complete, even though not everything had been resolved between us.

At the height of our estrangement, when we both felt betrayed and armored, sequestered in our warring camps, neither of us could have imagined that we'd ever attain this level of connection. If you'd suggested it, I would have insisted that it was impossible. Yet several decades later, I was the one at her deathbed. That's why I always tell people, "You can't be absolutely certain of the final outcome until both people are dead." And even after one person has passed, in circumstances where direct person-to-person reconciliation has been ill advised or inconceivable, it is still possible for the remaining family member to attain inner peace with a relationship that could not be resolved in life or in person.

My mother and I achieved real success in our reconciliation, yet I want to caution you against using us as a model for what you should be able to achieve in your own life.

Some of you may long for reconciliation; others may be certain that you don't want a relationship with the person or people you're estranged from, that your best course of action is to maintain firm boundaries and focus on living the best life that you can without them. Each situation is different, and there are circumstances in which keeping an abusive or toxic person out of your life is the wisest, healthiest choice, despite strong pressure—internally or externally—to do otherwise. You should never sacrifice your own well-being to maintain a psychologically devastating relationship.

I explored these questions in depth in *I Thought We'd Never Speak Again: The Road from Estrangement to Reconciliation.* The book doesn't provide one solution or a clear set of steps to resolving family estrangements, because relationships are far too complex for that. Rather, I describe four possible reconciliation scenarios. The first is the most coveted and difficult to achieve—interpersonal healing that is deep and transformative for both parties, where true intimacy is established or reestablished. The second scenario occurs when one person changes their perspective and is able to view the relationship differently even if the other person doesn't make significant changes. In the third option, both parties "agree to disagree" and create a limited but cordial relationship. And in the fourth and final option, a viable relationship with the other person remains impossible, and the route for resolution and healing is within yourself. Although this is not the outcome most people prefer, it, too, can bring peace.

To discover which path of reconciliation is right for you, I highly recommend that you read *I Thought We'd Never Speak Again.* You'll learn about the human qualities necessary to resolve estrangements and read moving, honest, intimate stories of people in a wide range of scenarios—from family conflict to restorative justice—demonstrating how they found peace after years of anguish over broken, damaged relationships. You can learn more here:

www.lauradavis.net/reconciliation

ENHANCE YOUR EXPERIENCE OF *THE BURNING LIGHT OF TWO STARS*

SEVEN GIFTS FOR READERS

Visit Laura Davis's website and join her mailing list to access the following bonus material:

- Photos of the main characters who populate the pages of *The Burning Light of Two Stars,* including original images from the day Temme was crowned Campus Queen.
- An exclusive slideshow of a 2001 photo shoot with Laura and Temme, taken in the lead-up to the publication of *I Thought We'd Never Speak Again.*
- Special access to a videotape of Temme's brilliant performance in the *Vagina Monologues,* as described in chapter 32.
- A wide-ranging historical audio interview Laura recorded with Temme in the StoryCorps van in Salinas, California, in March 2009. Many readers have asked to learn more about Temme's background. This interview, filled with great stories about her early life, provides an engaging and moving account of her history in her own rich, melodious voice.
- A downloadable PDF featuring several dramatic scenes from *The Burning Light of Two Stars* that ended up on the cutting room floor. It was painful for Laura to cut these scenes out of the book—especially the one in which she drops acid with her father, but the book was too long, and

some scenes just had to go. But if you'd still like a chance to find out more about Laura's relationship with her free-wheeling hippie dad, this is your chance.

- A free downloadable e-book that Laura created to help people meet life's toughest challenges: *Writing Toward Courage: A Thirty-Day Practice.* You don't have to consider yourself a writer to benefit from the inspiring quotes and provocative questions that fill this book.
- As a final gift, you'll start receiving weekly writing prompts in your inbox. These evocative quotes and probing questions, thoughtfully curated by Laura, are invaluable and thought-provoking to writers and non-writers alike. You can unsubscribe at any time.

www.lauradavis.net/readergifts

IF YOU LOVED THIS BOOK, HELP ME SPREAD THE WORD:

A book like *The Burning Light of Two Stars* makes its way into the hearts and hands of readers primarily through word of mouth: one reader telling another, "You've *got* to read this great book!" through their own networks, both on- and offline.

You, as a satisfied reader, are my best tool for spreading the word about the book. So, if you loved *The Burning Light of Two Stars,* I'd like to ask you to take a moment to tell others about it.

Here are a few specific things that can really help:

- Review the book. Reviews make a huge difference. Take a few minutes now, while the book is still fresh in your mind, to post a review. The two most important places for reviews are on Amazon and Goodreads. But feel free to review the book on whatever online bookseller you favor: print, e-book or audiobook. With Amazon, it's the number of reviews that matter, not the length, so your review can be short and simple. The more readers who post reviews, the more Amazon shows the book to people. And you don't need to have bought the book on Amazon to post a review. Just go to the book's Amazon page, click on the ratings at the top, then click, "Write a customer review." For Goodreads, click on the "reviews" at the top of the page and then on "Write a review." It's perfectly acceptable to copy and paste the same review in multiple places.

- Tell your friends on- and offline about *The Burning Light of Two Stars*. Post a recommendation or review on social media, in a newsletter or blog, in an online group, or bring it up in conversation with family, colleagues, or friends. You can go to this page on my website to find easy links for sharing the book on social media: www.lauradavis.net/media. It's easy to just click and go. Or use a picture of yourself holding the book.
- Ask your local library to carry the book.
- If you know anyone who has a podcast, TV show, radio show, newsletter, blog, organization, or big social media following where they talk about books on writing, aging, caregiving, relationships, sexual abuse, mothers and daughters, healing, or what it takes to be human—any of the themes in *The Burning Light of Two Stars*—recommend the book to them. Better yet, send them a copy. If appropriate, suggest that they invite me on as a guest.
- Suggest that your book club / class / church group / recovery meeting / grief support group read and discuss *The Burning Light of Two Stars*. If your group buys in bulk and invites me, I'll happily be a guest via Skype or Zoom. You can learn more at www.lauradavis.net/bookclubs.

Thanks so much for helping me to spread the word! It really makes a difference.

Laura Davis

ACKNOWLEDGMENTS

It took me more than ten years to write *The Burning Light of Two Stars*, and in that time, I was helped by so many people in so many ways. Specifically, I'd like to thank:

Joshua Townshend-Zellner, without whom *The Burning Light of Two Stars* would not exist. Joshua coached me through the last year and a half of this project. A brilliant actor and director who deeply understands the twists and turns of the creative process, Joshua believed in me and my story, and more than anyone, empowered me to birth this book into its final form. I am grateful for all that he taught me about storytelling and how to craft compelling, multilayered scenes.

Susan Brown, friend and colleague, nurtured this book in its infancy, always offering her incisive, deep knowledge about structure to my story. Susan believed in this project before anyone else did and helped me keep the flame alive when I wanted to quit. I'm particularly grateful for her warmth, tough love, hospitality, generous coaching, and most of all, her insistence that I must tell more of the truth as the story's protagonist. I'll never forget the day I was riding shotgun in her car when she told me, "This memoir is about the courage to *reveal*, Laura, not the courage to heal."

Debra Gwartney, gifted editor and memoir teacher, squeezed my unfinished book into her very full life for an editorial assist at a crucial time.

Ellen Bass offered her brilliance with language and sensitively and lovingly let me know that the book wasn't finished when I thought it was—and then generously taught me exactly what I needed to do in my next set of revisions. Here's to forty years of being coauthors, writing companions, and always family.

Carolyn Brigit Flynn and the members of our Wednesday afternoon writers' group: Marigold Fine, Judy Phillips, Ratna Jennifer Sturz, Barbara Thomas, Janet Croteau, Nancy Grace, Carolyn Davis Rudolph, Michelle Shulman, and Susan Rothenberg, for more than a decade sharing our lives, our words, and sacred space.

Marian Oliker and her wonderful Motion Theater class, for teaching me to tell stories spontaneously and on my feet, along with my beautiful performing partners: Santoshi Wagner-Anue, Deo Robbins, Rob Anue, Sheryl Loomis, Salima Cobb, Pilar Martin, and April Burns. And to Nina Wise, founder of Motion Theater, for creating a brilliant form of storytelling and artistic expression.

Ann Randolph, for her wonderful *From the Page to the Stage* workshops, and to all the writers and performers I met and worked with there, in particular Margaret Wrinkle, Johanna Courtleigh, and Ron Robinson. The seeds for several stories in this book were birthed in the safe space Ann so lovingly creates.

Natalie Goldberg, for the gift of three decades of writing practice, as both student and teacher.

Wilma Marcus, for telling me that my first draft of this story was definitely not destined to be a play, and that I should just go ahead and write it as a memoir.

Charlotte Raymond, my long-time agent, and her daughter, Alyssa Raymond, a brilliant editor, for friendship, hospitality, and the countless hours they dedicated to reading multiple drafts of this book. The whole Raymond family welcomed and hosted our family whenever we were in Massachusetts visiting our kids. We loved staying in their house, conversing in their living room, and savoring the delicious meals Alan cooked for us.

Nancy London, for being writing buddies and teaching companions, and for our sparky friendship. For her belief in this project over the course of so many years, for reading drafts and for sharing hours of conversation about our mothers, our shadows, and our lives.

David Colin Carr, for years of loving, supportive collaboration, companionship, and editorial support in early drafts of this book.

Karen Zelin, for four decades of sisterhood and friendship, always seeing me clearly, being a willing beta reader—anytime—and especially for our conversations at Tassajara, which helped me shape the final draft of this book.

Evelyn Hall, for journeys, healing, and enduring friendship.

Nona Olivia, for being the first person who helped me understand my relationship with my mother, and for sisterhood that sustains the soul.

Barbara Cymrot, for always showing up. And for consistently good advice.

Nancy Gertz, for support, perspective, sisterhood, and our great pandemic early morning phone calls.

Hollye Dexter, for being a colleague, cheerleader, editor, role model, and friend.

Amy Ferris, for being a fan of this project and my ability to pull it off when it was still a tiny seed.

Dale Thielges, for her support while Temme was alive, and her careful reading of this book with an eye toward issues surrounding caregiving, Alzheimer's, and memory loss.

Sandra Balderrama, for reviewing the scenes about my father and her mother, Ophelia Balderrama, my father's partner for the last seventeen years of his life.

Tova Green, for the joy of teaching together and for her unmitigated support of me and this book.

April Eberhardt, for exquisite guidance through the unfamiliar maze of hybrid publishing.

Robert Peters and his assistant, Ruth Jarvis, of Fresh Eyes Consultancy, a great web team who's kept my website going and growing for years.

Jen Petras, the best virtual assistant anyone could ever hope for. Thank you for your efficiency, cheerfulness, humor, and always figuring out the best way to do the job.

Neil Roberts, for the best tech help, day or night, in the universe.

Girl Friday Books, for partnering with me to publish this manuscript and bring it out into the world. Ingrid Emerick, for enthusiasm and integrity, Katherine Richards, for being unflappable, steady, and prepared no matter what I threw her way, Bethany Davis, for her amazing attention to detail, Georgie Hockett, for her commitment and deep knowledge of marketing, and Paul Barrett, for a beautiful design.

Becky Parker Geist and her team at Pro Audio Voices, for expertise and holding my hand through the audiobook production process. I love the way Becky supported my vision and brought all my secondary characters to life. It was a real pleasure to stand in my little sound booth recording together week after week.

For essential and generous help getting me set up to record the audiobook version of *The Burning Light of Two Stars*, my sons Eli Davis and Bryan Rawles (who built me a sound booth in my office closet) and Andy and David Sumberg, who calmly took my repeated, panicked calls about how to use Audacity.

Sue Campbell, for clarity, creativity, and optimism in our many book marketing consultations, and for always having the answers I needed.

Kim Dower of Kim from LA, my publicist, for falling in love with this story and helping me tell the world about it.

Vanya Erickson and Autumn Vandiver, for research and good cheer.

Cathy Krizik, my graphic designer, for responsiveness, speed, and amazing work, time and time again.

Claire Chao, for sharing resources and mutual support, indie author to indie author.

My writing students, past and present: You help make me who I am and stretch me to learn more so I can teach you. You inspire me with your open hearts, hard work, dedication to craft, and sacred presence in our beloved community. Thank you for trusting me and for your deep love of writing. And for your support of this book, always.

All my beta readers. So many people took the time to read the manuscript and give me honest feedback. I hope I've remembered everyone: Natalie Devora, Evelyn Hall, Talin Vartanian, Kat Lancaster, Keith Rand, Hollye Dexter, Enid Brock, Karen Zelin, Susan Doherty, Shauna Smith, Karyn Bristol, Nancy Gertz, Tova Green, Kimlin McDaniel Keith, Jennifer Meyer, Marlene Bumgarner, Kay Taylor, Natalie Devora, Melinda Iuster, Nancy London, Jane Richey, Dana Hemmert, Santoshi Wagner Anue, Kimberly Crum, Rita Scangetti, Betsy Blankenbaker, Betsy Fasbinder, Sandra Brown, Adrienne Drake, Dale Thielges, Elizabeth Becker, Julie Tave, Jackie Baritell, Nancy Brown, Abby Stamelman Hocky, Susan Levin, Nancy Rosulek and

Daniel Kramer, Joan Rippe, Debbie Owen, Janet Gellman, Carol Barry, Irene Hall, Vanya Erickson, Toni Taylor, Cathy Krizik, Cliff Friedlander, Jen Astone, Judy Astone, Renee Winter, Jan Landry, Nancy Guinter, Cindy Shulak-Rome, Claire Moore, Brenda Lange, Danilyn Rutherford, Sunny Shaw, Bing Shaw, Julie Olsen Edwards, Eileene Tejada, Howard Dillon, Mara Tuiletufuga Willis, Susan Doherty, Salima Cobb, Ratna Jennifer Sturz, Lis Bensley, Rachel Michelberg, China Gallant, Rhonda Levine, Rosa-Linda Fregoso, Roz Spafford, Lucie Eggleston, Elya Brayden, Terry Spodick, Beverly Pincus, Sherri Paris, Kate Dreyfus, Judith Randall, Esther Fine, Maril Crabtree, Sally Han, Gail Burk, Bonnie Pettus, Ros Nesler, Norma Wyse, Faith Wyse, Shoshana Helman, Gail Kingwell, Michaela Sieh, Melissa Thomson, Terry Stein, Susan Evans, Judy Slattum, Teresa Miller, Kristi Walsh, Sarah Dale, Kelly Hartley, Liz Stolar, Meg Soiffer, Marian Towar, Margo Fowkes, Sara Benvenento, Crystal Emerick, Olivia Bethea, Karen Bartholomew, Diane Hamer, Yasmin Kerkez, and Madeline Hawdon.

In particular, I'd like to thank:

Gail Burk, an astounding editor, whose fine eye and editorial prowess never fail to amaze me.

Sherri Paris, a generous and loving friend, who read the book three times, with great insight into the story and perspectives I could always value.

Roz Spafford, for amazing insight and impeccable editing, and for pointing out omissions I might have otherwise overlooked.

Denise Notzon and Dino Sierp, for information about the early days of *The Courage to Heal.*

Cousins Ian and Miriam Kent and Petrina Cooper, for providing crucial location details, many of which, unfortunately, ended up on the cutting room floor.

Paul Davis, my brother, for loving me across a lifetime despite my resistance to his love, for his insistence that this story be told, for our many great hikes together, and for his willingness to let me portray him as my foil in this book. I'm grateful to claim him as my brother.

Eli Davis, Lizzy Davis, and Bryan Rawles, my children, for their careful review of the manuscript and for allowing me to include them in this story. Bryan brought his video director's hat to this memoir, offering a unique lens into my plot that no one else provided. Lizzy

and Eli read the book twice and, each time, gave me thoughtful, funny, detailed notes and terrific line edits. As enthusiastic cheerleaders for this book since its inception, their contributions were unique and helpful. After I completed the final draft, Eli gave me one final amazing gift—he created an elaborate spreadsheet that tracked the dates, ages, and timelines in this story, something I desperately needed and was completely incapable of doing on my own.

Karyn Bristol, my beautiful spouse, for supporting and sustaining me for over thirty years. She has always believed in me and been the bedrock of our family. Karyn loved my mother and helped me stretch past my rigid, historical boundaries as I cared for her. Karyn supported my need to tell this story from the beginning, despite the fact that she, as a private person, would by necessity be in it. I am deeply grateful for this incredibly generous act of love on her part.

To my family, please forgive me for my depiction of events you remember differently or would prefer to forget.

I recognize that this book may be painful for some members of my extended family. *The Burning Light of Two Stars* brings out into the public eye, once again, difficult family issues that I've written about in the past. More than thirty years ago, my decision to write about incest in our family led to a painful estrangement between me and a number of family members. In the decades since then, we've worked our way back from the brink and rebuilt our ties, and I hope my choice to write this book doesn't break the connections we've worked so hard to reestablish. I apologize for any stress resulting from the publication of *The Burning Light of Two Stars*. I wrestled with the decision for a long time, but ultimately, my need to tell this story won out.

Finally, a deep thank-you to all of my mother's caregivers. Many people played vital roles in her care, loving and being there for her until the end. You know who you are. Thank you.

BOOK CLUB DISCUSSION QUESTIONS FOR *THE BURNING LIGHT OF TWO STARS*

Laura is available through Zoom or Skype to meet with book groups to discuss *The Burning Light of Two Stars*. If you're interested in having Laura as a guest at your book club, go to www.lauradavis.net/bookclubs.

1. Laura chooses to open her memoir with an account of her birth. She introduces the character of Vicki, her dead twin sister. Why do you think she made this choice? What significance does Vicki's presence—and absence—have in Laura's life?

2. In chapter 2, Laura shows ambivalence toward her mother's announcement that she's moving to California. At that point in the story, did you think her hesitation was justified? At what point did you realize just how fraught their relationship was?

3. Do you consider the conflict between Temme and Laura to be a typical mother-daughter conflict? Why or why not? How does Laura's relationship with her mother compare with your relationship with your mother—or your daughter?

4. What function do the letters between mother and daughter play in the story? Why were Laura and her mother able to express things in letters that they couldn't communicate in person? Have you ever expressed different parts of yourself through different modes of communication?

5. In her letter on Memory, Laura says her "head is spinning" because the correspondence with her mother contradicts her own beliefs about the past. How do you think you'd respond if you made the same discovery? Have you ever found something in your family's archives that disrupted your perspective on the past?

6. Laura says, "A truth teller can only tell as much of the truth as she can face at a given time." What do you think this means? What application does it have in your own life?

7. How do you think the tenor of the times Laura grew up in influenced her and the relationships within her family? How do you think the circumstances of Temme's growing up, as a poor child of immigrant parents during the Depression, influenced her choices, her perspective, and her mothering?

8. In the dinner-party scene, Laura describes being gaslighted by her mother—being told that what she felt and perceived weren't real. Has this ever happened to you? How did it impact your life and your self-confidence?

9. In chapter 23, Temme shrugs off Laura's attempt to hug her because she believes Laura is "faking it." What is the role of touch in the evolution of their relationship?

10. In chapter 38, Laura confronts her propensity to "build a case against Mom." Why do you think she does this? Have you ever been in a relationship where you gathered evidence against someone else? Or where another person gathered evidence against you?

11. When Laura describes her reconciliation with her mother, she says they were able to make peace, in part, because they "agreed to disagree." What is the difference between "agreeing to disagree" and caving in?

12. Laura quotes the author Debra Fruchey, who says, “Every time I look in the rearview mirror, the past has changed.” How has this been true in your life?

13. Geography plays a crucial role in the estrangement and eventual healing between Laura and her mother. How did geographical proximity and distance impact their relationship? Do you agree with Temme’s statement “We’ll never reconcile if we only see each other once a year”? In your relationships with others, what role has geography played?

14. Laura says, “I’d always assumed that reconciliation required a major reckoning about all the terrible things that had ever happened. But reweaving our relationship was more about the little things.” Do you think that healing a major rift requires that everything be put on the table? Or are there indirect ways to heal an estranged relationship?

15. Laura knows her mother isn’t a safe driver, but it takes her a long time to intervene. What gets in her way? Have you ever been in the position of having to limit the freedom and independence of a parent? How did you handle that responsibility?

16. After Laura confronts her mother regarding her racist comments about Jews being superior, Laura still finds a way to end up on Temme’s side. What does this scene show about Laura’s growth as a daughter?

17. Laura expresses mixed emotions about her choice to take her mother to get tested for Alzheimer’s disease. Do you think Laura’s guilt was justified? Was it necessary for Temme to get tested? Why or why not?

18. During their confrontation on West Cliff, what drives Laura to lose control? Are her actions understandable? When Laura says, “The woman who’d screamed at my mother had been waiting a lifetime

to come out," what does she mean? Have you ever "lost it" as a parent or a caregiver?

19. Laura describes the way Temme's final doctor streamlined her medical care and reduced her medications. She also describes the alternative—multiple doctors for every part of the body and repetitive trips to the hospital. What do you believe are the best healthcare choices for elderly patients?

20. Laura describes her mother as courageous. What evidence do you see of this over the course of the story? What did you admire most about Temme?

21. Which events during the trip to Florida demonstrate Laura's growth in her quest to love her mother? Have you ever had a similar breakthrough in a caregiving relationship?

22. When her mother is about to be kicked out of rehab and Laura has to find the next place for her to live, Laura asks, "What makes a meaningful life?" As caregiver or next of kin, how would you answer that question?

23. In the final scene in the book, Laura and her brother participate in a forgiveness practice. Can you imagine anyone in your life you'd like to do a "forgiveness practice" with? What would you say to them? What do you wish they'd say to you?

24. What are your three biggest takeaways from reading *The Burning Light of Two Stars*?

MEET LAURA DAVIS

Photo by Jace Ritchey

Laura Davis is the author of six groundbreaking nonfiction books that have sold more than 1.8 million copies around the world. Her classic bestsellers, *The Courage to Heal* and *The Courage to Heal Workbook,* paved the way for hundreds of thousands of women and men to heal from the trauma of sexual abuse. In 1997, Davis coauthored *Becoming the Parent You Want to Be,* a rich resource guide that helps parents develop a vision for the families they want to create. The first book inspired by her relationship with her mother, *I Thought We'd Never Speak Again: The Road from Estrangement to Reconciliation,* teaches the skills of reconciliation and peace building to the world, one relationship at a time.

In her long career as a communicator, Laura has been a columnist, talk show host, and radio news reporter. She teaches weekly writing workshops online and in Santa Cruz, California, and has taught memoir writing, Writing as a Pathway to Healing, and creative writing at Kripalu, Esalen, 1440 Multiversity, Tassajara, and the San Miguel Writers' Conference. Her Writing as a Pathway Through Grief, Loss, Uncertainty and Change retreats, created with Nancy

London, have built community and changed lives at Commonweal in Bolinas, California and the Mabel Dodge Luhan House in Taos, New Mexico. When there isn't a pandemic, Laura takes people on transformative Write, Travel, Transform adventures in Bali, Peru, Spain, Italy, Vietnam, and other international destinations. As founder of *The Writer's Journey Roadmap,* Laura sends out evocative writing prompts by email every Tuesday.

Laura lives in Santa Cruz, California with her spouse Karyn and their new yellow lab puppy, Luna. She enjoys swimming, hiking, mah-jong, making kombucha, motion theater, her grandchildren, and of course, writing.

To learn about Laura's workshops, subscribe to her weekly prompts, or to invite her to spend a digital evening with your book club, visit her website:

www.lauradavis.net

Seven free gifts for readers to augment your reading experience can be found here:

www.lauradavis.net/readergifts